Blue Water Kiwis

Blue Water Kiwis

New Zealand's naval story

1870–2001

Second Edition

Matthew Wright

This book is copyright and subject to international treaties.
No part may be copied, reproduced, or otherwise duplicated by any means, without prior permission of the copyright holder.

Copyright © Matthew Wright 2001, 2015 and 2019

The moral rights of the author have been asserted.

Cover photography copyright © Matthew Wright

Published by Intruder Books, Wellington, 2019

ISBN 978-0-908318-25-4 (Intruder Books)

Publication history
First published 2001 by Reed New Zealand Ltd
Republished with minor revisions for Kindle 2015 by Intruder Books
Republished with further revisions as a second edition in print 2019 by Intruder Books

This book is part of the New Zealand Military Series. Collect the set.

www.matthewwright.net
www.mjwrightnz.wordpress.com
www.facebook.com/MatthewWrightNZ

Contents

Foreword ... vii

Introduction ... 1

1 The Russians are coming! ... 5
2 The Great War ... 31
3 The 'locust' years 1921–39 ... 59
4 Second World War ... 76
5 Pacific crisis 1941–45 ... 111
6 Korea and the Cold War ... 150
7 Frigate navy ... 173
8 Age of reform ... 191

Notes ... 205
Glossary ... 226
Bibliography ... 228
Index ... 237

Foreword

Blue Water Kiwis was published in 2001 by Reed NZ Ltd, New Zealand's oldest non-fiction publisher. Although not specifically a history of the Royal New Zealand Navy — for its scope ran well before that service was founded in 1941 — *Blue Water Kiwis* was picked up during writing by the Navy as the book to mark its sixtieth anniversary, and I remain grateful for their generous and unstinting support.

This edition returns *Blue Water Kiwis* to print for the first time since the early 2000s. The text has been interpretatively revised and detailed. However, quotations from the original edition, notably eyewitness records, remain unchanged per original usage permissions. I have not updated the story into the twenty-first century. The themes I explored in the original text reached their natural end around the turn of the millennium, with the transition away from Cold War priorities. The story of the Royal New Zealand Navy into the twenty-first century is a different tale.

Matthew Wright

BLUE WATER KIWIS

Introduction

As the New Zealand cruiser HMS *Achilles* closed with the German armoured ship *Admiral Graf Spee* off Montevideo in December 1939, a sailor rushed across the deck carrying a tightly wrapped bundle. 'Make way for the Digger flag!' Over the next ninety minutes her gunners fired so fast that the paint on the guns blistered. The cruiser was a long way from home — and right on New Zealand's naval front line.

The battle highlighted the point that New Zealand's naval interests could be anywhere along far-flung commerce routes. The problem, inevitably, was finding ways of paying for the forces needed to protect those routes. New Zealand's struggle began in the 1880s, well before there was any thought of a Royal New Zealand Navy, when Britain's economy creaked under the strain of worldwide Pax Britannica, and Australia, New Zealand and Britain had different opinions about what constituted a threat. Both Dominions saw an enemy in Britain's ally Japan. By 1900 Australia was determined to follow its own course, but New Zealand preferred a more jingoistic line, strengthening the centre. Although the politics of these actions have often been examined, explanations to date have been unsatisfactory, particularly in regard to the 'gift dreadnought', HMS *New Zealand*.

New Zealand's relationship with Britain set the scene for a naval policy that did not change much for years, one that in many ways pivoted around New Zealand's self-image of itself as a loyal part of a wider British Empire. Even when the Dominion set up local forces, they were not independent like those across the Tasman, but a division of the Royal Navy; and the main focus of forward defence, during the inter-war years, was on strengthening the British ability to use Singapore as major base in the Pacific and Far East. Such outcomes stood somewhat at tension with a growing local view of New Zealand as a self-determining nation, but that was where New Zealand's naval direction took it.

Resourcing was always a problem; New Zealand lurched from downturn to downturn and defence remained bottom priority for successive governments. When war broke out in 1939 the Naval Division comprised just two major warships and a few smaller vessels. Prime Minister Peter Fraser pushed for the creation of the Royal New Zealand Navy as a separate entity in 1941, for political reasons; but the government could make little change in resourcing, and New Zealand's naval contribution to the war was crippled when both cruisers were put out of action in mid-1943.

The service 'came of age' in the late 1940s. Although a planned aircraft carrier never eventuated, the Royal New Zealand Navy was reasonably well resourced for the first time, and heavily involved in the Korean War. Six frigates and two light cruisers proved the minimum effective force, backed by the navies of allies. Links with Britain remained important for decades, alongside ties with the United States and Australia.

Peace did not come with the end of the Cold War. Conflict around the world switched to national and ethnic lines, creating the illusion of peace, but generating flashpoints that carried the risk of wider trouble. This was a particular issue for New Zealand. Ninety percent of New Zealand's trade by value was seaborne at the end of the twentieth century, and much of this passed through the trouble-spots of Asia. Apart from contributing to international peacekeeping efforts, the navy fulfilled roles ranging from fisheries patrol to humanitarian relief. Yet at the same time, funding steadily dropped — for all New Zealand's military forces it was a case of 'think smart'.

This book is a broad-brush history designed, in the words of Eric Hobsbawm, not only to 'discover the past, but to explain it, and in doing so provide a link with the present . . . What we want to know is why, as well as what.' Relevant data is, of course, essential to any explanation, and a secondary aim of this book is to dispel a few of the myths and legends that have developed about the Royal New Zealand Navy over the years. Contemporary records frequently paint a different picture of events from the commonly accepted 'truth'. Consequently, some material in this book may vary from what has been published elsewhere.

INTRODUCTION

Ultimately, New Zealand's naval history is a human tale. Policy, technology and even the outcome of most events invariably derive from human thought and endeavour — and the 'salty yarns' of sailors must take their place alongside official documents and reports. To understand the truths of New Zealand's naval story, then, we must look to the hopes, fears and dreams of all who have played a part in the tale.

I am grateful to the Royal New Zealand Navy for their support of this book during 2000–01. My particular thanks go to Richard Jackson of RNZN Public Relations for his unstinting assistance. I also thank the staff of the Alexander Turnbull Library, Archives New Zealand, the Wellington Museum of City and Sea, the Ministry of Defence Library, Canterbury Museum Library, Alexander Turnbull Library and Archives New Zealand for their generous and willing assistance with source material.

Matthew Wright
September 2001

BLUE WATER KIWIS

CHAPTER ONE
The Russians are coming!

At this moment, we are under the complete domination of Russia, our own guns in our own man-of-war being pointed against the city, ready to be opened upon us...

— *Daily Southern Cross*, 17 February 1873.[1]

Aucklanders opening the *Daily Southern Cross* one balmy February day in 1873 were amazed to read that their city had been held to ransom by a captured British warship. Helped by 'mephitic water-gas' and a 'submarine pinnace', Tsarists of the Russian cruiser *Kaskowiski* had apparently slunk into the Waitemata Harbour, taken control of a visiting British ship, and demanded £250,000 from the town authorities. This was more than the town could provide, but the Russian pirates got away with £131,096 17s 6d, leaving a prize crew behind in the British ship to extort further cash from the helpless Aucklanders as the day wore on. 'WHERE IS THE BRITISH NAVY?' thundered the newspaper's editorial.

It was scandalous, outrageous and — of course — a complete fabrication by editor D.M. Luckie. It should have been obvious from the name of the ship alone, but a few briefly believed the tale and for a day or two the adventures of the *Kaskowiski* caused a mild sensation. However, although the story was a practical joke, Luckie's intentions were serious, and he followed up the naval defence problem in subsequent issues of the paper.

Luckie had good reason for doing so. New Zealand had a major naval headache by the early 1870s. As a British colony the country relied entirely on the Royal Navy for protection. The threat from Russia in particular was — perhaps naively — perceived as a direct practical menace to coastal towns and cities, for which locally-based naval forces seemed the best deterrent. The nearest was the small Australian Squadron, based in Sydney since 1859. But although detachments were occasionally sent to New Zealand waters there was nothing permanent, and that brought a sense of vulnerability. Luckie milked the scenario of a rogue cruiser for laughs, but his melodrama encapsulated fears that were seriously held in many circles. Hopeful politicians looked to 'torpedo' defence and non-existent forts for protection, but Luckie wanted a true Australasian Squadron.

'Torpedo' defence and the Russian menace

Getting Britain to agree to local defences was a real problem. Victory over France in 1815 and the end of the war with the United States in 1826 left Britain in a pre-eminent position, and there was a widespread belief that conflict between 'civilised' nations had ended forever. In fact the world simply became more dangerous; warfare shifted from national to ethnic lines in the colonies and 'frontiers', near-constant 'brush fire' struggles that placed a strain on centrally funded defences. Indeed, the heroic image of a 'thin red line' holding off vast enemy armies was symptomatic; the line had to be thin because Britain could not afford to make it thicker. The Crimean War of 1853 and the rekindling of warfare between developed nations took its place alongside these local struggles, further stretching British resources. The point triggered arguments between New Zealand and the Colonial Office during the New Zealand wars of the 1860s.

These wars — in which the Royal Navy played a part — dominated government and public attention in the developing colony, and thought did not turn to wider defence until the end of the 1860s. But the settlers did not have to look far to find an enemy. Russia was the bogeyman of the British

Empire, and with justification. The Crimean War was followed by ongoing tension on the border between Russia and British Afghanistan – the so-called 'Great Game' – and 'war scares' flared regularly. Successive New Zealand governments feared that a war tying down British naval forces in the Baltic or North Sea might leave Britain's South Pacific colonies vulnerable to attack from Russia's eastern bases. The Admiralty disagreed, believing Pacific distances were too vast. In any case, a Russian fleet coming south would be cut off by British naval forces in Hong Kong. But raids or threats against shipping were another matter, and the British set up the Australian Station in March 1859 partly for this reason. The squadron was based in Sydney, geographically near the centre of the region.

The Admiralty — which viewed Australia and New Zealand as a single strategic entity — thought this was an efficient answer to Australasian defence problems, but again these views were not shared in New Zealand. If British warships could rush about the world heedless of prevailing winds, so could those of the enemy. Only ships on the spot could protect the country against a 'bolt from the blue'. To some extent this 'brick and mortar' philosophy reflected inexperience. As the Admiralty pointed out, war usually followed a period of strained relations. However, such thoughts cut little ice in New Zealand, where instant Russian nemesis on the heels of British imperial hubris seemed all too likely.

Dealing with the problem was another matter. New Zealand was in the depths of a thirty-year depression. Money was scarce, and in any case, only port-guard ships were allowed within the imperial naval structure. Coast defences were mooted as early as 1869, but the cost seemed prohibitive, and hints that Britain should donate old weapons fell on deaf ears. Colonel-General Sir George Whitmore demanded coast defence guns again in 1870,[2] while options discussed along the way included deploying 'Whitehead automobile torpedoes' to protect the harbours. However, progress had to wait until 1877 when a British mission led by Colonel Peter Scratchley and Sir William Jervois looked into Australasian coast defence. They favoured forts. The New Zealand government balked at the estimated price tag of £26,000, but ordered two dozen 64-pounders with 150 rounds each, which were put in storage at Port Chalmers amid vacillation over the best way to install them.

The government also ordered four 'spar torpedo' boats for harbour defence from private shipbuilders John Thornycroft. Manned by 'volunteer submarine miners', these tiny craft were armed with an explosive charge on a pole protruding from the bows, which had to be rammed into the enemy ship for effect. They were rather heroic vessels; even if their headlong charge into the side of an enemy vessel did not end in the crew being riddled by enemy small-arms fire, the chances of then surviving an the explosion of their own 'torpedo' which was separated from the boat only by a length of pole — seemed slim. They were given Maori names, though Rewi Maniapoto's suggestion that one should be named after the taniwha of Arai-te-uru was not taken up.[3]

Scratchley had a further look at colonial defences in 1880, but it took another crisis to get work started in earnest. Triggered by a territorial dispute over the Afghan border, the 'war scare' of 1884 sent panic rippling through the British Empire. A Russian squadron that appeared off China seemed to pose a threat to New Zealanders,[4] and there were calls for the South Pacific colonies to contribute to their own defence.[5] Requests for volunteers prompted a huge response — numbers soared from just under 5000 in March 1885 to more than 8000 only three months later. An alarmed government placed panic orders with British arms-maker Armstrong for torpedoes and asked Britain for a first-class cruiser.[6] Nothing came of this, but a call for public subscriptions drew a swift response and work accelerated on fixed defences in the main harbours.

The fort on Auckland's Mount Victoria was essentially complete by 1886, after a struggle to mount guns that weighed more than the available equipment could easily handle. Three 8-inch and two 7-inch rifles along with one 64-pounder were finally installed on 'disappearing mountings' in reinforced concrete pits — the entire gun was mounted on massive hydraulic arms that swung it into a pit for reloading. The guns had yet to be test fired in May when the Russian corvette *Vestnik* visited Wellington, prompting media speculation about the Russians' hidden motives. She left for Japan at the end of the month, and when Mount Tarawera rent itself asunder in a shower of ash a few days later, many attributed the booming reports to the corvette. The *New Zealand Herald* remarked that 'many people, both here [in Auckland] and at Onehunga', assumed the *Vestnik* had run into trouble somewhere along the coast and was firing her guns by way of distress signal.[7]

Work began on the Lyttelton fort on Ripapa Island the same year. Relief workers, contractors, prison labour from Lyttelton gaol, and even men from the Permanent Artillery laboured over the next ten years to complete the structure to a design by Lieutenant-Colonel Edmund Meyer Tudor-Boddam. The fort was based around two 8-inch and two 6-inch Armstrong breech-loaders firing from 'disappearing mountings', backed with 6-pounder Nordenfeldt pivot guns. 'Bomb proof' concrete and ten feet of earth with walls 'forming [a] solid rampant mass' made it resistant to gunfire. The guns were test fired in 1892, but the fort was quickly overtaken by new naval developments.[8]

Despite the forts and torpedo defences there remained a general feeling that local ships were needed. Premier Sir Robert Stout vented his feelings about this to the Australasian Squadron's Commander in Chief, Rear-Admiral Sir George Tryon, and instructed the Agent-General in London to secure a first-class cruiser for New Zealand waters. This came to nothing, and the only development was a new graving dock on Calliope Point for the Auckland Harbour Board, ceremonially opened in February 1888 by HMS *Calliope* and HMS *Diamond*. It had obvious naval use, and in 1892 the Admiralty acquired four acres of adjacent land as the nucleus of a naval base.

British naval policy, meanwhile, lurched from war scare to war scare. Media agitation after the 1884 scare prompted the 'Northbook Programme', which allocated £3,100,000 over the next five years for new warships and £2,400,000 for static works. This formed the background to defence discussions at the 1887 Colonial Conference, where the Admiralty agreed that Australia and New Zealand could pay for five fast cruisers and two torpedo boats to supplement the Australasian Squadron. The two dominions were expected to cover construction costs, plus interest at five percent, sharing this annual sum of £35,000.[9] New Zealand's actual contribution — starting in the 1891–92 financial year — varied between £20,304 and £21,534 per year.[10] The Australian contribution hovered around the £100,000 mark, proportions roughly reflected in the names given to the ships — *Katoomba*, *Ringarooma*, *Wallaroo*, *Mildura* and *Tauranga*. Later, New Zealand ordered two small coastal minelayers named after the wives of two of New Zealand's most prominent politicians of the day, *Ellen Ballance* and *Jamie Seddon*.

A further British 'scare' in 1888 prompted the Naval Defence Act 1889, which committed the extraordinary sum of £21,500,000 over three years on more vessels, including 10 first-class battleships, 38 cruisers and 22 smaller vessels. It embodied the new 'two-power' standard, pushed by Lord George

Hamilton, the First Lord of the Admiralty, by which the Royal Navy would be kept at 'such a scale that it should be at least equal to the naval strength of any two other countries'.[11] British power was judged against this for the rest of the century, colouring perceptions both in Britain and the far-flung colonies. The usual fear in the South Pacific was that one or more European powers would defeat Britain and acquire her colonial possessions, and one consequence of this in New Zealand was a vigorous effort to gain as many Pacific Island territories as possible. This led to difficulties over Samoa, which the Germans and Americans also wanted — the New Zealand government did not appreciate that Britain used the islands as a bargaining tool.[12]

Japan: ally or enemy?

Britain ended her traditional 'splendid isolation' and found a friend in Japan as the nineteenth century drew to a close.[13] An alliance was signed in 1902. The diplomatic initiative was in part a response to the Russians, but it did not go down well in the South Pacific, where Japan was viewed as a threat on a number of levels. The Australians worried that the link would free up migration. Nor could the military aspect be ignored, and during the build-up to the 1902 Colonial Conference, Queensland naval commandant, Captain William Creswell, urged Australia to take an 'active and personal share in her own defence'. An increased naval subsidy would lead only to stagnation and 'continued naval impotence for Australia'.[14]

These thoughts were unsurprising at a time when local self-identity and nationalism had taken its place alongside imperial sentiments, but they were also heretical, and Minister of Defence Sir John Forrest downgraded them to an offer to supplement the Australasian Squadron with eight cruisers. Even this received a frosty reception. The First Lord of the Admiralty, Edward Marjoribanks, the second Lord Tweedmouth, told delegates that 'there must be only one authority with full power and responsibility to the Empire to move the ships . . . to concentrate them where they can deal the most effective blow against the forces of the enemy'.[15] Still, Australia had made a point, and the Admiralty agreed to send the huge protected cruiser *Powerful*, two second-class cruisers, four third-class cruisers and four sloops to the South Pacific. Two were stationed in New Zealand harbours, and there were more exercises. None of this came cheaply — New Zealand subsidies rose to £40,000 and Australia's to £200,000.[16] New Zealand also acquired the old gunboat *Sparrow* as a training ship. Although well past the first flush of youth, she was commissioned for New Zealand under Captain G.S. Hooper. Renamed *Amokura*, she served until 1921 and more than five hundred sailors were trained on her.

There was further alarm in 1904 when Russia and Japan came to blows. Against every expectation, Japan gained dominance at sea and gave the Russians a drubbing on land. Newspapers on both sides of the Tasman voiced concern about the surprise reversal, and the Bulletin referred to Japanese victories at Mukden as the 'gravest cause for anxiety . . . it would be long before Asiatic power could so grow as to threaten the territory of Europe . . . but Australia is a lonely outpost of the white race on the very borders of Asia'.[17] The first official alarm was expressed in April 1905 when Vice-Admiral A.D. Fanshawe, Commander in Chief of the Australasian Squadron, warned of the danger from 'other' Pacific powers. The only real protection either dominion had was the 'capacity of the Royal Navy to maintain command of Eastern seas'.[18] From a geo-political perspective this point remained true until well into the twentieth century. But not everybody shared this opinion at the time. Sir Robert Stout felt the real threat to New Zealand was economic. However, his remarks to this effect in the *New Zealand Herald* provoked the editor to suggest that Britain had wooed Japan as a hedge against Russian power. Since the Russians had been eliminated, the alliance could be terminated with no loss to British interests.[19]

This thinking on both sides of the Tasman had its sequel three years later when the United States sent a battle fleet around the Pacific, mainly to assert its claims to the Philippines. The Prime Ministers of both Australia and New Zealand invited the fleet to visit amid clamorous popular applause.[20] 'As the champions of white ascendancy in the Pacific,' the *Evening Post* opined, 'America . . . represents the ideals of Australia and New Zealand far better than Britain has hitherto been able to do.'[21]

These Pacific developments were further complicated by dramatic changes taking place on the other side of the world. Admiral Sir John Fisher became First Sea Lord in October 1904 and launched a scheme to modernise the Royal Navy while slashing costs by 30 percent.[22] This would have been controversial at the best of times, but trouble was virtually guaranteed by

Fisher's 'domineering and combatative' personality.[23] Years later, Winston Churchill found it 'impossible to re-read [Fisher's letters] without sentiments of strong regard for him, his fiery soul, his volcanic energy, his deep creative mind, his fierce outspoken hatreds, his love of England'.[24] Fisher's reforms were entwined with a personal vendetta against the Channel Fleet commander, Admiral Lord Charles Beresford. Yet with the help of a band of officers nicknamed the 'Fishpond', Fisher transformed the navy into a lean fighting force which — as he put it in thunderously capitalised prose — was at 'INSTANT READINESS FOR WAR'.[25]

The war Fisher envisaged was wholly European, one in which he visualised Britain as potentially standing alone — in 1904 he dramatically warned that 'Russia might . . . call on her ally France, and at the same time give Germany the opportunity for which Russia's secret ally is eagerly waiting.'[26] Even after Russian naval power had been destroyed, he wrote that a 'Franco-German-Russian coalition of powers . . . it is as well to remember, did actually combine . . . to rob Japan of the fruits of victory'.[27] To Fisher, Germany was not the main enemy until 1907, when it became the 'only possible foe'.[28] The problem was that Britain simply could not afford to maintain a fleet large enough to fight everywhere. Fisher's answer was to find both tactical and operational efficiencies. His tactical thinking was an early expression of what later became known as 'blue water' strategy – looking to seal off key waters by stationing fleets at the entrances – the 'five keys [that] lock up the world'.[29] He put battle fleets into three of them — Portsmouth, Gibraltar and Malta — protecting Britain directly from invasion and stopping enemy fleets from leaving the North Sea and the Mediterranean. In the face of the Russo-Japanese war, the First Lord, Selbourne, persuaded Fisher to also reinforce the British fleet in Chinese waters, but when the Japanese victory at Tsushima broke Russian naval power, Fisher withdrew all British battleships from the Pacific.[30]

Operational efficiencies flowed from the same thinking. With potential enemies safely bottled up in local European waters, and with Japan now an ally, there was no need for Britain to have significant fleets elsewhere. There was still a role for some of the third-class cruisers and gunboats that had been thinly dispersed around the globe, if only as imperial police and to squash any trouble. However, Fisher scrapped the 156 sloops, third-class cruisers and gunboats that had been 'showing the flag' from Auckland to Aden, and from Esquimalt to the Cape of Good Hope, on the basis that they were militarily useless in any modern war at sea. This was essentially true in terms of that role; but they had other functions in peacetime, including acting as a visible presence of Empire. Maurice Hankey argued that Fisher's dramatic move was a deliberate cost-saving ploy to gain Cabinet approval of the scheme. But it meant the Empire was virtually denuded of visible ships,[31] and with that came a popular sense of vulnerability.

This was certainly so for the two South Pacific Dominions. Australia's response — perhaps predictably — was to call for a local fleet. Creswell put the case to the Committee of Imperial Defence (CID) in 1905, proposing a Commonwealth navy of three 'cruiser destroyers', sixteen torpedo boat destroyers and fifteen torpedo boats, which he described as a 'purely defensive line, that will give security to our naval bases, populous centres, principal ports and commerce'.[32] This stood little chance in the face of Fisher's reform juggernaut, but even the CID were cool. Attacks on 'floating trade', the CID explained, would 'offer to the enemy but slight prospect of any but very transitory success'. Only 'single vessels or small squadrons' posed any real threat. This view was also applied to New Zealand, where the CID argued that attacks would be by 'at most, two or three cruisers' landing no more than four hundred men.[33]

For Creswell this was like a red rag to a bull, and he now suggested Australia should develop its own military and industrial capacity. 'The initiation of a naval service should be the starting point of a policy to remedy this weakness,' he wrote. 'An axiom of our defence should be the production in Australia of every war requisite.'[34] The Admiralty viewed Australia and New Zealand as a single strategic unit, and this carried the implication that New Zealand would have to join in. However, that was the last thing on the mind of New Zealand's Premier and Minister of Defence, Joseph Ward.

Ward takes the stage, 1907–09

Described by his contemporary A.R. Barclay as running an 'indiarubber' government, Joseph Ward — Premier and Minister of Defence from 1906 to 1912 — has generally been dismissed as an impulsive character with a liking for abrupt policy turns.[35] His successor as Minister of Defence, Colonel James Allen, did not think Ward had any idea of naval policy at all,[36] a view echoed by historians who have seen Ward's activities as little more than a headlong rush to help a beleaguered Empire.[37] Coherent New Zealand naval policy has generally not been seen as starting until William Massey's government took office in 1913. In fact, the situation was virtually the reverse. Although Ward was an 'imperial patriot', he had a coherent naval policy where Massey did not. The issue was that he pivoted it around his vision for Empire, in which he stood against both Australian and British sentiment. Allen had different ideas altogether and proved a spanner in the works for both. Ward's main problem was applying his ideas in an environment where Australia and New Zealand were seen as a single strategic entity, and where Australia — by virtue of a larger economy and population — essentially held the whip hand.

Ward became Premier at a time when New Zealand's perception of the next enemy was changing dramatically. Russia had given way to Japan in 1904–05, but by 1907 Japan — though still held as a threat — had taken second place to Germany, specifically the fear that British defeat in home waters could be followed by piecemeal destruction of the colonies.

Sea force was the only protection, and Britain's fifty first-class battleships compared well with Germany's twenty. However, the stakes were zeroed in 1906 when Fisher launched HMS *Dreadnought* on an unsuspecting world. Earlier battleships mounted four heavy guns, a handful of medium calibre guns, and a dozen or more lighter weapons. Armoured cruisers such as *Minotaur* carried a similar multi-calibre mix of weapons of slightly smaller scale, on a hull that approached the scale and expense of a battleship. The problem that emerged in the first years of the twentieth century, as these mixed armaments became more ubiquitous, was that they worked well at battle ranges of a few thousand yards. However, the guns could fire considerably further. At these greater ranges, gunlayers could not differentiate between the splash of medium or large calibre weapons, creating fire-control problems.

The answer to that problem was a homogeneous main armament, towards which naval architects worldwide groped for some years. Both the United States and Japan authorised all-big-gun vessels in 1904, and there were rumours that Russia planned similar ships.[38] Fisher trumped them all with the *Dreadnought*, laid down late in 1905 and completed the following year amid such inspired theatrics that the public and politicians began measuring naval strength in terms of 'dreadnoughts'. This was unfortunate. Although turbine driven and capable of 21 knots, *Dreadnought* was less well armoured than earlier battleships, and her effective fighting power was not radically greater at the ranges possible with 1906-era fire control equipment. The real jump came with the 13.5-inch guns and centreline armament introduced in 1909, and even then it took the fire-control advances of 1912–14 to better realise the long-range fighting capabilities.[39]

Fisher nevertheless championed the *Dreadnought* as a wonder-vessel, and transformed armoured cruisers the same way. *Invincible* was basically an all-big-gun version of *Minotaur*, similarly protected against medium calibre shells fired at about 9000 yards. However, a 12-inch main armament gave her capital ship status and virtually ensured her employment in the battle line. *Invincible*'s first captain noted the pitfalls,[40] but Fisher, who felt armour was obsolete in the face of ever more powerful guns, regarded the type as 'better dreadnoughts' and managed to get three laid down even before *Dreadnought* had completed her trials. All this had a decisive effect on the way politicians in the Dominions viewed naval strength; suddenly the old measures had gone, and power was purely defined by the number of 'dreadnoughts', a race in which Fisher had, as far as the public were concerned, reset the score to zero. The fact that the older ships still retained valid fighting power was recognised within professional naval circles, but somewhat lost to the public and — with that — the whole issue became politicised.

Ward's naval ideas were particularly framed by his 'patriotic' world view, and the imperial federal concepts peddled by both Richard Seddon and Ward himself from the 1890s. As F. L. W. Wood has argued, these originated as a means of keeping out of federation with Australia; but the Empire-wide structure wanted by Seddon and Ward was unpopular in an Empire moving towards permanent alliance between independent nations.[41] Even so, Seddon's failure to find support at the Colonial Conferences of 1897 and 1902 did not stop Ward calling for an 'imperial council' at the 1907 conference. Unified defence was a key part of Ward's thinking. 'There is but one sea around our shores,' he argued, 'and . . . with one sea and one Empire, there should in reality be but one Navy.'[42] His proposals were turned down.[43]

Australia had better luck. Tweedmouth had been informed privately by Australian Prime Minister Alfred Deakin that Australia viewed the naval subsidy as a 'tribute', and grudgingly agreed that Australia might build a small fleet to supplement British forces.[44] Deakin believed he had formal approval and in October told Governor-General Lord Northcote that 'in order to unite with the mother country for defence purposes', he would cancel the subsidy and instead provide 1000 seamen and two 'P' class cruisers or better. The cruisers and 400 seamen would be kept in Australian waters under Commonwealth control.[45] When the Admiralty rejected this in December,[46] a surprised Deakin warned the House of Representatives that it would be 'dangerous for the Admiralty to insist upon a supremacy which, if mis-adventure fell, would place the whole responsibility on them'.[47] Opposition Leader Andrew Fisher agreed,[48] and the Australian government submitted the proposal once more. The Colonial Office entered the field; the Admiralty was forced to bow to pressure, and in February 1908 agreed to the Australian plans.

Ward had copies of this correspondence and was aware of Admiralty opinion that the Australian proposals might be more acceptable if New Zealand co-operated.[49] His response was a sudden announcement that the New Zealand subsidy would be increased from £40,000 to £100,000 a year.[50] He justified this as an effort to improve general naval defence;[51] which in conjunction with the timing suggests he had actually made the offer to torpedo Australian fleet proposals and improve New Zealand's standing with the Board of Admiralty. It worked. New Zealand's treatment subsequently stood out in contrast to Australia's — the agreement to allow Australia its own fleet was followed by a good deal of chain-dragging.[52]

A new 'naval scare' brewed in early 1909. Britain had ten dreadnoughts built or building, and the government proposed a further four for the 1909–10 programme. Germany had five built or building. However, although German naval strength was dictated by law, news that Krupp had ordered plant for manufacturing heavy gun mountings prompted fears of a secret German 'spurt'. The four Sea Lords had warned Selbourne of the risk as early as December 1907, and by January 1909 Jellicoe was able to write, without a trace of satisfaction, that their 'anxiety is now fully justified'.[53] The issue became a public hot potato, and in the face of Liberal proposals for four ships, First Lord Reginald McKenna — backed by Fisher's propaganda and a strong pro-navy media lobby — called first for six and then eight dreadnoughts for the 1909–10 programme. The issue was taken up by the Conservative opposition with the catch-cry 'we want eight and we won't wait'.[54] It was yet another instance of public sentiment fuelling naval policy, driven by emotion rather than practical need. And it worked.

Ward made his 'dreadnought offer' against this background, one Sunday in March 1909, without calling either Cabinet or Parliament. He did it on a day when the Governor-General — through whom the offer had to be addressed — was in Woodville. Ward was in an almost desperate hurry, and as the 'dreadnought' crisis lasted months, the move has been widely regarded by both Ward's contemporaries and by historians as Ward once again rushing, headlong and without much other thought, to the aid of his beloved empire. Ward's vague justifications certainly lend credence to this idea. He told the House that 'prompt action was absolutely desirable — was, indeed, essential — if the moral effect which we had in view was to be secured'. This was received with deep scepticism, and his failure to follow the correct procedure was brought up like a tolling bell whenever the offer was discussed.

In May, Ward tried to get himself off the hook, hinting that he had 'confidential information relating to the pressing danger of the situation'. This was assumed to mean the British naval crisis, and revealed as bluff when the correspondence was published in Australia and cabled to New Zealand. Massey again made political capital out of it, and even Plunket thought Ward had made an 'error in tactics'.[55] Neither Ward's contemporaries nor historians since have questioned the assumption that Ward acted out of personal patriotism.

In fact, Ward was again trying to politically undermine the Australians on the Imperial stage. He was still driving for policies by which the Dominions would support British naval power at the centre. His unilateral subsidy increase had not quite had the effect he wanted; he needed to do something bigger to make the point. And so he played his ace — the patriot card. As he later told Plunket, New Zealanders 'would take much greater pride and interest in knowing that HMS "So-and-so" and HMS "Something Else" were their ships and a visible tangible object lesson of their Dominion's part in the Empire's defence than in merely paying £100,000 a year in ignorance as to how the money was spent'.[56] Ward explained that he had been thinking of making an offer for some time for these reasons. What he did not say — but what is obvious from his actions — is that he hoped to release the same sentiments in Australia, creating a ground-swell of public opinion that ran against the government policy of a local fleet.

His hand was forced by the annual meeting of Australian Commonwealth leaders in mid-March 1909. On the 18th, Australian Prime Minister Andrew

Fisher remarked that Australia and Canada could best help British defence by offering to pay for a dreadnought each, as an indication that the 'relatively rich young Dominions' would be prepared to help the mother country. It was only a talking point; official Australian policy was veering hard towards bolstering local naval defence instead of the centre. However, the remark drew attention in the English press and was observed with interest in New Zealand.[57] Knowing that an Australian offer would trump his own, Ward made his own 'dreadnought' offer as soon as he heard the news. He could not afford to wait even a day to call Cabinet, in case the Australian government decided to make an announcement before the conference ended. In other words, his remarks about 'prompt action' and 'moral effect' sitting behind his precipitate actions were actually true; what he had not admitted, however, was that it was in order to subvert possible action across the Tasman, not a response to information from London.

The gamble paid off. With this single and very expensive gesture, one that played on the sense of patriotic sentiment held from London to Melbourne, New Zealand had seized the moral high ground in the public Imperial stakes. And although Australian government opinion veered towards a local fleet, that did not diminish the sense of Imperial patriotism held on both sides of the Tsman. The Australian stock exchange called on the Commonwealth parliament to make a similar offer. The Lord Mayor of Sydney opened a 'dreadnought' fund which received £55,000 within 24 hours. A few days later he called for a public 'dreadnought' subscription of some £250,000. In Perth there were heated scenes at a public meeting where a motion was passed that Australia should do all it could to help British supremacy. The Premiers of New South Wales and Victoria announced that if the Federal Government did not make a dreadnought offer, they would. They confirmed this a few days later with an official telegram to the Colonial Office.[58]

Ward had touched a deep vein of patriotic sentiment across the Tasman, and in the face of his initiative Andrew Fisher's 31 March announcement that Australia would spend £5,000,000 on twenty destroyers went down like a lead balloon. The *Daily Telegraph* argued that such a force would be useless unless attached to an overseas squadron, while the *Morning Herald* suggested that destroyers did not give immunity to attack. In New Zealand the *Evening Post* argued that Australia's real defence would still rest with the Royal Navy.[59] It was swiftly politicised: Australian Opposition Leader Alfred Deakin made a 'dreadnought offer' into an election issue — which he honoured when he won the 1909 elections.[60]

The 1909 Naval Agreement

As he had doubtless intended, Ward's offer also triggered patriotic sentiment in Britain, where the concept of a loyal young dominion offering such an extravagant gift went down very well with the public. In the face of this thinking it would have been churlish of the Admiralty to turn it down, and Ward certainly had good reason to feel pleased with himself as he left for an Imperial Conference in July. With a single stroke he had fired up patriotic sentiment on both sides of the Tasman, bolstered his own flagging popularity at home, torpedoed Australian local fleet proposals, and foisted his own ideas about imperial naval defence on a reluctant Admiralty.

His strategy quickly unravelled. Although Deakin had made the Australian dreadnought offer, thinking in Melbourne remained focused on a local fleet and Colonel J.F.G. Foxton was sent along to the conference to argue the toss.[61] He did not have to argue much; the Admiralty were keen to avoid further disagreement, and urgently needed to resolve Ward's offer, which ran against the preferred cash contribution and provided no long term answer to the Australian problem. The compromise was geared towards Australia. The gift ships would join two Pacific 'fleet units', each comprising a 'dreadnought armoured cruiser', three unarmoured cruisers, six destroyers and three submarines. One would be paid for and operated by the Australians — in effect their local fleet — and the second, based in Hong Kong, would incorporate the New Zealand gift.[62] A third unit on the Cape of Good Hope would be similar, minus the cruiser.

This proposal was not a turning point in Admiralty attitudes. It was a compromise intended to quell Australian demands and manage the gift ships. Under Fisher's iron hand, the Sea Lords had no intention of changing their policy of central focus and were merely 'remodelling . . . the squadrons maintained in Far Eastern waters' to form a new Pacific fleet which would consist of 'three units in the East Indies, Australia and China sea'.[63] Ward was 'rather sorry that the Admiralty has recommended that a [naval] unit be formed for Australia'. Although he thought the Germans would 'endeavour to starve England' rather than invade, even two or three dreadnoughts in the Pacific would not alter matters, he insisted, if a victorious German fleet emerged to attack them. A squadron stationed in Sydney could not even protect the entire Australian coastline. Unified defence had to fit his own federal model, not 'this piece-meal disintegrating system of trying to create a local Navy . . .'.[64] With an eye to the further future, Ward also thought the gift dreadnought would help when 'a great Power in the East', now 'happily attached to England', was 'detached from' its English alliance. However, once again his ideas fell on deaf ears. Admiralty proposals gave Australia the fleet they had wanted for nearly a decade.

Faced with the *fait accompli* of a Hong Kong unit and an Australian fleet, Ward realised New Zealand would be denuded of the second-line protection he had expected. This forced him to compromise his 'federal' principles and, purely for pragmatic reasons, follow the Australian lead. He agreed to support the plan provided that two China Unit cruisers, three destroyers and two submarines were stationed in New Zealand waters. First Lord Reginald McKenna agreed, although this would split the China Unit in two.[65] It was a decisive shift. Although New Zealand's local forces were subsequently administered under legislation passed in 1913, the 1909 arrangement defined the basic shape of the force until 1941 — specifically, a cruiser-based force that was part of the Royal Navy and which was stationed in New Zealand waters.

This compromise was not the only bad news from Ward's perspective. The gift ships were built as battlecruisers. Officially, conversion of the 'first class dreadnoughts' on offer into fleet-footed 'dreadnought cruisers' was not an issue.[66] The impetus came from Fisher, who thought the type was superior to dreadnoughts and wondered about having two additional *Invincible* class ships built with the gift money. In the event, the gift ships were built as slightly modified *Indefatigables*, their successor class.

On the surface, *Indefatigable* was a superb example of this new type of ship. The term 'battlecruiser' was not formalised until 1911, by Admiralty edict; until then they were variously labelled 'dreadnought armoured cruisers', 'dreadnought cruisers', and sometimes 'battleship-cruisers'. However, even before the terminology stabilised they had a glamour about them; ships of huge fire-power and great speed that presented to a naval-minded public as the heroic cavalry of the fleet. *Indefatigable* was also the most cost-effective capital ship of the period, her £82 10s 6d per ton comparing favourably with the £101 12s 0d per ton it had cost to build the *Invincibles*.[67] She was launched amid a good deal of hype — *Jane's Fighting Ships*, at the time ever the mouthpiece for Fisher's propaganda, hinted at secret features, and Fisher wrote to his friend Reginald Brett, Lord Esher, claiming the ship would 'make your mouth water . . . and the Germans gnash their teeth'.[68]

The technical reality, however, was quite different. In fact, *Indefatigable* was a mild re-design of *Invincible*, which had been intended to overwhelm armoured cruisers and act as a fast scouting wing for the fleet. The type did not meet the rule-of-thumb measure by which a heavy ship was meant to be protected against its own main armament and were not really intended to closely engage enemy heavy ships. The problem was not so much the thickness as the extent of the protection scheme. But even the thickness of the armour was a problem against the newer guns coming into service by 1909. The Controller, Captain John Jellicoe, certainly thought *Indefatigable* was 'very insufficiently protected' against heavy gunfire.[69] When he received 'secret information' in early 1909 to the effect that the Germans were building larger 'dreadnought cruisers' than the Naval Intelligence Department anticipated, he had the *Indefatigable*'s successors radically altered.[70] The first of the new type was the 26,475-ton *Lion*, designed before the 1909 Imperial Conference and laid down in September as one of the 'contingent' dreadnoughts of the 1908–09 programme.[71]

In short, Ward not only failed to get a 'first-class dreadnought' — he failed even to get a first-class 'dreadnought cruiser'. To some extent the reasons were political. Fisher disliked stationing capital ships anywhere other than the North Sea, and two *Indefatigables* were less important than two *Lions*. Second-rate ships had, traditionally, always been deployed to foreign stations; and to put two older-design 'dreadnought cruisers' there was not unusual. The decision placated Australia without undermining the policy of central control. However, there also seems to have been a practical issue: the availability of heavy gun mountings. British dreadnoughts required five twin mountings against the two needed for earlier battleships. Into this mix came the dreadnoughts being built for foreign nations; and by 1908 there was an average six-month delay beyond contract delivery dates. It would have been possible for ordnance firms to expand their plant, but — as Jellicoe pointed out — they were reluctant to do so in an atmosphere of arms reduction.[72]

There was a particular bottleneck in 1909. British gun-makers Armstrong, Elswick and Vickers had mountings under construction or on order for the eight 1909 ships, the four ships of the 1910 programme, and for four foreign dreadnoughts being built in British yards. The issue was compounded by the change in the *Orion*, *Lion* and subsequent classes to 13.5-inch guns. The two 'colonial dreadnoughts' came on top of this, and it seems likely that converting them to *Indefatigables* eased the problem. Propaganda circulating at the time — repeated in *Jane's Fighting Ships* and naval texts for decades afterwards — listed *Indefatigable*'s 12-inch guns as the latest Mk XI 50-calibre version.[73] In fact, they were the earlier Mk X 45-calibre weapons, as fitted to the later pre-dreadnoughts and early dreadnoughts. HMS *New Zealand* received the 12-inch Mk X guns #370 and #372–374 made by Vickers, and #380–383 made by Elswick, on BVIII model mountings.[74]

James Allen — naval maverick

None of the doubts about the *Indefatigable* design were known outside the Admiralty, and Ward returned to New Zealand amid clamorous popular applause. A new Naval Defence Act authorised an eighteen-year sinking fund of up to £2,000,000 for the gift ship.[75] This came on top of the expanded subsidy, meaning that New Zealand's naval expenditure virtually doubled in the three years from 1910 to 1913.[76] The government accepted the Fairfield Shipbuilding Company's tender in January 1910, and work began in anticipation of the official contract, which was not signed for six months.[77]

The book-keeping associated with this work was tortuous at best. Normal channels ran from shipbuilder to Admiralty, but for the new battlecruiser the Admiralty forwarded the accounts to the New Zealand High Commissioner, Sir William Hall-Jones, who then had to cable Ward for authorisation to pay. This made sense for larger items such as armour — for which Hall-Jones was billed £190,000 in August 1910. He passed the account on with the comment that he had learned confidentially from Jellicoe that 'the armour for the cruiser would be as per a recent pattern (much superior to Krupp armour)'. However, the same procedure was followed down to a request for £20 to fit an extra dipole switch in an onboard workshop. On another occasion, £1 — the equivalent of about NZ$160 in early twenty-first century terms — was refunded because some brass hooks had not been used. This again ran the gamut of red tape.[78]

Naming the vessel was another challenge. The obvious name, New Zealand, had been given to a *King Edward VII* class battleship commissioned in July 1905. Ward proposed *Zealandia* for the new battlecruiser in May 1910, but McKenna preferred *New Zealand* and suggested renaming the older battleship *Wellington* 'as this is a name which has been used in the Royal Navy previously and at the same time the Dominion would retain her double-link with the Royal Navy'. Ward preferred *Maori*, but this had already been given to a 'Tribal' class destroyer; McKenna was reluctant to accept a double change, and Ward suggested shelving the matter for twelve months. By the end of the year there were two ships with the same name on the lists, and the gift ship was referred to variously as HMS *New Zealand* (C), 'The New Zealand Armoured Cruiser', or 'The New Zealand Battlecruiser'.[79] McKenna warned Hall-Jones that in the absence of a better suggestion from Ward he was considering *Caledonia* for the older battleship, which kept an Imperial theme running through the names of the class. The issue was not finally resolved until late 1911, when the battleship was renamed *Zealandia*.

These courtesies belied deeper problems. Fisher retired in 1910, and his political counterpart, First Lord Reginald McKenna, lost the post in 1911 when a change of government brought the vigorous young Conservative MP Winston Churchill to the Admiralty as First Lord, matched with First Sea Lord Sir Arthur Wilson. The naval arms race was in full swing by this time. Britain formally abandoned the 'two power' standard in April 1909, in favour of a margin of sixty percent over that of the next strongest naval power, Germany — a number essentially measured in dreadnoughts. Both governments were well aware of the cost of the race, but neither could agree on an appropriate ratio; at the time, Admiral Alfred von Tirpitz would agree only to 4:3, not the 16:10 implied by the British policy. However, the British would not accept anything less. Nor would they agree that the two 'colonial dreadnoughts' should be included in the ratio. To this extent, the wayward naval policies of the two South Pacific Dominions continued to have an effect at the centre of Empire.

So the race continued, despite the increasing financial burden it was placing on both governments, and by 1912, both Churchill and Wilson were influenced by the nightmare scenario of a sudden German bolt from the blue, when British ships were absent for repair, refit, or on foreign service. Churchill believed that, in any case, the Germans would issue from Wilhelmshaven on the outbreak of war for a second Trafalgar.[80] Consequently the number of dreadnoughts had to exceed the number expected to fight on 'the day' by quite a margin. Yet finances remained tight, and in February 1911 Churchill suggested cuts in capital ship construction which could be made up by 'securing' the two 'colonial dreadnoughts'.[81]

This came to nothing, but by the end of the year it was clear that Admiral Alfred von Tirpitz would persuade the *Reichstag* to increase German construction, and the building programmes of both Italy and Austria-Hungary were gaining momentum. 'The naval increases are serious and will require new and vigorous measures on our part,' an alarmed Churchill wrote in January 1912; 'the addition to our Estimates consequent on the German increase will not be less than three million a year.'[82] Once again he saw the 'colonial battlecruisers' as the answer. Writing to Secretary of State Lewis Harcourt, he argued that the Australians would probably want to keep theirs, although this ship was 'so important to our fleet in home waters', and suggested Britain 'should reduce our force in Australian waters at the earliest possible moment to a minimum'. He thought Japan would be kept in line by a 'strong continuing bond of self interest'.[83]

At Harcourt's suggestion he put the idea to Cabinet. However, the British had little to worry about. Although a request for permission to relocate HMS *New Zealand* was not forwarded to New Zealand until April, Thomas Mackenzie — briefly Prime Minister — thought the ship 'should be stationed where Home Government consider her service of the most value'.[84] This brought Ward's original aim of strengthening the Royal Navy at the centre back to reality. However, the flip-side of the 1909 Naval Agreement — local protection for New Zealand — also dissipated under the same pressures. Fisher had persistently refused to authorise light cruisers, feeling this type was unnecessary in a fleet that included battlecruisers. He finally relented in the 1907–08 programme, but cruisers were short: in point of fact, the shortages continued until the war emergency programmes started to take effect in 1915–16. By 1912 the two cruisers intended for New Zealand waters were needed elsewhere. The Admiralty offered two old 'P' class cruisers in compensation. As Churchill later pointed out, more was unnecessary since there were no vessels of equal power to be countered in New Zealand waters.[85]

Inevitably, this was not received well in New Zealand, where the renewal of the Anglo-Japanese alliance in 1911 spurred further alarm despite CID reports that the deterrent effect of the Royal Navy would prevent all but a few cruiser raids.[86] Prime Minister William Massey could not be induced to comment, and when Allen was sent to London at the end of 1912 to discuss the issue, local papers took the opportunity to criticise Massey for lacking defence policy.[87] Allen blamed Ward,[88] but this was pure politics, and when Allen arrived in London he had only a vague plan that revolved around developing a local New Zealand force. The issue, ultimately, was one of perception: Admiralty opinion was that New Zealand was adequately protected from afar, but that was not shared in Wellington. The problem was crystallising that dissonance into a practical policy. Churchill thought Allen was 'full of very foolish and retrogressive ideas'.[89] Allen later admitted that 'from the first it was evident that the First Lord held opinions as to the attitude New Zealand should adopt which differed from mine'.[90] There was crackling tension behind the diplomatic language — so worrying to Harcourt that he secretly sent the minutes of one meeting to the Governor-General of New Zealand, explaining that he felt he should inform authorities of the actual situation.[91]

By the time Allen left London he had agreed only that the annual subsidy would be diverted to run the old Australasian Squadron cruisers *Psyche* and *Pyramus* in New Zealand waters.[92] The Admiralty offered to send a third old ship, but Allen wanted modern vessels, and an exasperated Churchill finally told him that Britain did not have any to spare. 'There are apparently no foreign cruisers of an equal type which require to be met within thousands of miles of New Zealand. If there were, we should immediately match them by similar vessels.'[93] Massey responded with a request for two *Bristol*-class cruisers. He was told that if New Zealand wanted such ships it would have to pay for them. Massey felt he had little option, and at the end of October announced that New Zealand would order one.[94]

The Naval Defence Act 1913 got the ball rolling. Some historians have interpreted this as a new policy designed to provide New Zealand with its first naval force. However, although Allen wanted such a force, the development was forced by British policy changes, and Massey's initiatives were essentially designed to restore the position reached in the 1909 Naval Agreement — local cruiser forces coupled with a contribution to central defence in the form of HMS *New Zealand*. In the end even this did not quite work out. The *Bristol* class cruiser was not ordered, and the only addition to the ancient gunboat *Torch* and the two 'unspeakably useless' P-class cruisers was HMS *Philomel*, an even older cruiser. She reached New Zealand waters in early 1914 under Captain P. H. Hall-Thompson and was commissioned on the eve of the war as a training ship.[95]

The visit of HMS *New Zealand*

HMS *New Zealand* was formally commissioned in mid-November 1912 under Captain Lionel Halsey, amid talk of a 'thank you' visit to the Dominion. It was controversial. The New Zealand government was keen to have the ship in local waters for several months, but the Admiralty — still haunted by the spectre of 'instant war' — was reluctant to have the battlecruiser away from British waters too long. Halsey was no stranger to the South Pacific — he had been captain of HMS *Powerful* for three years — and went in to bat for the New Zealanders:

> *I am fully aware that it is most necessary & desirable that we should return as soon as possible to England, but I think the people of the Dominion would be very disappointed if we did not go everywhere possible & give as many as possible a chance to see the ship & I feel sure it would be the means of creating a great wave of Imperial loyalty.*[96]

In the end a proposed three-month stay was slightly cut to ten weeks, with a promise from the Admiralty that 'nothing but the most serious emergency will be allowed to interrupt the arrangements for her cruise'.[97] Most of New Zealand's seaports made it into the itinerary. Other destinations came and went as interested parties litigated. At one stage there were proposals to 'leave out Australia altogether', while another suggestion to visit South Africa was thought likely to 'detract from the prestige of the prospective visits by HMAS *Australia* which are by the invitation of the South African government'. An alternative route via the Suez Canal brought its own problems. 'The hydrographer remarks that the passage through the canal necessitates *New Zealand* being kept light.'[98] Special procedures were in force to move an

Indefatigable class battlecruiser through the canal — draft could not exceed 28 feet. The route was still under debate as late as January 1913, weeks before New Zealand was due to leave, and she finally sailed via the Cape of Good Hope. It was May 1913 before inclining experiments with HMAS *Australia* refined the canal instructions.

When New Zealand reached Wellington on 12 April she was welcomed by a fleet of small boats. There were official visits that afternoon, and people flocked on board when the ship was thrown open to visitors the next day. Some 15,154 people poured through the ship on 16 April alone. Officers and men were feted ashore. Some officers went on a three-day tour of a sheep station near Picton, while other parties were ferried to Rotorua. Even the ordinary sailors were treated like royalty. The ship spent more than a week in Wellington before heading to Napier.

Patriotism in Hawke's Bay seemed even greater. Twelve thousand visitors flocked into Napier on 25 April to see the 'mighty engine of warfare', which anchored in the roadstead, and was welcomed by seventeen cadets standing on Bluff Hill. By 9.45 a.m. a thousand schoolchildren were heading out to the battlecruiser on board the government steamer *Tutanekai*. Heavy swells made their transfer difficult, but eventually the children were able to board her, and *Tutanekai* returned to a wharf still 'black with children'. The whole town was in festive mood. Offices were closed and there were parades, bands, sports events, dinners, displays and dances. People thronged the streets to catch a glimpse of the ship's officers and sailors. Around three hundred sailors landed late in the morning and formed a procession led by the Napier Pipe and City bands and the ship's band. Flanked by cheering spectators and followed by cars, they marched to lunch at the Drill Hall in Hastings Street.

The officers were entertained at the Masonic Hotel by Napier's mayor, John Vigor-Brown, and invited guests. Sports began on Marine Parade in the early afternoon, and around seven thousand spectators turned up to watch as teams from the warship were matched off against local enthusiasts in a good-natured succession of sprints, relays, leap-frog and a sock-race. While this went on Halsey was taken on a drive to other local towns, including Taradale, Hastings and Havelock North. That evening the officers were entertained at the prestigious Hawkes Bay Club while the sailors attended a stage show at the Municipal Theatre — which was electrically lit for the first time. There were dances and songs on the Marine Parade. More visitors flocked to the ship the next day. The editorial in the local paper that night compared the gift to the Australian policy:

> ... Australia has commenced the formation of what is styled a 'local navy'. Opinions may differ as to which arrangement is the more suitable, which is the more likely to serve as stiffening to the naval forces of the Empire when, if ever, the test of talking guns must be faced ... as lovers of peace, we of course hope that the guns of the New Zealand may never have to be fired in anger, and that the navies which Canada and Australia propose to maintain may never have to essay the bloody task of defending the shores of those countries ... but ... should any such necessity arise we may be sure the traditions of our race will not be shamed.[99]

The ship went on to a similarly frenzied public reception at Gisborne, then turned south and steamed into Lyttelton on 13 May for an equally tumultuous welcome. Though delayed by a storm she eventually sailed to Akaroa for exercises with HMS *Pyramus*. Bad weather also forced Halsey to abandon a planned stop at Timaru, disappointing crowds of well-wishers — he later received 'one or two nasty letters'. At Oamaru, the seas eased enough for the ship to put a team ashore for a game of football. A fleet of small boats braved heavy swells as New Zealand steamed up to the Otago Heads on 31 May. She stood off the heads for three days until the weather calmed down, and Halsey was given a riotous reception in Dunedin. 'Enthusiasm ... seems to increase,' he later wrote to his mother, 'and it is awfully hard to keep going with all that one has to do.'[100] He made a special trip by train north to Timaru, stopping at Oamaru to unveil a memorial to the ill-fated Antarctic expedition of his friend, Antarctic explorer Captain Robert Falcon Scott.

New Zealand anchored off Wanganui early on 16 June and was met by *Tutanekai* and a local vessel, the *Himitangi*, with 700 children on board. Once again the crowds turned out in force, and there were lunches, ceremonies, sports meetings and special displays. One enterprising Wanganui shopkeeper even built a sugar model of the New Zealand for his window. Largesse from enthusiastic officials and the public alike included a cannon ball recovered from the wreck of the trader *Guide*, a decorated letter from the mayor and councillors, and a parcel of game — five deer, two swans, thirty-two pigeons, a hare and twenty lambs. The ship finally weighed anchor at 3.30 p.m., disappointing many who had hoped she would stay long enough to make an evening searchlight display; but she turned back and as dusk fell at 5.30 p.m. the display went ahead.[101]

Next morning HMS *New Zealand* arrived off New Plymouth. The wind had dropped and in bright sunny weather a record crowd estimated at 20,000 packed the shore to watch the battlecruiser arrive. Many of them later went on board — *Tutanekai* was joined by six local vessels and a huge number of smaller boats — but many people had to be satisfied with simply circling the battlecruiser. Halsey landed and was welcomed by the mayor. Later he turned the tap that officially opened the Taranaki Oil Well Ltd refinery — one of the first 'energy projects' in the province. Nearly 40,000 people lined the Auckland wharves to farewell the battlecruiser at the end of the tour. 'The extraordinary enthusiasm displayed by every person is wonderful,' Halsey later wrote. He was overwhelmed by this attention. 'It is all very embarrassing,' he explained; 'I feel much more like a king than a poor naval officer.' By his own estimate he made at least sixty speeches, which he found discomfiting. 'I don't like being the man of the hour at all.'[103]

There was no question about the degree of attention lavished on the ship, its commander and its crew. Of 47 official presentations made to the ship during the world tour, 30 came from New Zealand, including cups, trophies, two boar's heads, pictures, shields and items of memorabilia. Officers and crew were deluged with personal presents — flowers, souvenirs, clothes, knick-knacks, and a range of other items. Halsey's cabin became a virtual 'conservatory of flowers'. Gifts came from both Maori and European. Halsey himself was presented with Maori ceremonial clothes, carvings, rugs, a stamp album, and other pieces. One of the most important was a piupiu, a warrior's skirt of rolled flax, which the *Evening Post* reported as coming from Mana Hiniona, but which Halsey always attributed to Te Heuheu Tukino. Either way, it was presented on 21 April with the strict instruction that it had to be worn during battle — though Maori never promised that it would protect the ship from damage, which appears to have been a 'lower deck' legend.[102]

The ten-week visit by the battlecruiser had been an astonishing moment in New Zealand's history, because it marked one of the few times that an entire population had been roused to common public activity. Two out of every five New Zealanders had been on board, and many others had at least gone to see the vessel.

In many ways, the mass public enthusiasm shown over the visit of the gift ship transcended that of any other historical public event in New Zealand, except perhaps the public celebrations at the end of the two World Wars. The historical question is why. Some explanation for the contrast with more dramatic moments of large-scale public expression, later in 1913 and again in 1981, also has to be found. Public response at those times was driven by dissatisfaction with the *status quo*. The visit of HMS *New Zealand*, by contrast, was a joyous affair that brought the public together in common celebration.

What was happening? The answer can be found in the mind-set of the period. New Zealand was at the height of its 'jingo' era, an exaltation of imperial patriotism by which New Zealand was 'our country' but Britain 'our nation' and 'home', even for the rising proportion of the population who had never been there. As in 1909 when the offer was made, the tour of the gift ship keyed in to this national mind-set, a mood further bolstered by the socially-defined militarism of the period that had yet to be blown away by the slaughter of the First World War. This transcended politics, transcended the simmering issues associated with unionism that were running beneath the social surface of New Zealand in 1913, and brought New Zealanders out in droves to celebrate.

CHAPTER TWO
The Great War

> *Spent the day preparing for war. Steaming north destination unknown...*
>
> — Lt Commander Alexander D. Boyle, HMS *New Zealand*, Thursday 30 July 1914.[1]

Nobody expected war as the northern summer of 1914 unfolded in a glorious panoply of sun and the social whirl. And yet, before the end of it, the continent — with its world-wide empires — had been drawn into a conflict of a scale and lethality never seen before in the history of the world. In a way it was inevitable: Europe, by this time, was a powder-keg. The fuse was lit on the volatile brew of long standing economic rivalry, national ambition, old territorial grievances and complex alliances with their mechanistic mobilisation and war plans by the assassination of Archduke Ferdinand of Austria in Sarajevo on 28 June. It was not, of itself, a war-inciting moment; but it set in motion a series of events driven as much by pride, intransigence, and the automaton-like nature of mobilisation and war plans — which reflected long-standing German work on train timetables, among other things. Into the mix also came the idea that any war would be over quickly; to fight did not appear to be too great a risk, and the potential gains, certainly for Germany, seemed clear. So Europe lurched, inexorably, into conflict even as its diplomats and governments declared their hopes for peace.

By chance, months earlier, the First Lord of the Admiralty, Winston Churchill, had requested a test mobilisation instead of the usual July fleet review. This brought the Home Fleet up to full operation. It normally comprised the First Fleet of fully commissioned warships, backed by the Second and Third fleets, which were variously manned by sailors from barracks ashore, the naval schools, and reservists. All now assembled for exercises. On 26 July, with every prospect of conflict breaking out, the First Sea Lord, Prince Louis of Battenberg, ordered that the fleets were not to disperse.

New Zealanders R.T. Down, 25-year-old Lieutenant Alexander D. Boyle, Sub-Lieutenant Penrose L. Barcroft — known to his friends as Nick — and Midshipman Edward G.B. Coore were on board New Zealand when she joined the force off the Isle of Wight after hastening back with the other battlecruisers from an official visit to St Petersburg.[2] Boyle went ashore to play golf on the 27th as the fleet lay in Portland Harbour. 'No further news,' he scribbled in his diary.[3] On the 28th, Battenberg turned down Churchill's recommendation that the *New Zealand* should be sent to the Mediterranean to reinforce Vice-Admiral Sir Ernest Troubridge's armoured cruisers against the German battlecruiser *Goeben*. *New Zealand* began coaling that day at 5.30 a.m., taking on about 1000 tons. There was 'still no news about sailing or of our future movements',[4] but the Admiralty issued an official 'warning telegram' and Cabinet gave Churchill authority to take formal 'precautionary' steps. He and Battenberg decided it was time to send the Home Fleet to its war station, although such a move was provocative in this moment of crisis.

The news electrified the fleet. Most of the ships had men ashore. There was a scramble to get them back as night drew on. *New Zealand*'s complement was recalled aboard by squads 'piping' around the streets of Weymouth and Portland. The shrill whistling 'caused quite a sensation and woke up Weymouth who cheered the men as they left'.[5] All but eleven men were located. The ship had steam for 20 knots by 6 a.m. next day, and gradually the huge First Fleet left Portland Harbour.[6] They passed through the Straits of Dover at night, without lights — fearing a pre-emptive German destroyer attack, though war had not yet been declared — and into the North Sea. Boyle assumed their destination was Scapa Flow, but still felt there would be no war. 'I can't tell you why,' he confided to his diary on 30 July, 'but I do.' He was also realistic. 'I am probably quite wrong.'[7]

His thoughts were not surprising. The last all-encompassing war between Britain and a European power had ended 99 years earlier. It seemed incredible that another might break out; despite the way Europe was lurching into conflict, surely diplomacy would find answers. Even Churchill wondered whether 'armies and fleets could remain mobilised for a space without fighting and then demobilize'. He had barely had the thought when, as he later wrote, 'another Foreign Office box came in. I opened it and read "Germany has declared war on Russia." There was no more to be said.'[8]

The fleet reached Scapa Flow in miserable rain late on the 31st, and *New Zealand* at once began coaling. Tensions remained high, but Britain was not yet at war, and even the next day Boyle still hoped against hope.

> *I still feel there will be no war. I can't see how Germany can possibly take on Russia, France and ourselves even with Austria and possibly Italy. I wonder very much if my ideas will come true. I am the only person on board who thinks this way. If we were not ready and Germany knew it I think there might be [war] but as it is I can't see how it can be. It will be the end of Germany if there is. I think we are as ready as we can be for anything. They say everything is cut and dried at the Admiralty.*[9]

Boyle's optimism was quickly dashed. Germany began mobilising against France that day. By 2 August, Churchill considered war certain and formally mobilised the fleet. The same day German forces entered Belgium as part of the plan to bypass French defences, and Britain — which had guaranteed Belgian neutrality in 1839 — issued an ultimatum. In fog-bound Scapa Flow, orders went round to man half the guns. Boyle admitted his hopes of peace were becoming 'shaky' as the day wore on. The Germans indeed rejected the ultimatum, and at 11 p.m. on 4 August, as the chimes of Big Ben and the sound of singing crowds filtered through the open windows of the Admiralty offices, the 'war telegram' went out to the fleet — 'commence hostilities at once with Germany in accordance with remainder of War Standing Orders'.[10] All imperial warships around the world reverted to Royal Navy command, including *Philomel* — commissioned in New Zealand training service less than three weeks earlier. Admiral Sir John Jellicoe, the rising star of the Admiralty and part of Fisher's so-called 'fishpond' of favoured officers, was ordered to take command of the First Fleet and elements of the Second at Scapa Flow, renamed the Grand Fleet for the duration.

New Zealand's main naval contribution was manpower. Many Kiwis served on HMS *New Zealand* during the four and a half year 'war to end all wars'. The battlecruiser fought for the dominion by proxy, a patriotic focus of national and imperial pride for most New Zealanders. She was one of the few heavy ships in all three major North Sea battles. New Zealanders also took a lead role in the Dover patrols, less spectacular but more up-front naval activity that put them directly into the line of danger.

South Pacific and the Middle East, 1914–17

Naval forces in the South Pacific were on alert as the crisis intensified. The first warning telegram on 4 August advised that the ultimatum would expire at midnight and 'no acts of war should be committed before'. British merchant shipping was ordered to 'abandon regular tracks; complete voyages without bunkering if possible; reduce brilliancy of lights on arrival in United Kingdom; call early for orders', and to 'pass [this message] to all British ships'. Another message advised that 'in view of terms of our ultimatum they [Germans] may decide to commence operations . . . you must be ready for this'.[11]

War was a few days old when *Philomel* abandoned a shake-down cruise into the Marlborough Sounds, collected reservists in Wellington, and sailed for Auckland where she joined *Psyche* and *Pyramus* to escort *Monowai* and *Moeraki*, carrying some 1400 troops against German-owned Samoa. It was no cake-walk; the powerful German East Asiatic Squadron under Vice-Admiral Maximilian Reichsgraf von Spee had left Tsingtao (Qingdao) on 3 August and its location was unknown. The Admiralty thought it 'most improbable' that von Spee might know about the intended troop movement,[12] and there was no chance of the three old New Zealand cruisers defending the convoy; but they went on the basis that the battlecruiser HMS *Australia* would meet them at Suva. This did not happen. However, the force reached Noumea on 30 August without incident.

Von Spee was actually in the Marianas when the New Zealand convoy crossed to Samoa. He popped up off Apia on 14 September, believing HMS *Australia* was there and planning to engage her with torpedoes before he was sunk. In fact the harbour was empty, but he declined to attack the island. Von Spee was quitting the Pacific; Japan's entry into the war against Germany on 23 August made the region far too hot for comfort.

The New Zealand Expeditionary Force was readied for sailing to Egypt in late September. In the absence of firm news about von Spee, Massey's government balked at sending the troops without escort. The Admiralty argued that the Tasman was too far from coal sources for von Spee to get there, and as the only alternative was a six-week delay — during which time the Australians could use their fleet unit to get their own contingent across — Massey and Allen decided to send the transports with minimal escort. An alarming message from the Australian Governor-General aborted the attempt soon after the ships left Wellington. Aware of Australian delays, and in the face of Massey's threat to resign if an escort was not provided, the Admiralty despatched the armoured cruiser *Minotaur* and the hybrid Japanese cruiser *Ibuki*. The ships left Wellington on 16 October, joined Australian forces at King George Sound, and headed for Aden. Midway across the Indian Ocean the convoy discovered that SMS *Emden*, a detached light cruiser of von Spee's squadron, was nearby. She was defeated in a single-ship action by *Sydney*.

The New Zealand cruisers did not go to South Africa with the convoy. *Philomel* and *Pyramus* were ordered first to Singapore and then to Suez on 30 October, and *Philomel* went on to refit at Malta. This began an extensive Middle East service. She patrolled the Gulf of Alexandretta in early 1915, and — much as British naval crews had done in the same waters a century earlier — lost no opportunity to get at the enemy. It did not take long. Hall-Thompson observed a good number of pack animals transiting the coast towards Alexandretta, and on the night of 8 February '... sent an armed boat away with orders to land a party of two officers and fifteen men in a dry river bed and endeavour to intercept and catch ... one or two of the animals and inspect their packs'.[13]

The landing was unopposed, but as the men approached the pack track they were ambushed from three sides, and the 'retreat along the river bed was enfiladed'. Hall-Thompson opened fire with the cruiser's guns to cover the retreat. A number of the troop were later mentioned in Hall-Thompson's despatch, among them Lt RNVR Pirie Gordon and two Able Seamen, Gardiner and Stanbury, who 'carried a badly wounded man on his back during the whole retreat under heavy fire'. The men had to wait until darkness before they could be re-embarked. New Zealand Able Seaman J.T. Moreton was among the dead, reputedly the first Kiwi casualty of the war.[14]

More adventures followed when *Philomel* and the collier *Silverwing* were detailed to tow two gunboats to the Persian Gulf. They left in good weather, but on the night of 22 April the wind shifted and by 8.55 a.m. the next morning the gunboat *Sakkhara*, behind *Philomel*, was 'getting deep in the water aft and lifting her bow ominously'. Hall-Thompson decided to head for Safaja and sheltered waters, but at 10.28 a.m. the gunboat 'suddenly listed heavily to port'. She sank at 11.05 a.m. Hall-Thompson pressed on with the *Silverwing*'s tow *Cynthia*, but she too sank at 4.38 p.m., fifteen minutes after listing to starboard. This time the little gunboat turned turtle as she went down, revealing that 'one of the butts of the bottom plating, near the stern, had opened up, and this was the undoubted cause of her loss, and in all probability also the cause of the loss of the *Sakkhara*'.[15]

Philomel spent the rest of the year in the Middle East, moving to a beleaguered Aden in July when the town seemed likely to fall to Turkish siege. She spent several months in the vicinity, landing men to bolster the defences and suffering casualties to Turkish fire. Once this crisis was over the old cruiser was sent to Muscat 'with all despatch' — a technical term demanding three-fifths power. However, Hall-Thompson found that 'owing to [the] foul condition of [the] ship's bottom' he could 'not make passage at 3/5 horsepower' and had to cut back to 100 rpm 'which would normally give about 13 knots but produced about 11'.[16]

The cruiser spent most of 1916 around Muscat. She was in urgent need of a refit, but the work was postponed until January 1917 when she was inspected in Bombay. This revealed that *Philomel*'s problems were worse than imagined. Carpenter V. Rolling discovered that the hull was in good order above the protective deck, but the boiler bearers were buckled and the main transverse bulkheads were very thin, requiring repair to meet the 'strain which would be involved if large quantities of water were suddenly brought on them'. The inner bottom plating under the boilers was in poor condition. 'I think that if [the] ship was holed from any cause the inner bottom plating would not withstand the pressure which would be brought on it,' Rolling reported. He doubted that the plating could justifiably be repaired given the age of the ship — doing so would mean taking the boilers out. The upper deck plating was in poor condition and the ventilating trunks 'generally in a state of decay'.[17]

This was not the only bad news. Engineer Lt Commander H.W. Stedston discovered that the entire propulsion train was in a pitiful state as a result of deferred repairs, and thought it was a 'question for most grave consideration as to whether the utility of the ship would anywhere near justify the great cost which would be involved to make the ship efficient from an engineering and shipbuilding point of view'.[18] These discoveries were not surprising; the 26-year-old cruiser had essentially been on her last legs when she was sent to New Zealand in 1914, and had been worked extensively since. She was patched up for a journey to Wellington and paid off soon after arriving there in April. Recommissioned with a small maintenance crew, she was stripped of her guns and became a depot ship — a feature of the Wellington seascape for the rest of the war.

North Sea Kiwis, 1914–18

New Zealand's naval front line remained the North Sea. Defeat of the British fleet in home waters would have allowed the Germans to force peace terms to the financial and political detriment of the Empire. HMS *New Zealand* — the concrete expression of New Zealand's pre-war naval policy — was right on this crucial front line. She remained a focus for patriotic sentiment in the Dominion as a result. A few New Zealanders served on her during the war, and more than four hundred served on other Royal Navy ships during the conflict.[19]

The first days of the struggle were packed with tension. There had been an apparent brush with German forces as the fleet sailed north on the eve of the war. Admiral Sir John Jellicoe was appointed Commander in Chief the day before war broke out. Renamed the Grand Fleet, the force put to sea and spent 4 August 'searching for hostile ships' amid 'Beautiful clear weather'. They found nothing. The expected show-down, it seemed, would not happen that day. 'Spent night at guns,' Boyle told his diary, 'as we will do all the war.' Nick Barcroft led shifts on the 4-inch guns, 'looking out for destroyers'.[20]

As the days wore on it became clear that the High Seas Fleet under Vice-Admiral Frederich von Ingenohl would not emerge for a 'second Trafalgar'. Although the fleet assembled at the mouth of the Jade River on 1 August, German High Command regarded a fleet engagement as risky, and the fleet went back to Wilhelmshaven. Ironically, the opening months of the war were the only moment when a challenge might have been feasible. There were only twenty British dreadnoughts and four battlecruisers in the North Sea to counter fifteen German dreadnoughts and three battlecruisers. This was not an effective margin, particularly as the Germans could choose a moment when they were at full strength and the British were not. Although five capital ships were due to join Jellicoe's Grand Fleet by October-November,[21] their crews would take some time to work up. Jellicoe had to bring in the eight *King Edward* class pre-dreadnoughts, including *Zealandia*. However, the Germans did not seize the moment, and for the first few weeks the British chopped around the North Sea without hindrance, 'turning backwards and forwards to avoid submarines'.[22]

The first battle came at the end of the month. Harwich-based submarine commander Roger Keyes' boats were threatened by daily German antisubmarine patrols from Heligoland. He was a man of action, and his 'simple and daring' plan for pouncing on them, which he put to Churchill on 23 August, might have come from a *Boys Own* annual.[23] The idea of taking the fight directly into the enemy's territory harked back to the days of Nelson. The next day he discussed the scheme with Churchill, Harwich surface force commander Commodore Reginald Tyrwhitt, and First Sea Lord Louis Battenberg. The First Sea Lord suggested backing the raid with *New Zealand* and *Invincible* under Rear-Admiral Sir Archibald A. Moore. The sortie was authorised for the 28th. When Jellicoe found out, he added Vice-Admiral Sir David Beatty's three battlecruisers and Commodore W.E. Goodenough's 1st Light Cruiser Squadron. With good timing it would be possible to rush in and out while low tide kept heavy German forces trapped behind the Jade River bar. British plans even extended to an air attack on anchored German cruiser forces.[24]

The attack went ahead on 28 August. However, lapses in Admiralty staff work meant Beatty and Tyrwhitt were initially unaware of each other's presence. The air attack was cancelled at the last minute. However, Tyrwhitt's cruisers went into the bight at dawn, where they found and engaged the German light forces. The two battlecruiser forces rendezvoused at 5 a.m. and — as Boyle told his diary — 'steamed round in a square at our rendezvous waiting for news'. Around 10.15 a.m. *Invincible* fired on a submarine. *New Zealand* got away a single shot with a forward four-inch gun. Boyle also saw the German boat clearly through his range-finder. 'Got X-turret trained on her,' he later wrote in his diary, 'but she dipped before I could fire.'[25]

The plan soon went awry as the Germans rushed more light forces into the fray. Tyrwhitt's new flagship *Arethusa* was badly damaged, and at around 11.30 a.m. he called for support. Beatty sent Goodenough, but initially hesitated to commit the heavy ships. His Flag Captain, Ernle Chatfield, urged action. Around 11.35 a.m. Beatty wheeled his forces around and rushed into the mist, reaching the battlefield about an hour later.[26] Halsey caused a slight stir on board *New Zealand* when he arrived in the conning tower wearing the piupiu. His 'officers and men . . . [were] so startled at seeing me in this extraordinary clothing that they appeared to be quite incapable of carrying on with their very important personal duties and I had quickly to explain why I was thus attired'.[27]

Confusion reigned as British forces arrived, each unaware of the other. Goodenough's ships tried to ram the British submarine E-6. When Beatty neared the 'Saucy *Arethusa*', the latter's crew initially mistook his battlecruisers for Germans. However, his arrival was timely, as George Smith of the destroyer *Forrester* recalled. *Arethusa* came into view flanked by two German cruisers, 'spitting steel, fire and steam like a firework display . . . We came up on the disengaged side. I'll never forget that sight. The brand-new flagship looked like a scrap-heap.'[28]

From *New Zealand* the enemy was almost completely hidden amid 'thick fog caused by all the destroyer smoke'. Coore later wrote that it was 'very hard to distinguish anything owing to the haze'.[29] Boyle saw 'shells falling amongst the destroyers and the light cruisers firing as fast as they could at something'. He could not see the target, but eventually 'found that they [Harwich force] had captured a German light cruiser . . . She was in a frightful state . . . two out of three of her funnels were lying flat and both masts gone, well down in the bows and burning. It didn't look as if there could be many people aboard alive. We passed fairly close to her and went on at full speed in chase of other cruisers.'[30]

Around 12.40 p.m. *Lion* opened fire at a target that was invisible from *New Zealand* in the mist. This was the cruiser SMS *Ariadne*, which staggered off blazing into the mists. About this time *New Zealand* apparently came under attack from a German submarine. Then Halsey thought he saw two mines in the sea near the ship. Visibility was still appalling, but at 12.58 p.m. 'the flash of one gun was observed bearing about port 20', and A-turret 'got a round off at the flash', experimentally at 8000 yards because the range-finders could get no result. The German cruiser soon loomed into better view through the murk. Boyle, in X-turret on the quarterdeck, waited for the order to fire.

As she drew aft all turrets commenced mine in the stern last and then all I could see was the mast heads and occasionally the bow and stern the rest of her was enveloped in black smoke from bursting shells. She was only 4000 yards off. We fired for 20 minutes getting off 82 common shell at her, until her guns were silenced. X turret only fired 14 [shots] as the smoke from the other guns made it impossible to see half the time. The main cage of the left gun got jammed in the middle and that gun only fired 4 rounds. Not one of our shells hit . . . they nearly all went over. I could see her after guns firing till the end. When the smoke cleared you could see all her funnels down and masts gone and she was burning amidships.[31]

The cruiser was SMS *Köln*, and at 1.05 p.m. *New Zealand* fired two torpedoes at her. One 'caused a vast explosion, and flame burst up high'. The 'cease fire' gong sounded around 1.12 p.m. and the men had time to look more closely at the battered German ship, which by Coore's account still had a mast and two funnels standing. As they watched she appeared to fire a shot, and *Lion* reopened fire. After two salvoes the German cruiser sank by the bows, and Beatty signalled a general withdrawal. They had, as the papers later put it, singed the Kaiser's moustache. Surprisingly, although German heavy ships were able to cross the Jade River bar at noon, none arrived on the scene until about an hour after the British had departed.

Boyle thought *New Zealand*'s crew 'behaved very well indeed', adding that 'the cheer that went up when they heard that her guns had stopped firing was something worth hearing. P.O. Harrington my right gunlayer got very excited when first it started and flung his cap . . . cursing loudly. He is a very hot blooded Irishman.' However, he was less impressed with the technical performance. *Köln* had weathered the fire of the entire British battlecruiser force for twenty minutes, and survived a torpedo from *New Zealand* to boot. 'It was a very inglorious victory considering our superiority and I think the Germans very very gallant fellows . . . I trust some of them were saved.'[32] Coore was disgusted by *New Zealand*'s shooting, griping afterwards that 'far too many rounds were fired'.[33] Some 82 shells had been loosed, compared with 63 by *Princess Royal*, 68 by *Queen Mary* and 18 by *Invincible*.[34] Coore blamed the poor weather, but the performance was symptomatic of more general problems. It was partly because the battlecruisers lacked practice facilities, but there was also a belief that the battlecruisers did not need to practise. Being the dashing 'cavalry' was apparently sufficient.

Other problems also emerged during this first serious clash of the war. All the battlecruisers suffered from the blast of their own main armament. Boyle observed afterwards that: 'The blast of our own guns did considerable damage amongst the officers' cabins and messes.'[35] Cross-deck firing by the off-side wing turret was particularly difficult — the blast erupting from the muzzles tended to damage the deck planking. At many angles of engagement the ship was only capable of six-gun broadsides.

The British were at their nadir during the months that followed. Eight capital ships were taken out of service for various reasons during the latter part of 1914, and the super-dreadnought *Audacious* sank off Lough Swilly after striking a mine. The passengers and crew of the liner *Olympic* watched her go down. Churchill believed the disaster had to be kept from the Germans and persuaded the press not to say anything.[36] However, as H.C. Wright of HMS *Orion* later recalled, the news circulated as 'rumbling rumours which, being neither confirmed nor denied, increased public curiosity'.[37] Faced with demands to front up with the *Audacious*, the British disguised a merchant as the missing battleship. The fleet nicknamed her the 'lame duck', but:

> On the bow the name Audacious *stoutly defined its identity . . . Taking its place with the Second Battle Squadron the dummy battleship blithely carried out its clandestine role . . . One morning, through the first glimmering of daylight, a brand new battleship was discovered swinging around the buoy where the faithful imposter had acted out its important role . . . This was the first glimpse of HMS* Erin.[38]

For the Germans this was a golden opportunity to challenge British sea power, but they were poorly served by intelligence, and life for the Grand Fleet returned to the dull pattern of patrols and harbour duties. Boyle spent his 27th birthday at sea on board *New Zealand* as the battlecruisers — now based at Cromarty — sortied on rumour of a German raid. 'No letters!' he recorded glumly. 'No presents!'[39] Winter storms made life miserable. Gales ripped across the anchorage on 5 December, 'raining and blowing like nothing on Earth. Almost too bad to send any boats ashore. Nobody left the ship.' He had some leave a week later, braving 'beastly cold' weather to go ashore with Coore and another officer to 'flight duck with people called Duff'. He found they came from Hawke's Bay and had connections with his own family in Christchurch.

Battenberg resigned as First Sea Lord in late October amidst public dismay at his German ancestry, and Cabinet reappointed Fisher. Now aged 74, the old war-horse stormed back into the Admiralty, showed the bemused Sea Lords how he had taught a countess to dance, and tore into his duties with undiminished verve. He was at his best in the mornings when, as Churchill remarked, his 'drive and life-force made the Admiralty quiver like one of his great ships at its highest speed'.[40] When von Spee defeated a British cruiser force under Rear-Admiral Christopher Cradock off Coronel, Fisher and Churchill despatched two battlecruisers to catch them — risking defeat in home waters but ending the worst raider threat to New Zealand.

On 4 November, German battlecruisers under Vice-Admiral Franz Hipper shelled Yarmouth. The success of this raid spurred the Germans to devise a scheme to draw out part of the British fleet with Hipper's battlecruisers and ambush them with the High Seas Fleet. It almost worked. On 16 December, Hipper issued from the Jade with his 1st Scouting Group, supported by fourteen dreadnoughts, nine pre-dreadnoughts and a horde of lighter vessels. British intelligence — which had access to German codes — failed to note that virtually the whole High Seas Fleet was at sea. Beatty had four battlecruisers, which Jellicoe reinforced with six dreadnoughts of the Second Battle Squadron under Vice-Admiral Warrender. Difficult visibility and conflicting reports of German movements brought them close to encountering the High Seas Fleet. Wright, on board *Orion*, recalled the moment:

> *The Germans were steaming towards their own coast — we were steaming in the opposite direction to intercept them. We loaded, and trained our guns on the German ships and awaited the order to open fire. The King George V [Warrender's flagship] ordered 'Withhold fire'. Rear-Admiral Arbuthnot of the* Orion *said 'Those ships are enemy ships — permission to fire.' Warrender said 'Withhold fire — train guns fore and aft.' So the Germans got back to base . . . But it was divulged eventually that the High Seas Fleet was waiting over the horizon. Warrender had the responsibility of the 2nd Battle Squadron . . . He was no coward.*[41]

The cruisers were part of Hipper's screen, appearing briefly in thick weather as he pushed his way past the British. As Wright explained, the Second Battle Squadron could have 'given a good account of itself', but they would almost certainly have been overwhelmed. Churchill later tried to deflect criticism by pointing out that Warrender's force was at least a knot faster than the High Seas Fleet.

In January 1915 British intelligence warned of a further German sortie.[42] Beatty had five heavy ships, *New Zealand* among them. Hipper could muster three, supported by the armoured cruiser *Blücher*.[43] Jellicoe sailed from Scapa with the Grand Fleet. Beatty intercepted the Germans off the Dogger Bank around 8 a.m. on 23 January. The Germans were limited to 23 knots by the *Blücher*, and Beatty gave chase, calling for 29 knots although this was well in excess of what his ships could achieve. The *Lion*, *Tiger* and *Princess Royal* managed 27, which was two knots faster than *New Zealand*'s design speed, but the latter's stokers worked like demons and the older ship kept pace on an indicated output of 65,250 horsepower, 'giving a speed of about 27 knots'.[44] Meanwhile Halsey 'got many messages from all over the ship' hoping he might wear the piupiu again.[45]

This was the first battle ever fought between the heavy ships of the day. Nobody knew quite what would happen. Around 9 a.m. the 13.5-inch gunned British battlecruisers opened fire at the unprecedented range of 22,000 yards, and as his force surged up, Beatty ordered his leading ships to fire on opposite numbers. *New Zealand* engaged *Blücher* at around 9.30, which was a one-horse race although the battlecruiser could not 'fire with any degree of rapidity' because of the range.[46] Meanwhile Captain Henry Pelly of the *Tiger* mistook the instruction and, with *Lion*, concentrated on Hipper's flagship *Seydlitz*. This left *Moltke* able to fire without interruption on the *Lion*, which eventually came under attack from all the German battlecruisers. A 12-inch hit from *Derfflinger* at 10.18 a.m. displaced the belt armour and allowed seawater to flood into the port feed tank. British fire was relatively ineffective, though a spectacular hit on *Seydlitz* knocked out both after turrets and almost destroyed her.

While this went on the crippled *Blücher* swung in a circle. Her target was *New Zealand*, but none of her 8.2-inch shells came near. Complete British victory seemed imminent, but around 10.45 a.m. saltwater contamination forced *Lion*'s engineers to stop the port engines, and the flagship fell back. Six minutes later, Beatty thought he saw a submarine off *Lion*'s starboard bow and, by flag, ordered his ships to turn eight points to port. This took them across the stern of the fleeing German squadron. Worried that the Germans might drop mines, Beatty ordered a further change of course to northeast at 11.10 a.m. By this time the *Lion* was well behind, listing ten degrees, and seeing his fleet apparently swinging to attack *Blücher* Beatty added 'attack the rear of the enemy'. But the signal was hauled down with the earlier message to turn northeast, and consequently read 'attack the rear of the enemy, bearing NE'. This happened to be the *Blücher*, so the entire force abandoned their pursuit. Beatty tried to signal again, but was too far behind.

Hipper's battlecruisers consequently got away. *Blücher* did not. She was outgunned by *New Zealand* alone, and under the fire of the entire British force was hit around seventy times at ranges down to 6000 yards. By the time she struck her colours, at around 11.50 a.m., she was a 'regular shambles', her guns 'pointing in all directions'. She rolled over and sank about forty minutes later, leaving hundreds of sailors floating in the icy North Sea. Many died; the British picked up about 180 including the captain, but rescue efforts were hampered by a Zeppelin that 'dropped its bombs indiscriminately on the drowning Germans and the British rescuers'.[47] The 'battle of the Dogger Bank' was heralded as a British victory, but within the Admiralty there were heavy recriminations. Beatty's second-in-command, Rear-Admiral Sir Archibald Gordon Moore, aboard *New Zealand*, drew flak for letting the German force get away, but Fisher's wrath fell on Pelly — physical leader of the British line. 'Any fool can obey orders,' he stormed.

Australia arrived during April; Churchill wanted her in the North Sea, and the Australian government agreed, though it is debatable whether they would have done so if von Spee's cruiser squadron remained at large. Policy had turned full circle; for reasons unconnected with Ward's policies, *New Zealand* and *Australia* were stationed where Ward intended.

The long-awaited fleet action took place at the end of May 1916. *New Zealand* was in the thick of it. She had collided with *Australia* in fog north of Horns Reef in late April, but suffered only minimal damage and was back with the fleet by late May when reports came in that the Germans were planning to bombard Sunderland. Jellicoe ordered the fleets to sea on 30 May. Beatty's six battlecruisers and four fast battleships of the Fifth Battle Squadron reached a point off the Jutland Bank near the coast of Denmark about 2.30 p.m. the next day, and turned north to rendezvous with Jellicoe. At that moment a chance inspection of a neutral merchant by Beatty's light cruiser forces brought Hipper's outer cruiser screen into sight.

Beatty rushed towards the Germans, leaving the Fifth Battle Squadron behind — Rear-Admiral Hugh Evan-Thomas was not signalled until his ships were ten miles distant — and consequently Beatty's six battlecruisers alone closed with Hipper's five, opening fire at around 3.45 p.m. when the range closed to 15,000 yards. *New Zealand* was the fourth ship in line, behind *Tiger* and ahead of *Indefatigable*. British gunnery once again fell below par. Within a few minutes both *Tiger* and *Princess Royal* were hit. *Lion* was hammered by Hipper's flagship, *Lutzow*, and a shell slammed into Q-turret, wreaking havoc among the gun crew. About twenty minutes later a cartridge fell from one of the guns and caught alight. Though mortally wounded, turret commander Major Francis J.W. Harvey ordered the flash doors closed and the magazines flooded, saving the ship.

At length *Queen Mary* began hitting *Seydlitz*, but the pounding the Germans were handing out began to tell, and Beatty opened the range to around 20,000 yards, where only *Von der Tann* — whose guns could elevate further — remained in action. Around 4.05 p.m. *Von der Tann* landed a salvo on the *Indefatigable*'s quarterdeck, just as Beatty ordered a turn towards the Germans. The British battlecruiser failed to make the turn, trailing smoke and apparently sinking by the stern. Another salvo slammed into her fore turret. Observers on *New Zealand* watched in horror as their sister ship disappeared in a gush of flame and a monstrous cloud of brown smoke, topped with a 50-foot picket boat — intact but upside down. When the smoke cleared only the forepart remained visible, canted over and sinking fast. Over a thousand men died. The Germans could not believe what they had done:

> This is the first time we have ever seen a warship blow up. It is a bewildered moment before we realise that the armored [sic] giant is torn to pieces and that everything above the waterline has been hurled high into the sky. The long black barrels of the cannons are seen somersaulting in mid air. The huge store of oil is flung up and then rains down. It spreads upon the water and catches fire. Into this oceanic cauldron drop red-hot fragments of steel... For a long time a great ball of smoke hovers over the scene of disaster as if over the crater of a volcano.[48]

New Zealand almost suffered the same fate a few minutes later when an 11-inch shell slammed into X-turret, 'filling the turret with thick yellow fumes' and knocking a piece of 9-inch armour into the 'danger space' on the rollers. The blast was 'also felt in the centre sighting position and working chamber, but luckily no one was hurt'.[49] Although this did not impede the turret, other splinters on the roller caused problems, and the guns only fired two rounds before the crew had to clear the debris. The turret was out of action for about 25 minutes. Fortunately there was no fire; because of wartime munitions-handling procedures, which bypassed safety systems and left a trail of munitions through the system, flash from burning cartridges could easily have passed down into the magazines. As matters stood, *New Zealand* continued firing on the 'fifth ship', thought to be the *Seydlitz* — actually *Von der Tann* — and straddled her at 14,000 yards. Smoke quickly obscured the range, so she shifted to the fourth German battlecruiser.[50] About this time Evan-Thomas's four battleships — cutting corners to catch up — opened fire on *Von der Tann* and then *Moltke* with their 15-inch guns. Barcroft recalled how 'jolly glad we were to see them as things were getting a bit warm'.[51]

Things soon got warmer. Beatty sent his destroyers to attack Hipper's line just as Hipper's torpedo boats surged to attack the British. There was a brisk melee, during which three British destroyers were disabled and *Seydlitz* was hit with a torpedo. A few minutes later, at 4.26 p.m., five shells from *Derfflinger* and *Seydlitz* slammed into *Queen Mary*, and a massive explosion tore the ship apart. *Kapitän zur See* Moritz von Egidy of the *Seydlitz* heard a gunnery officer call: 'Number three going up in the air,' and heard Captain Richard Foerster shift their aim to the next ship, 'as precisely as though at drill'. But it was not a moment to miss:

> . . . *When I glanced over at the enemy through the torpedo telescope, my heart jumped to my throat. There, at a distance of ten miles, a huge immovable grey column stood up against the dull blue sky. It must have been two thousand feet across and ten thousand feet high. In its lower part black masses were whirling around. At the top, like an aureole, were glowing, darting spurts of flame. Beside its base something like a torpedo boat was sliding along. A torpedo boat? No, it was number four of the enemy's line, the* Tiger, *but it seemed like a tiny boat beside that immense column . . .*[52]

Observers on *New Zealand* saw *Queen Mary*'s stern rising high out of the water. Her propellers were still turning, but 'when abreast of us, there was another explosion, after which there was nothing left of her'.[53] Debris showered down, spattering sea and ships. A ring-bolt from the doomed battlecruiser was subsequently found on *New Zealand*'s deck.

A few minutes later *Princess Royal* was briefly shrouded in spray and smoke, and observers on *Lion* thought she too had been sunk. 'Chatfield,' Beatty reputedly said to his flag captain, 'there seems to be something wrong with our bloody ships today.' Moments later he ordered a turn towards the Germans. Now Beatty's advance cruiser squadrons sighted the High Seas Fleet coming up from the south. Intending to lead the Germans towards Jellicoe, Beatty swung his ships around and steamed north, but omitted to tell Evan-Thomas. As a result the four super-dreadnoughts did not turn for another ten minutes, and came under the fire of the High Seas Fleet. For a few minutes they fought a spirited duel with both Scheer's and Hipper's ships. Count Felix von Luckner, commanding a turret on the dreadnought *Kronprinz*, recalled that the 'ocean seemed to rock with explosions'. They were:

> ... showered with the 38 cm projectiles of the enemy dreadnaughts [sic] ... All around us rose columns of water as high as towers, as though the water were being sucked up into the sky ... Our ships ran through the colossal barrage, shaking incessantly from the explosion of projectiles in the water.[54]

Shooting fell away as the range opened. *New Zealand* fired sporadically 'on any battlecruiser appearing in the mist', and at 5.58 p.m. sighted the Grand Fleet off the port bow.[55] Poor visibility prevented Hipper seeing the approaching Grand Fleet, but he encountered the Third Battlecruiser Squadron ahead and east of Jellicoe's force. After a brief engagement *Invincible* disappeared in a great burst of flame as her midships magazines exploded.

Jellicoe became increasingly agitated as he steamed south on board his flagship *Iron Duke*. His scouts had failed to let him know where the Germans were, but he had to deploy the fleet from its six-column cruising formation into line. After some thought he decided to swing on the port column, letting most of his battleships fire full broadsides on the leading German vessels, which could only reply with a few forward guns. Deploying on other columns risked reversing the situation.[56] The High Seas Fleet was stretched out chasing Beatty, when von Luckner saw:

> *To the larboard three of John Bull's more ancient armored [sic] cruisers suddenly appear . . . Our salvoes strike home. Up in the air go two of them with their armored [sic] hulls torn to pieces and clouds of smoke where formerly ships and men have been . . . The climax of the battle now comes suddenly. Ahead on the horizon appears a semicircular sea of fire . . . The whole of the British fleet has entered the fight, the full line of Britain's superdreadnaughts [sic], the mightiest sea force in the history of naval warfare.*[57]

Jellicoe's decision paid off as the Grand Fleet pounded the advancing Germans with an extraordinary volume of fire. In just a few minutes a dozen hits were scored on the *Markgraf*, *König*, and the German battlecruisers. As the van of his fleet crumpled under the onslaught, Scheer had only one option — an emergency turn, long practised for such an eventuality. Less than twenty minutes after coming under fire, the High Seas Fleet was moving southwest. Firing fell away. Jellicoe angled the Grand Fleet due south, intending to cut Scheer off from his base. Incredibly, Scheer turned back towards Jellicoe. Later he argued that he was intending to upset Jellicoe's plans, but in fact he probably did not know where the British were in the murk and was trying to feel his way around their rear.

The result was disastrous; Scheer's 'T' was crossed a second time and his leading battleships again came under a massive cannonade. In desperation Scheer ordered a second emergency turn and sent his battlecruisers forward to draw British fire. This 'death ride' put them — as *Derfflinger*'s fire control officer Georg von Hase put it — '*in absoluten wurstkessel*' ('absolutely in the sausage boiler').[58] Scheer followed this with a mass torpedo boat attack, and Jellicoe — following his own prior dictum — turned away, opening the range and presenting narrower beam-on targets to the torpedoes. The combination allowed the High Seas Fleet to slip away into the mist, but Jellicoe had not issued the order without reason. It preserved his fleet at least risk, and he was still between the German force and their bases: he knew they would have to renew the engagement to get home.

Around 8.20 p.m., as the setting sun peeked beneath the overcast, the British battlecruisers spotted the German pre-dreadnought squadron to the west, and *New Zealand* fired some of the last heavy shells of the battle. Nick Barcroft was impressed:

Light was very bad for both sides now and we fairly shook them. It only lasted about a quarter of an hour, but during this period they never got a hit on any of our squadron while we were simply pelting them. We got about twelve direct hits on our opposite number who caught fire and was a sheet of flame and smoke from end to end and when it cleared away he had disappeared, sunk we hope. But he may have got away into the fog. But I don't think so. The remainder (two now) then also bolted and that was the last we saw of them.[59]

This was an exaggeration; but the moment marked the last heavy firing of the daylight action. Scheer — hoping to break past the British under cover of darkness — set course for Horns Reef and the nearest of the three channels through the German minefields protecting the Heligoland Bight. Jellicoe thought Scheer might choose a less risky path through one of the westerly routes and set course accordingly, but hedged his bets by stationing light forces in his rear. As the High Seas Fleet barged across the rear of the Grand Fleet in the dark, it ran into these forces and a string of fire-fights broke out. However, none of the commanders successfully reported Scheer's course to Jellicoe. 'Room 40' wireless interception in London picked up messages suggesting Scheer was heading for Horns Reef, but forwarded only summaries and failed to pass on a critical signal asking for air reconnaissance over that area. Jellicoe apparently had intended to turn for Horns Reef at 2.30 a.m., but was so certain the Germans were to the west of him — given the lack of evidence reaching him that they had broken through — that he held on. A Zeppelin passing west seemed to confirm his thoughts. In fact, Scheer reached Horns Reef at around 3.30 a.m. and got away.

Britain consequently did not fight a second 'Glorious First of June', and higher numerical losses smacked of defeat. In New Zealand there was a good deal of alarm. The coalition government led by Ward and Massey offered to buy the Japanese battlecruiser *Kongo* to help replace losses. This actually had a deeper impute in Wellington than mere patriotism. In 1909

Ward had viewed a gift dreadnought as a hedge against Japanese ambition once the German threat was gone. To strengthen the British with another gift, this time actually at the expense of the Japanese, was a more effective application of the same thinking. However, Britain declined to take up the offer, and in any case the ship was not for sale. Nor was any reinforcement necessary. Although the 'Jutland controversy' raged into the 1920s, ultimately devolving to an obsessive over-analysis of trivia,[60] the fact was that Jellicoe had out-manoeuvred Scheer and sent him packing, while preserving his total command of the seas. By any measure, Jutland was a strategic victory — thanks essentially to Jellicoe — and despite popular period expectations of a new Trafalgar, keeping command of the sea was all that mattered to the British as far as the wider war was concerned. The Germans knew they had received a drubbing and were 'astonished to find how small our own [losses] had been'.[61] Scheer abandoned his efforts to whittle down the Grand Fleet, and although the High Seas Fleet was back at sea in August, it sailed only rarely from then on. The blow to morale and long periods of enforced idleness of the crews in harbour was one of the factors behind the fleet mutinies of late 1918, which became wider revolution and brought Germany to armistice.

HMS *New Zealand* fired 420 12-inch shells during the battle, more than any other heavy ship on either side, but apparently scored only four hits, three of them on *Seydlitz*, a success rate of less than one percent. The result underscored the dismal state of battlecruiser gunnery at the time.

Jutland was also her swan song. Investigations indicated that the magazine explosions which sank the battlecruisers and the armoured cruiser *Defence* were likely caused by wartime munitions handling procedures, which had been accepted by the officers and improved the rates of fire, but which also bypassed safety protocols and left a trail of high explosives from the turret into the magazines. This meant that a penetrating hit on a turret risked destroying the ship. However, suspicion also fell on the adequacy of battlecruiser armour. This was known to be below par at certain ranges, particularly given the way heavy gun-power had risen. To avoid embarrassment over the authorised lapses in operating procedure, the official explanation blamed the armour. But the cover-up was moot in any event, because the improved armour-piercing shells introduced after Jutland, along with the ranges at which battles were being fought, meant that even armour schemes and the thicknesses previously thought adequate were no longer going to cut it.

All the battlecruisers were docked over the next few months for modifications to meet the armour issue. However, the best that could be done within the limits of their design was to add plates in a few critical areas, notably around the magazines, largely to catch splinters from shells penetrating the main armour system. Manpower and equipment shortages meant that *New Zealand* even missed out on some of these improvements.[62] Fisher fumed and spluttered about the fall from grace of what he called his 'New Testament' vessels, but in the end even he relented. In 1919 — aged 79 — he looked to a different future. 'The greatest possible speed with the biggest practicable gun was, up to the time of aircraft, the acme of sea fighting,' he explained in his memoirs. 'Now, there is only one word — submersible.'[63]

Submarines certainly provided a salutary lesson during the war. U-boat captains at first surfaced with colours flying and invited their targets to surrender, as required by international law in the time-honoured tradition of eighteenth century frigate. But in 1915 the German *Admiralstab* (Admiralty) changed the rules. Submarines began attacking without warning from beneath the waves. The strategy sent shock waves around the world, and the loss of the liner *Lusitania* threatened to bring America into the war. The policy was called off, but Germany re-implemented it in early 1917, and within months Britain was at crisis point. Jellicoe, as First Sea Lord, initially refused to implement a convoy system, and Britain came within a whisker of the starvation Fisher had predicted in 1904. Fisher himself was appointed to head a committee investigating underwater sound-detection systems in 1917. Members included Ernest, Lord Rutherford, the New Zealand scientist who had split the atom and who now turned his formidable talents to applied physics underwater. Convoys were implemented, and efforts focused on baiting U-boats into action with 'Q-ships', innocent-looking merchants with concealed armament designed to take advantage of the fact that U-boat commanders still preferred to sink merchants with their deck gun.

New Zealanders served on the Q-ships. Perhaps the best known was Aucklander William Edward Sanders, who volunteered for the Royal Naval Reserve in 1915. He reached Britain the following year, serving in three ships before being given the *Prize*, a schooner captured from the Germans at the outbreak of war. While patrolling south of Ireland in April 1917, Sanders' command was spotted by U-93, under Lieutenant-Commander Freiherr von Spiegel, who surfaced to attack. Sanders went through the deception routine, even sending a 'panic party' to apparently abandon ship. Von Spiegel nonetheless delivered a ferocious cannonade for nearly twenty minutes before closing in. Despite the rising toll of damage to his ship, Sanders held his fire until the German boat was about seventy yards distant. Then he raised the White Ensign and opened fire. At that range the guns were decisive; the U-boat slid past, apparently sinking by the stern. Only three of her crew were picked up, Spiegel among them.

It turned out that the German boat did not sink; but it had been a dramatic action by any measure. Sanders was promoted to Lieutenant Commander and awarded the Victoria Cross. He did not enjoy the honour for long. *Prize* was repaired and by August was back at sea, this time with the submarine D-6. They hoped to use the Q-ship as bait while the British submarine attacked. Heavy swells frustrated D-6's efforts to manoeuvre into firing position when they found U-48 on 13 August. Sanders engaged the U-boat directly, but only managed to get two hits before it slid away. They could not relocate the German boat. In fact U-48 was quietly stalking the Q-ship and attacked in the early hours of the following morning, while D-6 was alongside recharging her batteries. The first the British knew of the attack came when the Q-ship exploded in a sheet of flame, heeled over and sank with all hands.

Kiwis on the Dover Patrol had an adventurous war. Christchurch-born Charles Williams served on destroyers in the waters between Britain and France. These were frequented by German light forces helping U-boats slip out to the Atlantic. Williams was aboard HMS *Broke* in April 1917 swhen she was caught by six German destroyers off Dover, supported only by *Swift*. In April 1918 Williams volunteered for another of Roger Keyes' escapades, a daring raid on the Belgian port of Zeebrugge intended to deny it to the U-boats. Williams distinguished himself again during the assault on the Zeebrugge mole and survived the war to find work on the *Tainui*, but was among those lost when she foundered in heavy seas near Lyttelton in September 1919.

The *Wolf* and the Sea Devil

Once the German East Asiatic Squadron had been sunk, New Zealand's only direct wartime threat came from raiders running the North Sea blockade. The first to reach New Zealand was the *Wolf*, under Captain Karl August

Nerger. The converted steamer was equipped with 5.9-inch guns, torpedoes, mines and a floatplane, and left Hamburg in November 1916. Nerger broke through the blockade by stealth, and during a cruise that lasted fifteen months captured or sank fourteen merchants. His exploits drew admiration even from his enemies. 'A great ship,' one of his prisoners later wrote. 'A great cruise. A great commander.'[64]

Nerger arrived in New Zealand waters in June 1917 and anchored off Sunday Island, one of the Kermadecs, for an engine overhaul. The Germans were soon found by the steamer *Wairuna*, whose crew were puzzled to see an apparent tramp lying at anchor. The Germans reacted quickly. *Wairuna*'s wireless operator Roy Alexander was about to have afternoon tea when he heard a low-flying aircraft and rushed on deck to see a biplane with German markings. The 'observer could be clearly seen dangling a long, pear-shaped bomb over the side', while a 'strange ship' stood off with guns trained.[65]

Wairuna was stripped and sunk, taking her cargo of New Zealand hides, flax, wool and kauri gum to the bottom. A few days later the steamer *Winslow* appeared and was also captured. Nerger now steamed for New Zealand, where *Wolf* laid 25 mines near the Three Kings Islands, and a second field of 35 off Farewell Spit. Nerger crossed the Tasman to lay another minefield off the Australian coast, and began steaming along the Sydney–Suva track. He found a benzine-laden schooner, which he pillaged and sank, and a few days later located the sailing vessel *Encore*, carrying 900,000 linear feet of Oregon pine. The hungry Germans found she was also stocked with 'cases upon cases' of canned food. 'When he sighted these luxuries coming alongside, one German officer was heard piously thanking his Maker that, coal or no coal, the *Encore* was an American ship and not a British tramp.'[66]

By this time the raider had been at sea for seven months and was reliant on coal and food looted from her victims. Prisoners' fare was mainly black bread 'in a delicate colour combination of dark blue, streaked through with patches of moss green', often accompanied by 'preserved meat and rice or dried potatoes'. The potatoes 'looked, tasted, and smelt like warmed-up superphosphate'.[67] The rice came from a cargo captured in the Indian Ocean and was 'issued continually', either as a substitute for vegetables, or mixed with cinnamon 'as a sweet dish'. Later, an American capture provided a vast supply of prunes, which were cooked with meat to make a 'sugary soup' that Alexander noted was 'an acquired taste'.[68]

By early August *Wolf* was cruising the Brisbane–Port Moresby route, where Nerger captured the *Matunga*, whose cargo included 500 tons of Westport coal. The two ships put into isolated Offak Bay, New Guinea, where *Matunga* was stripped and *Wolf* overhauled before the raider set off for Singapore and the long journey back to Europe. It was not easy; *Wolf* had been too long out of dock. The crew had to struggle against leaks, fuel shortages and a disastrous lack of fresh food. She nevertheless ran the British blockade and returned to Germany in February 1918 with scurvy-riddled crew and prisoners, ending a journey of some 64,000 miles.[69]

Wolf's mines floated undetected in New Zealand waters until December 1917, when the 4770-ton freighter *Port Kembla* went down after striking one off Farewell Spit. New Zealand authorities initially put the loss down to sabotage, but then a bottle dropped by one of *Wolf*'s prisoners — Captain Meadows — floated ashore warning of the fields. Three trawlers were promptly pressed into service as minesweepers and eventually found most of the sixty mines. However, they were too late to save the *Wimmera*, which ran into the field off the Three Kings in mid-1918 and sank with the loss of 26 lives. The news prompted a major search and a government request for aircraft to help patrol local waters.

Perhaps the best known South Pacific raider remains Count Felix von Luckner, whose exploits became famous in the 1920s when he dictated his 'salty yarns' to Lowell Thomas.[70] His accounts were presented with a very healthy spin, intended to present von Luckner as an honourable man, friends with everyone – including his enemies, who were merely other sailors, all chums really. The image presented was one of a long-standing career sailor, nice guy and honourable officer who professionally pursued a war strictly by the rules, without animus and who saw it, in effect, as an elevated form of sport. This was not quite true, though the fact remains that no-one died as a result of von Luckner's wartime cruise. 'It is better sport to capture men than to take their lives,' he later wrote. He also despatched 86,000 tons of allied shipping to the bottom during his 224 days at sea, and his adventures gained him the nickname 'Sea Devil'. He joined the Imperial German Navy at twenty, and in late 1916 was offered command of the captured American clipper *Pass of Bahama*, renamed *Seeadler*.

The ship broke through the British blockade disguised as a Norwegian trader. Von Luckner later claimed that neither he nor his 64-man crew could speak a word of the language, though other accounts suggest a Norwegian-speaking crew had been specially selected.[71] In any event, *Seeadler* was intercepted by HMS *Avenger*, an auxiliary cruiser which before the war had plied New Zealand waters as the *Aotearoa*, and the inspection crew were completely fooled. Von Luckner's first victim was the steamer *Gladys Royal*. Searching for new targets, he offered ten pounds and a bottle of champagne to anyone on board — prisoners included — who spotted a ship. Nobody suspected the clipper was a warship, and von Luckner captured three steamships and a number of sailing ships. *Seeadler* was soon crowded with prisoners. Capturing a French clipper gave von Luckner the opportunity to free them, but he knew they would raise the alarm and decided to make for the Pacific.

Magellan's ocean was less fruitful. Von Luckner found only three ships in five months. The cruise came to an abrupt end in July 1917 when *Seeadler* approached the Society Islands for fresh food and water. They had been several days at Mopelia when a freak wave smashed the clipper against the reef. She was a total loss. The refugees made themselves comfortable, but von Luckner decided to sail to the Cook Islands in the ship's whaler. Christened *Kronprinzessin Cecile*, the 18-foot open boat leaked even after repairs. However, von Luckner and five picked men set out in the hope of capturing a ship and returning to Mopelia. They reached Atiu after three days, but found nothing. Nor was there a ship at Aitutaki, where they were recognised as Germans.

Von Luckner then decided to head for Fiji, a bold decision that relied on remarkable seamanship and a healthy dose of luck. The men suffered from exposure and then developed scurvy. In mid-September they reached Katafanga, in the Fiji group, where they spent several days recovering before approaching Wakaya. Here they found several schooners in harbour, but their cover story about being Dutch-American sailors crossing the Pacific for a wager was not believed. Hearing reports from Wakaya, Inspector Arthur Howard and Sub-Inspector Harry Hills of the Fijian police force suspected they were German and chartered the steamer *Amra* to investigate. They were just in time. Von Luckner and his men were on board a schooner when *Amra* arrived. Howard, Hills and half a dozen Fijian policemen rowed across. Their only weapon was Hills' revolver and a pistol, and von Luckner's men were well armed with grenades and machine guns. A very nervous Hills implied that canvas-covered objects on *Amra*'s deck were guns. Von Luckner and his men surrendered. Later the Count was furious to learn they had been bluffed.

After a period in a Fijian jail, von Luckner and his men arrived in Auckland on board *Talune*. They were held in the Devonport torpedo yard for protection against an angry public, who believed them responsible for sinking *Wairuna*. Secretly transferred to Wellington, von Luckner stood trial but was able to convince his captors of his innocence and the case was dismissed. He was imprisoned on Motuihe Island in the Hauraki Gulf, while his crew went to Somes Island in Wellington Harbour, although one was transferred to Motuihe.

Von Luckner's fellow prisoners were Germans from Samoa, interned for the duration. They had assembled a good deal of escape equipment, but had no specific plans. Von Luckner soon came up with a scheme to capture the camp's motorboat *Pearl*. Under cover of producing a play, he organised supplies, ammunition, and a large German ensign. They also stole some New Zealand army uniforms. With his keen sense of post-fact justification, von Luckner later claimed he would not fight out of uniform, though in reality the clothing was probably part of the escape plan. Stormy weather provided cover for the attempt on the night of 13 December 1917. Barracks were set alight, telephone lines to the mainland were cut, and von Luckner, Lieutenant Kircheiss and seven merchant navy cadets made good their escape. Von Luckner had been on Motuihe only three weeks.

News of the escape shocked New Zealand. A search of the Hauraki Gulf failed to find the Germans, and it was thought *Pearl* had foundered in high seas. In fact, the Germans reached Red Mercury Island and then spotted two traders, *Rangi* and *Moa*. Von Luckner hoped to seize both, sink one, and sail away in the other. *Rangi* proved too fast, but he got the *Moa*. This 127-ton scow under Captain Bourke had a crew of five and an 11-year-old passenger. Von Luckner told them that as civilian prisoners of the Kaiser, they were eligible for payment for their period of captivity, and set course for the Kermadecs where there was a government stores cache, raising sail despite a storm. *Pearl* sank under tow and most of *Moa*'s deck cargo went over the side, but they reached the Kermadecs on 21 December. Volcanic gases made it dangerous to leave the prisoners near the cache, and von Luckner decided to take them to nearby Macauley Island and radio for someone to pick them up. As they were about to depart, the armed steamer *Iris* arrived. She had sailed directly from

Auckland on the assumption that von Luckner would make for the cache. The Germans clapped on sail and attempted to flee, but the *Iris* opened fire, and von Luckner had to surrender.

He spent a fortnight in Mount Eden jail, a 'hard bad prison' as he recalled, then the Germans were distributed among various camps.[72] Von Luckner and Kircheiss went to Fort Jervois, now a prison camp under Major Leeming, who von Luckner recalled was 'one of the best fellows I have ever met'. Bored by prison routine, Leeming soon joined the Germans at regular card games. Von Luckner lost no time finding ways to escape. He noticed that empty tar barrels were regularly thrown from the quayside and picked up by a coastal schooner. He planned to hide in one, armed with a knife. Once picked up, he would leap out 'like a jack-in-the-box', taking the crew by surprise and returning to collect Kircheiss before sailing for Mopelia. It was an outrageous plan which von Luckner could hardly have got away with, though he was an expert boxer and as strong as an ox.[73] In any case he was transferred back to Motuihe before he could carry it out. Later he claimed he could not dishonour Leeming by escaping while his prisoner, and was waiting until the commander went on leave.

At Motuihe, von Luckner discovered that fresh escape plans were well advanced. Armed with three stolen pistols, the prisoners intended to hide in a cave. When the furore died down they would seize a passing ship and make good their escape. Von Luckner scheduled the attempt for 18 November 1918 — then cancelled it when the armistice was signed on the 11th.

Von Luckner left New Zealand in March 1919, and was showered with honours when he got back to Germany — including a PhD, which he found amusing.[74] *Seeadler*'s crew came home in January 1920. They had seized a passing schooner and left Mopelia, but were wrecked on Easter Island and interned in Chile. During the 1920s von Luckner popularised the scout movement in Germany, and gained a significant public profile on the back of his wartime adventures, which he re-cast to suit the image of a cheerful sea captain for whom everybody, enemy or not, was really a friend.

This was reinforced in a biography penned by Lowell Thomas, and was doubtless genuine as far as it went. But it was also disingenuous. Like Nerger, Karl von Müller of the *Emden*, and other German raider commanders of the war, von Luckner had played by the rules of the day as far as possible; but he was also a loyal German and had done whatever was needed to fulfil his duty and prosecute the war. Later he developed ties with senior Nazis, notably Reinhard Heydrich. However, during the early inter-war years, when wartime Germans were still widely portrayed as the dastardly Hun, von Luckner's wartime exploits and his careful re-spinning of them afterwards struck chords.

That was particularly true in New Zealand where von Luckner's dramatic escapes had always been seen as carrying a level of derring-do and personal *Boys' Own* style courage. When von Luckner returned to New Zealand on board his yacht *Seeteufel* in 1938 he was treated as a national hero. And — to give him his due — he had not caused a single casualty during his raiding career. While he knew he was exaggerating at times when telling his tales, such expressions, perhaps, represented what he had hoped his war might have been. He expressed the sentiment years later, when he was reputedly asked whether he feared the danger of his wartime exploits. 'Of course not,' he replied. 'We were all gentlemen then.'

CHAPTER THREE
The 'locust' years 1921–39

The end of the 'war to end all wars' did not significantly change New Zealand's naval position. Millions had died, the map of Europe had been redrawn, the old monarchies had fallen, and the balance of world power had shifted. Yet in the South Pacific the old naval problems remained. Japan was still a worry to both Australia and New Zealand, the more so as war ended and a Sino-American naval arms race brewed. These concerns about Japanese ambition were at last shared by Britain, which allowed the alliance with Japan to lapse in 1922.

Britain again remained the linchpin of any defence strategy, and the New Zealand government continued to explore ways of supporting wider imperial defence, while securing local forces to meet secondary threats in New Zealand waters. However, four years of war had exhausted the home country financially, morally and spiritually. The Royal Navy was shrinking even before the Five Power Treaty of 1922, usually known as the 'Washington Treaty', fixed its size at less than half the wartime level. Direct defence of New Zealand waters was also in trouble; the cruisers had gone, with the exception of the worn-out *Philomel*.

Historians have traditionally seen the resolution of all these issues as an extension of the 1913 policy, modified by reliance on the 'main fleet to Singapore' strategy. In fact, the approach adopted in the 1920s was an extension of 1909 thinking, by which New Zealand operated a cruiser-based division of the Royal Navy but looked to ways of supporting British power at the centre. After the war, a modification of the 1909 compromise — focussing that support on the British-driven strategy for Pacific defence — seemed a useful way of reconciling New Zealand's ideas with the fact that Canada, Australia and India preferred having their own navies.

The Jellicoe mission

Ward and Massey, as joint leaders of the wartime coalition government, went to London in 1917 to argue for a post-war naval settlement that continued the themes both had been peddling for over a decade. Imperial co-operation seemed essential — Ward thought the burden of worldwide defence could not be handled by Britain alone. At the same time New Zealand's local waters needed direct defence. How this might be met remained a moot point. Gift ships had never been a real option. The Admiralty wanted cash contributions, and dominions other than New Zealand wanted a greater stake in their own defence. War experience seemed to underline this approach; the Australian fleet unit had integrated so smoothly with British forces in 1914 that there seemed good reason for other British possessions to adopt the same line. New Zealand, once again, seemed to be in a minority of one.

The issue came up again in 1918 when Massey — pushed by Allen — leaned towards a local fleet. The Admiralty still wanted financial contributions. Again, no decision was taken other than to agree that the dominions could discuss their needs with Britain. Canada rejected Admiralty ideas in August, and the Admiralty suggested that an officer might advise the dominions after the war. The Australians thought Jellicoe was the man for the job. He was on half-pay, and offered the task in November 1918.

This sounded promising, but the Admiralty was lukewarm about the venture. Jellicoe was on the outer, and unable to discover their plans for post-war naval strategy and strengths, and his efforts to get this information during a cruise on HMS *New Zealand* failed. He knew that thinking revolved around a base in Singapore, and that early post-war schemes for a fleet of 41 capital ships had been dashed, but — as he wrote later — 'no definite suggestion as to the strength of the co-operation of the various Dominions could be put forward by me without some knowledge of the strength of the future navy that was needed for the whole Empire'. As the Admiralty would not tell him, his only recourse was to 'form my opinion . . . and to base my recommendations on this opinion'.[1]

The mission had clearly been set up to keep the Dominions quiet. It was also another slap in the face for Jellicoe, and perhaps fortunate that the journey on board HMS *New Zealand* served the dual function of thanking New Zealand for its contribution. His itinerary ultimately took in India, Australia, New Zealand and Canada. He was promoted Admiral of the Fleet shortly before reaching Bombay, a singular honour which only highlighted the way he had been sidelined. He was in Sydney on 19 July when peace was formally declared, and reached Wellington in August to a riotous reception. *New Zealand* and her distinguished guest were feted with undiminished enthusiasm. This gave Jellicoe the distraction he needed to avoid dwelling on the depressing task of preparing proposals that were almost certainly going to be ignored by the Admiralty. He worked diligently, borrowing papers from the Minister of Defence, Naval Advisor and other officials. He consulted Massey, Ward and Allen, and by 2 September — when the battlecruiser was anchored near Picton — he had virtually finished his task.[2]

Jellicoe's proposals linked to a wider scheme for Australasia and the Far East, for which he envisaged a fleet of eight battleships, eight battlecruisers and ancillary ships based on Singapore. A proportion would be held in Australasian waters and paid for by the two dominions. New Zealand's portion would become a 'New Zealand Division' of the Royal Navy, growing to three light cruisers, six submarines, a 'submarine parent ship', and smaller craft. Jellicoe did not think dockyards were needed but recommended converting *Philomel* into a training ship.[3] He also wanted an air component, including five flying boats, a supporting carrier and an Auckland school. At £81,750 per annum this was less than a third the price of rival air force proposals put forward by visiting RAF Colonel A. Vere Bettington,[4] which in any case stood little chance in the face of naval priorities.[5]

The total costs of Jellicoe's scheme — including a schedule to repay the HMS *New Zealand* loan — were projected to start at £461,307 in 1920–21, peaking at £1,319,841 in 1927–28, but dropping to £1,123,434 after the *New Zealand* loan was paid off.[6] The scheme was essentially a revision of the 1909 naval agreement, updated to cater for post-war changes, but driven by the same thinking. As in 1909, Jellicoe viewed local forces in both Australia and New Zealand as integral portions of a British Far Eastern fleet. Again as in 1909, this reconciled the Australian need for an independent fleet with the British need to maintain unity. Jellicoe also took into account the ability to pay — New Zealand's share was five percent of the cost of the Far Eastern fleet. In New Zealand at least, the ideas made good sense, enabling the country to make its long-desired contribution to central defence while supporting the defences needed for local waters.

New Zealand and the Washington Conference

To some extent, the Admiralty's failure to give Jellicoe insight into their policies was inevitable. The future was also unclear to them. By 1918 an alarming naval race had brewed between Japan and the United States. Britain was in neither the fiscal condition or the moral mood to play along. The 'war to end all wars' had been won at the cost of a generation, and the parlous state of Britain's post-war finances dashed early plans for a fleet of 41 battleships. In August 1919 the British government initiated the 'ten year rule' — by which the armed services should plan on not having to fight in the next ten years. The idea came from the Treasury. The Admiralty disagreed, and the argument bubbled into virtual warfare over the 1921–22 naval estimates, which the government wanted to slash to £60 million from the Admiralty's recommended £85 million. At stake were the Admiralty's response to the Pacific naval race, four enormous and very fast battlecruisers that were more heavily armed and better armoured than any battleship. Four even more powerful battleships were projected to follow.

Paying for them was another matter. Britain was in no position to start building a fleet at £10 million a ship, particularly as new docks were likely also required. Massey hoped New Zealand might contribute financially to the new ships, and believed the 1921 Imperial Conference had laid the groundwork.[7] However, other nations faced the same strictures, and when Britain proposed a naval arms limitation conference in July 1921 the suggestion fell on fertile ground. The British government added £2.5 million to the 1921–22 Estimates for the battlecruisers, but this was only a bargaining counter.

Delegates from Japan, Britain and the United States convened in Washington in November to deal with a raft of issues, including renewing or replacing the Anglo-Japanese alliance. The British contingent included representatives from the dominions, which had become individual members of the League of Nations in 1919 and in theory had separate voices. However, the New Zealand government despatched Sir John Salmond, former Solicitor General and High Court judge, to speak with Britain and the other dominions 'as constituent portions of an undivided empire'.[8] Delegates concluded five separate treaties, including an agreement relating to poison gas and another dealing with customs tariffs in China. From New Zealand's perspective the two most important were the Five Power Treaty and the Pacific Treaty. The latter, signed by the British Empire, the United States, Japan and France, replaced the Anglo-Japanese alliance and was designed to define the interests of the signatories in their various Pacific Island territories, and to establish mechanisms for resolving disputes.[9]

United States Secretary of State Charles Hughes opened the conference with a spectacular proposal to scrap all new construction and disarm the main powers to a ratio for Britain, the United States and Japan of 5:5:3. There would be a ten-year 'battleship holiday', and new ships would be limited to 35,000 tons and 16-inch guns. Hughes thought Britain should retain four additional capital ships to compensate for the age of her battle fleet. However, Japan's new battleship *Mutsu* was also on the chopping block. A compromise allowed Japan to finish *Mutsu*, while the United States completed three 16-inch gunned ships, and Britain was allowed to build two new battleships.

The naval agreement — formally known to diplomats as the Five Power Treaty, or the Treaty for the Limitation of Naval Armament, but usually known as the 'Washington Treaty' — was signed on 6 February. Salmond was realistic. 'Its primary purpose and significance is financial,' he reported. 'It is not an agreement to preserve the peace, nor is it designed for that end.'[10] However, it did mean new security for New Zealand, limiting the Japanese fleet and — via Article XIX — restricting the militarisation of the Pacific Islands. No new bases were permitted within a widely defined area.[11]

HMS *New Zealand* was one of the ships named for scrapping in Section II,[12] and Salmond thought her loss would be a 'matter of natural regret in the Dominion whose name she bears, and by the gift of whose Government and people she was added to the British Fleet'.[13] Actually the list simply acknowledged and extended a scrapping programme begun in 1919, of which the battlecruiser was already a part. In the face of harsh post-war finances and growing obsolescence, Britain's 12-inch gunned ships were decommissioned as the war ended. Several ships named for disposal in the treaty had gone to the breakers before negotiations began.[14] *New Zealand* was among them. She had survived because of her second world tour, but was decommissioned on her return to Britain in March 1920 and laid up in reserve, more than a year before the Washington Treaty was proposed. She was formally prepared for disposal from December 1921 — two months before the treaty was finalised — paid off altogether in April 1922 and sold that December to A.J. Purves, who on-sold her to the Rosyth Shipbreaking Company, a firm established specifically to break up *New Zealand*, *Agincourt* and *Princess Royal*.[15]

A few components were saved, including her electro-mechanical fire-control computer and some of her 4-inch guns. The latter were sent to New Zealand and mounted at Fort Dorset and Godley Head.[16] Various other mementoes made their way back to the Dominion, including the ship's auxiliary steering wheel. The loan remained. Capital repayments began in 1922, but the economic indifference of the 1920s made the burden difficult to meet, and was compounded when that became depression in 1929. Repayments were suspended in 1931, and although these were eventually resumed, the final instalment was not paid until the 1944–45 financial year.[17]

The New Zealand Naval Division

In many respects the 1922 naval treaty system merely formalised post-war realities. Britain's strategy for dealing with global commitments and a reduced navy — involving a defensive war in the Far East until the fleet arrived — had been developed by late 1920 and was endorsed by the CID in mid-1921, well before the treaty. The plan required a major naval base in theatre, and although Hong Kong was initially considered, the decision was made to build at Singapore. The Quadruple Treaty for settling Pacific differences, also signed in Washington, made little difference to this approach. 'The strategic situation in the Western Pacific has changed for the worse,' the CID warned, 'and the necessary preparations for a possible rapid concentration of the main fleet in the East must be pressed on with.'[18]

Although the combination of treaty and Admiralty policy changes torpedoed Jellicoe's wider scheme, local aspects of his report were still applicable. Officially the Admiralty preferred contributions to central defence over local navies, and Canada's decision to abandon its surface forces seemed promising to the Sea Lords. If the Dominions had to develop local forces, the Admiralty explained, they wanted squadrons that could be rapidly expanded in wartime, help set up worldwide oil fuel supplies. They also expected support 'by certain Dominions and India in the development of Singapore as a naval base'.[19] New Zealand would also have preferred cash contributions but, as in 1909, the enthusiasm for local forces in Australia meant there was little option but to follow suit. What followed was a compromise, splitting scarce funding, usually to the detriment of the local aspect.

Jellicoe was appointed Governor-General of New Zealand in 1920, and as Governor-General was also Commander in Chief of the armed forces. He perhaps should not have been involved with the minutiae of them as much as he was, but his input into the Naval Division was inevitable given his background and interests.[20]

The 1913 Naval Defence Act created the legislative apparatus to let the government set up the New Zealand Naval Division by successive Orders in Council. This was not done without debate. The Liberals, briefly under T.M. Wilford, condemned the new Division as 'unwarranted, unnecessary and absolutely useless'.[21] However, the Liberal-favoured return to central contributions seemed unfeasible in the light of the shift elsewhere to Dominion forces. Jellicoe's plans also had to be amended. New Zealand had no oil fueling facilities in 1920, and Jellicoe's idea of relying on commercial ports had to be shelved in favour of an expanded Devonport base. Until oiling facilities could be developed the new Division had to deploy coal-burners. Submarines were dropped, but more ships were needed to 'show the flag' in the Pacific Islands. Two sloops were earmarked. The first, *Veronica*, arrived in September 1920. Her sister ship *Laburnum* arrived two years later. They were never part of the Division: although Britain made overtures, the sloops remained Royal Navy ships on overseas duty.

The coal-burning cruiser *Chatham* arrived at Devonport in late January 1921, with artificers and dockyard hands on board to help resurrect *Philomel*, moored in Wellington since staggering back from the Middle East in 1917. They were able to get the old cruiser seaworthy for a final voyage to Auckland, under Commander John Walsh. Once at Devonport she was converted to an accommodation and training ship. The training scheme, however, was not particularly successful — by 1924, when the scheme was reviewed, only 80 sailors had actually been recruited. It was a dismal result, but perhaps not too surprising in the wake of the First World War. *Chatham*, meanwhile, went on a familiarisation cruise around the country before her first voyage to the Pacific Islands, one of the main tasks expected of the Naval Division. All this happened in advance of the paperwork — the Division was officially authorised by special Order in Council and formally came into existence in June 1921.

The 'locust' years

Political controversy dogged the New Zealand Naval Division for most of the inter-war years. The Labour Party, under Harry Holland, called the Division a 'laughing stock' in 1922.[22] The situation was complicated by another British change of position at the 1923 Imperial Conference, when Beatty — as First Sea Lord — told delegates that the Admiralty now welcomed local naval development. It was a pragmatic admission of financial realities. Churchill, later, described these as the 'locust years', a term that could also have been applied to New Zealand's defence spending of the same period.

Work got under way to get Devonport ready for the first oil-fired cruiser, due to reach New Zealand with a Special Service Squadron early in 1924. Plans were also laid to acquire a small oiler. However, a second cruiser fell foul of Massey's intention to part-fund the Singapore naval base. He hoped to advance £100,000 per annum for the next two years while the Divison was relatively cheap, and made the offer at the Imperial Conference. It went down well with Australia and India, but Canada saw little sense in the strategy. Ramsay MacDonald's minority Labour government, which came to power in Britain later in 1923, also disliked the idea. Singapore went on hold. Massey then came under pressure to use the £100,000 for a second cruiser. At the Imperial Conference in 1923 he was promised one would be sent when needed, but seemed reluctant. The issue was kicked along when the Special Service Squadron arrived under Vice-Admiral Sir Frederick Field, who pointed out the practical problems associated with a single cruiser which had to be docked for repairs from time to time — and urged New Zealand to acquire three.[23]

HMS *Dunedin* came with the squadron and joined the Division, replacing *Chatham*. By this time oiling facilities at Devonport had been completed, and oil was available in a few other ports. The gaps were filled by the Royal Fleet Auxiliary *Nucula*, taken over at Suva in 1924. The New Zealand Parliament approved a second cruiser in October. Almost simultaneously, however, MacDonald's minority Labour government in England was defeated in a general election and the Conservatives under Stanley Baldwin restarted Singapore. New Zealand could not fund both the second cruiser and the base. Pushed by Jellicoe, Massey wavered towards the cruiser, but wondered about taking out a loan for a spectacular £250,000 one-off grant for the base. It was, in its own way, the HMS *New Zealand* strategy all over again.

Domestic politics continued to dog the New Zealand Naval Division. The apparent failure of the training scheme attracted Parliamentary debate late in 1924, and a move to withdraw the scheme was defeated by only six votes. The Estimates that year topped £330,000 — a significant sum for a country beset by post-war recession. Massey died in office in May 1925, but the cruiser versus Singapore debate was inherited by his successor, J.G. Coates. The Navy League urged Coates to authorise a third light cruiser, arguing that the '. . . serious economical [sic] position in which the Old Country finds itself is tending to make it impossible that they should longer undertake the lion's share of the Empire's defence . . .'[24]

The Royal Naval Volunteer Reserve (New Zealand Division) was formed by legislation during the early 1920s, and by the end of the 1926 financial year included 18 officers and 120 ratings.[25] They were expected to man minesweepers in wartime, and a 'Castle' class minesweeper was procured to train them. Christened HMS *Wakakura*, the ship reached New Zealand in early 1927 and was converted for the training role at Devonport.

Diomede arrived in January 1926. Again there were calls for a third cruiser,[26] but Coates was pressed by the British to contribute £225,000 per annum to Singapore instead. He agreed, but refused to take over the two sloops in New Zealand waters, and in late 1926 told the House he would be guided by the Admiralty during the coming Imperial Conference. What followed was a compromise. Coates 'sought the advice of Admiral Hotham',[27] attended meetings with other imperial leaders at Downing Street, and moved on to the Admiralty, the War Office and the Air Ministry.[28] He launched the new policy in April 1927. A third 'D' class cruiser was out, but he announced that the two existing ships would be replaced by the new 'B' type, costing around £70,000 more per annum to run. Devonport would be expanded to suit. Meanwhile, he committed £1,000,000 to the Singapore naval base, by instalment.[29]

A few months later Britain, the United States and Japan met in Geneva to discuss new treaty limits on cruisers. High Commissioner James Parr and Jellicoe represented New Zealand. Arguments hung on the special British need for cruisers to patrol the far-flung Empire; this was not accepted by the Americans, and when the Admiralty seemed determined to hold to its 70-cruiser figure the conference broke up in disarray.

The New Zealand Naval Division saw its first active service in January 1930 when the Samoan League rebelled in Western Samoa, a New Zealand mandated territory. *Dunedin* was despatched to show the flag and back up local authorities. The cruiser carried a DH-60 Moth floatplane, and 31-year-old Flight Lieutenant Sidney Wallingford of the New Zealand Permanent Air Force. The aircraft was virtually unarmed — there were mounts for a Lewis gun, but it had to be aimed and fired with one hand while the pilot flew with the other. Wallingford and his crew were billeted ashore, where the aircraft was stored on a makeshift ramp under armed guard. He flew 90 hours during the two months the cruiser was in Samoan waters, mostly reconnaissance and ground co-operation, though he did drop a small bomb made by naval armourers, unfortunately on the wrong target.

Hawke's Bay earthquake, 1931

The Hawke's Bay earthquake of 1931 was a regional and national calamity; it remains New Zealand's most lethal natural disaster. But is also marked the high-water mark of the New Zealand Naval Division's inter-war activities.[0] an object lesson in the value of military forces in the civil defence role, and of the importance of having adequate resources. All the armed forces took part in relief work, but the Permanent Air Force had to borrow aircraft,[31] and the army relied on commandeered trucks. Only the Naval Division was able to provide assistance from within existing resources.

As it happened, the navy were there when the disaster occurred. The sloop HMS *Veronica* was on a coastal survey, and had arrived in Ahuriri harbour several hours early. Harbourmaster H. White-Parsons boarded the ship to see Commander Horace L. Morgan, and they were sitting in Morgan's cabin at around 10.47 a.m. when 'suddenly we heard a terrific explosion'. Thinking the magazines had gone up, both men rushed on deck, where White-Parsons saw:

The corrugated iron walls of the stores on the wharf were bursting asunder and disgorging bales of wool. The railway lines were twisting and bending under our eyes, and, with a crashing sound, the wharf a few yards in front of us gave way and fell into the harbour. The bed of the sea rose beneath us, and the stern wires gave way.[32]

The harbour bottom slammed into *Veronica*'s keel, and five of the six hawsers holding her to the quay snapped. The quayside astern — where Morgan had intended to moor — slumped and broke.[33] Water rushed from the harbour, and as *Veronica* threatened to cant over Morgan rallied the crew to secure the ship. At 10.54 a.m. he signalled Commodore Geoffrey Blake in Auckland by morse, then made arrangements to land parties with medical supplies, food and rescue equipment.[34] During the afternoon they were joined by seamen from *Taranaki* and *Northumberland*, which were in the roadstead and whose crews put themselves under Navy authority.

By chance, both cruisers were due to depart Devonport for exercises with the Royal Australian Navy on the morning of 3 February. They were fully manned, supplied and fuelled, and had steam up when Morgan's SOS came in. After a second signal at 11.27 a.m. revealed the 'precariousness of the situation',[35] Blake cancelled the manoeuvres and contacted Dr C.E. Maguire, superintendent of Auckland Hospital, asking for doctors, nurses, and medical supplies. The response was a 'genuine triumph of organisation'.[36] Eleven doctors and seventeen nurses arrived within ninety minutes. They were joined by the Reverend G.T. Robson MC, chaplain of HMS *Philomel*. Surgical and medical stores, an X-ray plant provided by Philips Lamps, 54 stretchers, 5 marquees, 34 tents, 400 blankets, 125 beds, 200 ground sheets, 80 shovels and 21 picks were collected on the dockside by 2 p.m. and loaded within half an hour.

The two cruisers immediately put to sea, working up to 24 knots and rounding North Head by 3 p.m.[37] Blake also ordered *Laburnum* to Auckland, where she refuelled and loaded medical supplies in case they were called on.[38] The Australian Prime Minister, J.H. Scullin, offered the services of a Royal Australian Navy cruiser then in Tasmanian waters.[39]

Veronica's initial contact was with the Navy authorities; the first 'all stations' alert about the quake was broadcast by the MV *Northumberland* at 11.20 a.m. At 12.50 p.m., *Veronica* sent a formal general distress signal by Morse, each word repeated twice:

> GLUD to CQ: *Serious earthquake at NAPIER. All communications destroyed. Medical assistance urgently required.*[40]

Cabinet met early in the afternoon to discuss the emergency, and soon after 2 p.m. Prime Minister George Forbes signalled Morgan directly, anxious for 'any information as to extent medical assistance required'. Morgan's terse response left no doubt. 'As much medical assistance as possible. Whole town wrecked and fires raging.'[41]

Both cruisers hastened south through the night. Their crews were divided into rescue parties during the voyage and given basic training in stretcher-bearing and first aid.[42] Galley hands baked bread, while others set up the X-ray machinery in the torpedo flat.[43] The cruisers reached Napier at 8.30 a.m., slowing well out to sea after receiving reports of shoaling. They felt their way in and anchored about three miles offshore. The navigating officers, Lieutenant Commanders Harper and Clarke, spent that day carrying out a thorough survey of the harbour approaches. They found that the bottom had been lifted generally by five feet, and with this information were able to bring the cruisers a mile closer inshore on 5 February.

The navy made an enormous contribution in the disaster area over the next few days. One observer even suggested that there was 'without doubt, an entire absence of organised effort until the Navy arrived'.[44] This was not actually true. The Army, Permanent Air Force, police, fire brigade and medical services all played an important part, as did many of those who survived the quake. However, the influx of hundreds of fresh, disciplined men who were not facing the loss of all they knew made a real difference. The marines set up headquarters at the Byron Street Police Station under Royal Marine Captain

Hardy Spicer of HMS *Dunedin*. 'The first two days were the worst,' Spicer later recalled, 'for the men had no sleep whatever.' Royal Marine Captain J.C. Westall of the *Diomede* later explained to reporters that they 'acted as firemen, took part in demolition work, cooked meals for refugees, were food distributors, water carriers, tractor drivers, policemen, searched for the dead and carried bodies to the morgues, carried out sanitation work, and even acted as nurses . . .'[45]

Many of the sailors were deeply affected by the overwhelming depth of the human tragedy. Survivor Mary Hunter was helped a few days after the quake by a marine who was 'really shaking with horror'.[46] One sailor told a survivor he had 'never seen such appalling sights'.[47] Even sixty years later, Able Seaman A.E. Ball-Guymer recalled the horror of the days in Napier and Hastings:

I went into [the] hospital . . . there must have been an open verandah, because there was an old lady, that I had to take a slab off . . . She must have been in a basket chair talking to another patient in bed, and she was . . . dead as a doornail . . . Well I just about spewed my heart up, you know . . . I went for a walk and I saw a bath . . . I went over and had a look, and good God, a young woman . . . naked in the bath. She must have been caught. Whether they had put the body there, got it from somewhere else I don't know. She was in a proper big bath . . .[48]

The cruisers were hammered by an aftershock soon after arriving. Ball-Guymer had returned to the ship for the night and was 'sleeping in the Sick Bay flat'. He had 'just got in the hammock and [was] just getting comfortable . . . [when] The quake hit the bottom of the ship . . . It must have been quite a jolt.' Water splashed through the open scuttles of the stoker's mess deck.[49]

The navy stayed in Napier for the next week. *Veronica* left shortly after noon on 10 February. The harbour was too shallow for her to manoeuvre, so she was towed out to the cheers of Napier townsfolk. Damage to her rudder meant she had to be steered by hand, and she was escorted to Auckland for dockyard inspection by *Diomede*. *Dunedin* followed the next day.[50]

Veronica left New Zealand waters in February 1934, was paid off on her return to Britain, and sold the following year for scrap. Her bell was saved and returned to Napier where it was installed in the Sun Bay, the earthquake memorial on the Marine Parade. Ironically, *Diomede* ultimately also became part of a human tragedy. She was patrolling the Atlantic north of Pernambuco in November 1941 when she was torpedoed and sunk by U-124; there were only 67 survivors from her complement of 450.[51]

Fresh challenges, 1930–39

New Zealand's naval forces faced a series of political challenges during the 1930s. The change began in 1928 when 57 nations signed the Kellogg Peace Pact, designed to promote further disarmament. The following year a Labour government came to power in Britain, and incoming Prime Minister Ramsay MacDonald called a new naval conference largely to resolve international issues over cruiser strength. This was held in London in January 1930. The Admiralty reduced their demands for cruisers to fifty — with implications for the New Zealand Division — and an alarmed New Zealand government, briefly under the ageing and ailing Joseph Ward, called on Jellicoe for aid. MacDonald's government refused to allow him to participate, and New Zealand was represented only by High Commissioner Thomas Willford.

New Zealand's position seemed further threatened by initial British proposals — slashing the fleet to a dozen or so battleships, cutting displacement limits to 25,000 tons and 12-inch guns, abolishing submarines, and reducing cruiser strength to fifty. All this was financially driven; by this time Britain was plunging into a severe economic depression. In the end capital ship numbers were cut to the 15:15:10 ratio envisaged in 1921. Cruisers were divided into light and heavy categories, the latter on a ratio of 18:15:12 for the United States, Britain and Japan respectively. Japan essentially came out ahead in the resulting London Naval Treaty, signed on 22 April, a point that caused considerable alarm in New Zealand and Australia. Prime Minister Charles Forbes made the point at the 1930 Imperial Conference.

New Zealand had good reason to be concerned. Long-held worries about Japanese ambitions seemed to be coming true by the late 1920s. Civil war broke out in China, and Japanese forces intervened at Shantung in 1927 and 1928. Hamaguchi Osachi, who became Prime Minister in 1929, seemed more moderate, but he could not halt the tide. Devastated by depression and racked with food shortages, Japan was ripe for revolt, and military expansion was widely viewed as a solution. In 1930 Hamaguchi was assassinated. The following year a coup was abandoned only at the last minute. When a Japanese railway in Manchuria was bombed that year, the Japanese army used the event as a pretext to occupy the province without political authorisation from Tokyo. Fear of Japanese ambitions in the Pacific were further underlined in 1933 when Japan withdrew from the League of Nations. A New Zealand Committee of Imperial Defence was formed under Major-General W.L.H. Sinclair-Burgess to co-ordinate the national response.

For New Zealand these developments were accompanied by worrisome internal problems. The indifferent economy of the 1920s gave way to depression. Coates, now Finance Minister in the Forbes government, argued that government books had to be balanced at any cost. State wages were slashed 20 percent between 1931 and 1932, pensions were cut 30 percent, public works expenditure by three-quarters, and hospitals were plunged into a deep funding crisis.[52] These initiatives merely intensified the downturn.[53] Defence was also hit. Although efforts to cut naval funds were ameliorated by the developing Pacific crisis, there were cutbacks and the Singapore grant was questioned. This had already slumped to £100,000 per annum. The government nonetheless agreed in late 1932 to replace the cruisers, and a three-year expansion programme was authorised at Devonport. Most of the work involved reclaiming land for a new 12,000-ton capacity oil tank, and extending Calliope Dock.

Thinking turned to an air force as a cheaper way of bolstering local defence. Coates and Forbes took initial steps in this direction, but demurred from a major shift. The real change came in 1935–36 when Labour came to power on a wave of popular support. In January 1936, Grey Lynn MP John A. Lee called for an independent and expanded air force. To Lee, naval policy was merely subservient to British whim, as evidenced by *Dunedin*'s despatch to the East Indies during the Abyssinian crisis. As far as he was concerned New Zealand faced no direct threat, and blockade could not starve the country. Air power was the real future, though this did not mean abrogating New Zealand's imperial duties — he envisaged strong local defences able to fly to the aid of a beleaguered Empire.

These ideas were discussed by Cabinet in May 1936, where the decision was taken to limit defence spending to £1.1 million, and there was talk of concentrating all spending on air forces. In the end this was tempered by existing naval obligations — the air force vote was increased at the expense of the army. From New Zealand's perspective the main issue, as had been the case since the Russian threat of the late nineteenth century, was inadequate British preparation for war in the Pacific. An unsuccessful coup in Tokyo in February 1936 appeared to underline the point. But there was also danger further afield; Savage told the House in 1936 that 'the general European situation is not one to make us feel that we can afford to be indifferent to defence matters'.[54] The problem was paying for defence when the focus had to be on restoring the economy.

Meanwhile the new cruisers arrived. *Diomede* went to Sheerness after her East Indies service and exchanged crews with HMS *Achilles*, which was commissioned into New Zealand service in March 1936 under Captain I.G. Glennie. She reached New Zealand in September after a journey out that included a period with the Home Fleet in the Mediterranean, and a tour of the Pacific Islands. *Leander* commissioned into New Zealand service in April 1937, replacing *Dunedin*; she spent three months working up in British waters arriving in Auckland in August 1937. That year *Nucula* was laid up as a storage hulk, made redundant as local oil facilities improved.

International tensions rose during 1938 on both sides of the world as Japan prosecuted war against China, while Hitler entered Czechoslovakia and Hungary. In April the New Zealand Chiefs of Staff completed a five-year plan recommending expansion of all three services. Government implemented only the air force component. Meanwhile the Admiralty wanted New Zealand to man up to two dozen small auxiliary ships for local anti-submarine and minesweeping duties. The New Zealand Naval Board thought only half a dozen were feasible within manpower constraints, and in any case nothing was actually done, with the result that only four trawlers were available to sweep minefields laid by German raiders in 1940, and there was no defence against submarines.

The European crisis deepened during 1939. By July, Poland had become Europe's new *casus belli*. Hitler did not think war would follow, but his navy prepared for the worst, and on 2 August the supply ship *Altmark* left Germany for the United States, taking on 9400 tons of oil in Texas and heading for the South Atlantic. The U-boats went to war stations, and on 21 August the armoured ship *Admiral Graf Spee* put to sea under *Kapitän zur See* Hans Langsdorf. The older armoured ship *Deutschland* followed three days later.

Preparations began in New Zealand about the same time. The armed forces went on precautionary alert on 24 August. Three days later, all service personnel were recalled from leave. Air Force and Territorial mobilisation orders were issued on 28 August. Local Royal Naval Volunteer Reserve members were called up on 29 August.

War seemed inevitable as the Polish crisis developed. The New Zealand Naval Division was put at the disposal of the Royal Navy, and the two sloops were recalled first to Singapore, then to England. *Leith* sailed on 28 August and *Wellington* left five days later, after arriving from the islands. The two cruisers were also readied for war, and on 29 August the Admiralty requested *Achilles* for service in the West Indies. The message arrived at 9 a.m., and five hours later the cruiser sailed from Devonport under Captain W.E. Parry with 567 men on board, 321 of them New Zealanders.

On 1 September — when the Germans rolled into Poland — the Governor-General issued a formal proclamation of emergency. Britain declared war on 3 September after Germany failed to respond to an ultimatum; and New Zealand, after little debate, followed.

CHAPTER FOUR
Second World War

> *Am engaging Enemy, one pocket battleship. Ships in company* Achilles, Exeter. *Enemy's course 080°. My position 175 degrees 22 miles from 34.5 49W.*
>
> — Commodore Henry Harwood, HMS *Ajax*, 7.12 a.m., 13 December 1939[1]

The New Zealand Division cruiser HMS *Achilles* was well out into the Pacific when war broke out, destination unknown to her crew, though shipboard rumour gave the sailors the 'impression that we were going to the Caribbean'.[2] In fact the orders were changed on 2 September, before war was declared, and *Achilles* instead made course for Chile, which she reached ten days later. She had the job of finding and capturing any German merchants on the west coast of South America. Their number theoretically included the *Lahn*, a German freighter that left New Zealand waters the week before war was declared, but the German ship did not show up.

The switch to wartime 'cruising stations' brought a change of routine, and the ship went to action stations at dawn and dusk. This invariably prompted a scramble, as Able Seaman H.H. Beesley recalled:

> . . . *you tore like hell to wherever your action stations were. My action station was P1HA [port-side anti-aircraft gun], at cruising stations I was up in the Director. When the Director crew were trying to get up and*

The Second World War

I was trying to get down, there were more fingers trodden on and toes kicked out of ladder rungs than you can imagine, but we got there in record time anyway.[3]

Chile was neutral, and the cruiser spent the next few weeks 'up and down the coast of South America' playing cat-and-mouse with German merchants which by international law had to be given a 24-hour start from any harbour, 'so it was leapfrog all up and down the coast'.[4] They forced seventeen German merchants into port. Lieutenant K.F. Connew recalled one pursuit which ended inside the three-mile limit and had to be abandoned. 'Into the port they went, and we went in and anchored not far from them . . . they shook their fist at us and called out . . . and we just told them how lucky they were because they had got in there just in time.'[5] After six weeks the cruiser entered Valparaiso, which to Connew was 'the most beautiful city I think I have ever seen'. The crew went on 'a magnificent three days' leave while *Achilles* refuelled:

. . . and we saw a civilization that we never knew existed . . . they have got buildings and streets and squares and a civilisation that has been going on for over 500 years, it is just an amazing place . . . Eventually we sailed and went up and down, up again, and down the West Coast of South America . . . into Callao . . . the Port of Lima . . . I can remember going to Lima, half a dozen of us, and we eventually came back in a taxi. It appears that the road from Lima to Callao is straight . . . We got our taxis to race, maybe it was the Peruvian beer . . . but it was a lot of fun at the time . . .[6]

Achilles' visit to the neutral harbour was a chance to meet the enemy. R.B. Harvey, Milton Hill and Ivan Alderton 'came across a couple of German cadets' outside a cinema and 'they very politely spoke to us'. The young Germans had come from the sail training ship *Lawhill* and had no money, so the Kiwis took them in to have a look at a news reel. They collected 'a couple of frowns' from some Polish cadets but, as Harvey recalled, the Kiwis 'didn't have any personal animosity to these German people . . . we weren't in a nasty mood with them . . . We thought it was quite intriguing that we should be able to speak to them seeing as our countries were at war.'[7]

The Battle of the River Plate

While *Achilles* patrolled Chilean waters, more dramatic developments unfolded in the South Atlantic, where the loss of *Clement* on 1 October alerted the Admiralty to the fact that a German armoured ship — initially thought to be *Admiral Scheer* — had reached the area. In fact she was the *Admiral Graf Spee*, under *Kapitän zur See* Hans Langsdorf, but this was not known to the British at the time. At any event, a raider of that power could not be allowed to run loose and they despatched 22 warships to find her, including the three cruisers of the newly-formed South Atlantic Station under Commodore Henry Harwood.

Harwood's force was the weakest of the hunting groups, and in early October *Achilles* was sent to reinforce them. The New Zealand ship anchored on the night of 19 October halfway through the Straits of Magellan. 'I have often said that that was the day I heard silence,' Connew recalled:

> ... It was so quiet that one could hear a chap talking on the foc'sle while you were standing on the quarter deck. It was an uncanny experience, the snow and the ice came right down to the water's edge, and there was ice in the water as we went through. It was quite an amazing thing. We didn't show any lights, or anything like that. We just stood there and were amazed that we were in such a place in the world.[8]

Achilles reached Port Stanley on 20 October, refuelled and steamed north. Initially she worked with *Cumberland* and later *Ajax*, but on 23 November was ordered to operate independently to the north. There was no sign of the German ship. In fact, after sinking four vessels in the South Atlantic, Langsdorf had swept into the Indian Ocean, where he sank a small tanker on 15 November. The British rushed forces around the Cape of Good Hope. Meanwhile *Achilles* searched for the *Lahn*, which had gone into a Chilean port and then escaped to sea.

Langsdorf returned to the South Atlantic at the end of the month and sank the *Doric Star* on 2 December. Harwood judged that the German raider was on its way to the River Plate, a busy waterway bustling with fat targets. He calculated that the ship could be there by 14 December, and ordered his own force to concentrate, with the exception of *Cumberland*, which was refitting at Port Stanley. Although his force was out-gunned by an armoured ship, Harwood had laid specific plans to tackle such a vessel, variously by night or by day, and had every intention of engaging despite the odds. The armoured ships were among the *Kriegsmarine*'s few heavier vessels, and he had merely to damage his quarry so it could no longer continue raiding. And if the German ship did prevail over his squadron, the loss of his cruisers was not going to dent overall Royal Navy superiority over the *Kriegsmarine*.

Behind all loomed the spectre of Vice-Admiral Sir Ernest Troubridge, who at the outbreak of the First World War had been in command of four armoured cruisers in a position to engage the German battlecruiser *Goeben* as she steamed east through the Mediterranean. At the behest of his flag-captain, Troubridge declined on the basis that the German ship was superior to his entire squadron. There was a court-martial. Troubridge was acquitted; but the fact that tradition demanded engagement despite such odds essentially ended his career. A quarter-century later, in a new war, Harwood had no intention of following suit.

Achilles and *Ajax* made a rendezvous with *Exeter* on 12 December. After weeks alone, the crew of *Achilles* saw it as:

> ... [a] moment of great excitement ... We came together and we just couldn't believe that there was another warship in this great ocean we were in. There they were, the three of us, together. We stopped ... and lowered a boat, and ... Captain Parry went across to the flagship ... They didn't tell us what they discussed or anything like that, but the Captain came back on board and we set sail again ...[9]

All three cruisers were 350 miles east of the Plate by dawn next day, 'a beautiful day, the sea was like glass',[10] practising Harwood's strategy for splitting German fire by dividing into two groups. At 6.14 a.m. *Exeter* spotted smoke on the horizon bearing 310 degrees — the German armoured ship, arriving exactly where Harwood expected. 'The tip of her mast was the only thing to be seen,' Beesley recalled. 'It was full action stations ... *Exeter* was despatched out to the port and within minutes there was a flash on the horizon and in a suitable time the shells started landing.'[11] *Achilles* manoeuvred 'as required to conform with *Ajax*'s motions',[12] and the New Zealand ensign — the 'digger flag' — rose to the masthead.

Langsdorf assumed the two light cruisers were destroyers, perhaps part of a convoy escort, and decided to engage the heavy cruiser, opening fire at 6.18 a.m. at a range of 19,800 yards. The first shells fell 300 yards short of *Exeter*, which opened fire at 6.20. *Achilles* opened fire a minute later, followed by *Ajax*.[13] Langsdorf concentrated on *Exeter*, which was hit at 6.23 a.m., knocking out B-turret and sweeping the bridge with splinters. This was the first of a series of hits that eventually forced her from the battle. Meanwhile the two light cruisers steamed northeast. At around 6.30 a.m. they came under fire. Connew:

> ... *walked around to the port side of the ship and to my amazement 50 yards off the ship a splash went up which must have been at least 50 to 60 feet in the air ... I stood there and watched ... and we learned later that it came from an 11-inch shell which had been fired at us from the* Graf Spee *which was around about 20 miles away from us. We just couldn't believe that their gunnery was so perfect that they could land a shell about 50 yards off the* Achilles.[14]

Chief Electrician R.B. Harvey was at his action station in a turret lobby when the battle started, and ran into a crewman who had seen *Graf Spee*'s first shells pass overhead.

> ... *I said 'What's going on Henry?', he said, 'They are going over,' and that's all he said. You could just about see the hair standing on his head, he had looked out the gun house door up top and said he had seen shells going overhead. It was the real thing from then on and so we just got cracking, and ... being the age I was like many of them in the gun house and lobby, you have got the drill that you have been taught to do and it's more or less automatic ... The fear doesn't seem to come to the fore front, you have got a job to do and you do it. It's not until about an hour and a half later ... we decided 'crikey!' a shell could have come through here. There was only an inch [of] metal around this jolly place that we were in, it didn't though and so we were fortunate ...* [15]

Both light cruisers turned away slightly to open the range, and *Ajax* catapulted her aircraft to help spot the fall of shell. By 6.45 a.m. both ships had worked up to revolutions for 31 knots, though exact speeds could not be determined because *Achilles* did not stream her log during the action.[16] Parry handled the cruiser 'like a motor boat' in an effort to foil the German gunners, 'running, firing a few, running out again'.[17]

Minutes later two shells, 'presumably 11-inch projectiles, burst in the vicinity of the ship at a distance of approximately 20 yards, abreast the forebridge and superstructure'.[18] Fifty-five splinters whistled inboard. Five tore through the three-eighth-inch plating protecting the forward director control tower.[19] 'I was conscious only of a hellish noise,' gunnery officer R.E. Washbourn later recalled. 'I ordered automatically: "A.C.P., take over."'[20] Able Seaman A.C.H. Shaw, Ordinary Seaman L.W. Grant, Telegraphist F. Stennett, and Ordinary Telegraphist N.J. Milburn died. Sergeant S.J. Trimble, a Royal Marine from Ireland, was seriously wounded but stayed at his post for the rest of the action. There were more casualties as three shell fragments ripped through the quarter-inch plating protecting the lower bridge, and a further three tore into the forebridge. Captain Parry was wounded in the legs, and Chief Yeoman of Signals L.C. Martinson was seriously hurt. Other shell fragments howled around the forward port 4-inch gun where Beesley stood at his action station.

> . . . *young Ian Grant who was alongside of me copped it in the chest. He died immediately . . . [another] chap . . . dropped to the deck. He was shot all around the buttocks . . . I picked him up, threw him over my shoulders like a sack of coal to get him down to the Sick Bay. I couldn't go down the ladder forward . . . so I turned around backwards and sat his arse on the coaming which didn't help him at all, and he called me all the bastards he could lay his tongue to. Anyway I deposited him in the Sick Bay and came up.*[21]

The remaining fragments caused a good deal of damage. Ten peppered the three-quarter-inch and three-eighth-inch side plating in the wake of the central store, galley flat and ship's canteen, ripping holes up to three inches in diameter above the waterline. Another smashed through the funnel casing and penetrated the inner .116-inch plating. Six fragments ripped into the fore superstructure, and others shattered a screen door over the wireless telegraphy office, damaged the signal deck superstructure, ripped through the steel tube of the foremast, smashed a hole in the cutter's davit, and shattered the ventilating trunk on X-gun deck.[22] It was a close shave. Connew was volunteered to help ditch the depth charges on the quarterdeck:

> *If by chance a shell ... had hit the quarter deck or the depth charges they would have blown our stern off ... We rushed down to the quarterdeck. .. we had to jump over the cordite boxes [ejected from Y-turret] ... there seemed to be hundreds of them, and we got to the depth charge rack. Davis-Goff ... [said] to me 'have you got a knife on you?'... These depth charges are set by a depth gauge and also by a set of forks, which hold the detonator clear of the depth charge ... We set them to 500 feet and took the key out, then I took the fork off the detonator ... and we rolled them over the side. They were safe because we weren't in 500 feet of water, the plume from our propellers was up about 30 feet in the air, God knows how fast we were going. The depth charges rolled over the side.*[23]

Harwood decided to close in at 7.10 a.m., when the range was about 16,000 yards. *Graf Spee* turned away, making smoke, but a few minutes later emerged from the screen and reopened fire, hitting *Ajax* with an 11-inch shell that passed through X-barbette, exploding in Harwood's cabin. Both aft 6-inch turrets were knocked out, and *Graf Spee* avoided torpedoes fired by the cruiser moments later. A return torpedo salvo forced the two British cruisers to manoeuvre violently and at 7.32 a.m. *Achilles* actually crossed *Ajax*'s wake while avoiding the German 'tin fish'.[24]

On board *Achilles* the gunners worked like clockwork, pulling shells from the hoists, ramming and going through the firing drill just as if at practice, 'except that everything seemed to be done at an amazing speed'.[25] Their weapons became so hot that the rammers had to push them out by hand after each salvo. This was not the only problem. As Harvey recalled:

> *... [the] driving bands on shells at that time were protected with tarred hemp and [they had] difficulty ... removing it down in the shell room ... They couldn't send the shells up until the tarred hemp was off. They could not find the knife or they didn't have the knife, a special brass knife. They got a pussers dirk eventually ... but an awkward situation ... from then on they supplied shells to the ships without the grommet on ...*[26]

For *Achilles* to get to the ordered speed of 31 knots in the waters of the Plate was challenging; the physics of shallow-water operations robbed all the ships of much of their potential speed. Parry also called for rapid alterations of power that far exceeded operating guidelines. However, the engineers worked miracles, pressing the steam plants beyond design parameters. In the boiler rooms the blast of the guns sent flame pouring from the gratings with every salvo, but the engineering staff did not shy from their duties.[27] Shallow-water hydrodynamic effects also meant that both cruisers kicked up great rooster-tails of spray, which impressed Beesley:

> ... the wake we were creating would be as high as X-turret ... If we could have stopped dead, that wave would have swamped the whole of the upper deck ... it was a glorious sight. I will never forget it. To my knowledge I was the only bugger looking at it. Nobody was around me. Everybody had closed up in their turret. I just happened to take a walk and there was this great stern wave.[28]

At 7.40 a.m. *Exeter* had to withdraw, heavily damaged and down by the stern. *Ajax* had only three guns in action and reportedly just 20 percent ammunition remaining, so Harwood decided to disengage. Both light cruisers made smoke and sheared off to the east. As they turned, a shell slashed through *Ajax*'s mainmast. *Achilles*' guns fell silent, their paint blistered from the heat of 82 minutes of constant firing.

The cruisers had hit *Graf Spee* twice with 8-inch and eighteen times with 6-inch shells. The Germans had fired 60 percent of their 11-inch ammunition. Langsdorf discovered that there was a good deal of superficial damage and that the armoured belt had failed in one place. The main problem was that the fuel processing system, desalinator and galley facilities had all been damaged. The loss of the fuel processor was serious and essentially forced him to make for the nearest harbour. He chose Montevideo, in Uruguay, as opposed to Mar del Plata in Argentina.

Ajax and *Achilles* followed at a respectable distance, but at around 10.10 a.m. *Achilles* came within range of *Graf Spee*, which opened fire. The Kiwi cruiser 'turned away at full speed'.[29] About an hour later a merchant came into view. Hoping to distract his pursuers, Langsdorf signalled the freighter to stop and radioed in clear to the British warships: 'Please pick up lifeboats of English steamer.'[30] However, the merchant's crew refused to abandon ship, and Langsdorf did not want to attack while the crew were on board — particularly given his own need for haven in nearby Montevideo — so he had to give up the diversion. This signal, using *Graf Spee*'s call sign, was the first indication to the New Zealanders that they had been fighting *Graf Spee* and not *Scheer*. Harwood, meanwhile, signalled *Cumberland* to join them 'with all despatch' from the Falklands.[31]

There was another brief exchange of fire at 12.37 p.m., but they did not break contact and all three ships steamed west for the rest of the afternoon without further incident towards the coast, coming in sight of Punta del Este and Lobos Island. *Ajax* now swung south to cover a possible escape channel around English Bank, while *Achilles* continued to hound *Graf Spee*. As evening drew on the New Zealand cruiser came closer to *Graf Spee*, which by 8.48 p.m. was 'well silhouetted' by the setting sun. Seven minutes later the Germans opened fire into the dusk, loosing three salvoes and straddling the cruiser — 'one went in front of the ship, one to the stern and one to the side'.[32] *Achilles* responded with five broadsides, then turned away at full speed, making smoke. *Graf Spee* continued to shoot in a desultory fashion until 9.43 p.m., but the effort was apparently intended to drive the New Zealand ship off rather than decisively engage. By 10.02 p.m. the raider was north of English Bank, and at 10.48 passed east of Whistle Buoy off Montevideo. Parry abandoned close pursuit and began a 23-knot patrol between English Bank and Flores Strait.[33] Langsdorf brought his damaged ship into Montevideo just after midnight.

Next morning the New Zealanders held a service for their four dead, including Able Seaman A.C.H. Shaw of Ngongotaha and Ordinary Seaman I.W. Grant of Tainui.[34] They died a long way from home. Yet the South Atlantic was New Zealand's real front line. Protection of local coasts could do nothing to save New Zealand cargoes from predation elsewhere. The New Zealand Naval Board advised the relatives of the dead, and kept the relations of the injured men posted — as late as 29 December, the Board wrote to E.M. Martinson advising that her husband had 'been transferred to the Falkland Island hospital and is continuing to make satisfactory progress'.[35]

Achilles suffered a good deal of damage during the battle, mostly from the blast of her own guns — rents and tears caused by 11-inch splinters paled into insignificance by comparison. The ventilating trunks had been bent by 6-inch blast, leaving the ship no longer gas tight. Three doors on the upper deck were badly distorted. The deadlights and scuttles in fore and aft superstructures had been blown off the plating. All internal fittings were damaged. Furniture had been tossed around in cabins, and there was major damage to instruments and equipment. Joints were broken below decks, while a 4½-inch supporting pillar in the CPO's mess was fractured under the deck-head and badly distorted. Some of this could be made good by the ship's company, with the exception of the square ports in the fore and aft superstructure.[36]

News that three cruisers had driven off the German armoured ship was a fillip to a British public jaded by three months of 'phony war'. Harwood was knighted and promoted to Rear-Admiral on the evening of 14 December. The First Sea Lord, Admiral Sir Dudley Pound, told him that the battle had 'reversed the findings of the Troubridge court-martial and shown how wrong that was'.[37]

Politics intruded that day. Uruguay was neutral, and under international law *Graf Spee* had just 24 hours' grace. Langsdorf and German Ambassador Otto Langmann asked for fourteen days. The British Ambassador, Eugene Millington-Drake, initially argued for immediate departure, but was then asked by Harwood to delay the German ship to allow reinforcements to arrive. International law required a belligerent to wait 24 hours after a merchant had departed, so Millington-Drake persuaded SS *Ashworth* to put to sea that evening. This proved an unnecessary precaution. Uruguayan authorities allowed the Germans 72 hours. It was a tense time for the New Zealanders. Connew recalled:

During those 3 days that we sat there waiting for her to come out . . . we used to go up to the entrance to the harbour and have a look at her . . . that was when we were most frightened. During the battle things happened too fast for us to be actually frightened [but] . . . during those 3 days if anyone dropped a spoon on the deck everyone jumped about 5 feet . . .[38]

On 15 December, as the British refuelled, Langsdorf released his prisoners and buried his dead. In an urgent signal exchange with Germany he was told not to accept internment. He believed the British had rushed heavy forces into the vicinity — his gunnery officer thought the battlecruiser *Renown* and carrier *Ark Royal* were visible through the rangefinder. In fact, heavy British forces were some way off. *Cumberland* arrived after a 34-hour passage from the Falklands — averaging 29 knots — but she was scant reinforcement, and Harwood estimated his chances at only 30 percent.

Tensions rose sharply during 17 December. American radio commentators who had rushed down to the Plate described the cruisers as the 'suicide squadron'. *Graf Spee* weighed anchor in the early evening and put to sea in company with the German tanker *Tacoma*. *Achilles* went to action stations at 8.02 p.m. and eight minutes later spotted the smoke of the *Graf Spee* bearing 340 degrees. Beesley described the mood as 'tense'.[39] *Ajax* catapulted her aircraft. However, Langsdorf declined an engagement. *Graf Spee* dropped anchor four miles offshore, near the Recalada pontoon marking the channel to Buenos Aires. A skeleton crew took to the boats, and at 9.10 p.m. the armoured ship blew up with a great splash of smoke and flame.

The two cruisers approached the blazing wreck; Connew recalled that '. . . we felt we had won a great battle'.[40] Commodore L.S. Stanners recalled how 'once we heard that the *Graf Spee* had blown herself up, the release of tension was tremendous'; he remembered the way:

> . . . the ship's companies of *Ajax* and *Achilles*, who by this time were lining the fo'csle, the forward turrets, the bridge, every possible vantage point, cheered each other and cheered themselves hoarse. It was well after dark before we in fact reached the vicinity of the blazing ship, and we circled her for a while and then slipped quietly back out to sea.[41]

The German armoured ship settled in shallow water. *Tacoma* crossed the Plate to Buenos Aires with the rest of *Graf Spee*'s crew, but the next day the Argentine authorities decided to intern them. Langsdorf had chosen to scuttle in view of his ammunition shortage and the belief that heavy British forces lay outside, and was criticised for not going down with his ship. In fact he felt responsible for his crew, and when they were interned — to his dismay — he believed he could do no more. Later that evening he spread an old Imperial German Navy flag on his bed, lay down on it, and shot himself.

The British ships returned to the Falklands. Harwood shifted his flag briefly to *Achilles* after *Ajax* sailed for England at the beginning of 1940, and they entered Montevideo where the 'English element' welcomed them. Beesley recalled they were not the only ones in the town:

> There were still a few German sailors around who were waiting . . . to be interned I believe. People thought there might have been fisticuffs ashore when we met up with each other but there was nothing like that at all. These guys were Imperial Naval ones, they weren't Nazis . . . On the odd occasion where we did see each other, we saluted each other and carried on.[42]

Achilles finally returned home to 'one of the grandest welcomes that you could have had anywhere' after a cruise of 52,333 miles.[43] Her crew marched up Queen Street before crowds estimated at a hundred thousand, passing under 24-foot banners bearing greetings from around the country — a touch hastily orchestrated the week before by Auckland's mayor Sir Ernest Davis. Commercial photographers Stewart and White immortalised the moment, capturing Parry 'taking the salute of the cheering crowds'.[44]

New Zealand's other services joined the general adulation. 'All ranks of RNZAF are proud of the *Achilles* and her gallant achievement,' the Air Department announced in a general signal, 'and extend a hearty welcome to all ranks on their return to New Zealand waters.'[45] Afterwards, some of the crew visited Wellington, and others went to their home towns where they were riotously received. Connew returned to Westport where he was presented with a gold watch; 'the Mayor marched up the street with me, and . . . My name seemed to be in the paper every day about anything I did'.[46]

Raiders and alarms — New Zealand waters

Leander was sent to Fanning Island as war loomed in August 1939, returned to New Zealand in mid-September, and was then sent to inspect Auckland and Campbell Islands for German shipping. She was back in New Zealand by the beginning of November.[47] Her retention prompted a brief spat with the British. The Admiralty wanted the Kiwi ship and proposed to replace her either with an old 'C' type cruiser, or three destroyers and an armed merchant. The New Zealand government balked — at some £450,000 the cost of the Admiralty's proposed forces would have exceeded that of a third cruiser and ancillary ships. In the end *Leander* was retained to escort the First Echelon overseas, joining the First World War battleship *Ramilles* and the heavy cruiser *Canberra* to take the convoy to Sydney, where *Leander* was relieved by *Australia*, and returned to New Zealand waters.

The British still wanted *Leander* elsewhere, but amid rumours that a German armed merchant cruiser was at large the New Zealand government was eager to retain her in local waters during the early months of 1940. *Achilles* was in refit at Devonport until May, and the British armed merchant *Hector* — which arrived as a stop-gap — was not quite the same as a light cruiser. However, *Leander* was earmarked to escort the 'fast convoy' component of the Second Echelon part-way across the Tasman in early May, and the government buckled to pressure to send her to the Middle East. *Leander* sailed with the two Australian heavy cruisers and the fast liners *Aquitania*, *Empress of Japan*, *Empress of Britain* and *Andes*, refuelling in Sydney on 5 May and heading for Bass Strait. Three more liners, including *Queen Mary*, joined the convoy in Australian waters.

Repairs to *Achilles* took some time. One of her gun barrels needed replacing. A spare was available at Devonport, and the old barrel was sent back to Woolwich.[48] Parry was promoted to Commodore 2nd Class, becoming Commodore Commanding New Zealand Squadron and First Naval Member of the New Zealand Naval Board as well as captain of the cruiser. Meanwhile, volunteer reservists were called up for local duties. Some 793 were on the rolls by 1939, and some 542 of them were mobilised by the end of the 1939–40 financial year.

As in the First World War, the biggest immediate threat came from German raiders. Germany had prepared several merchants as *Hilfskreuzers* (auxiliary cruisers), a term usually abbreviated to HSK. Ship No. 36, generally known as *Orion*, escaped the British blockade in April 1940. Kapitan Kurt Weyher brought her into the Pacific, and by 13 June was in New Zealand waters. He had been ordered to lay his cargo of 228 mines near Auckland, and did so one cloudy night between Great Mercury and Cuvier Islands. *Achilles* and *Hector* passed nearby while Weyher was doing this, but neither spotted the German vessel in the darkness.

Five days later the field scored its first victim, the 13,415-ton steamer *Niagara*, carrying £2.5 million worth of gold (about $222.5 million worth in early twenty-first century money). She hit one of the mines and went down on the night of 19 June. *Achilles* and the RNZAF's fast launch rushed to the rescue. The government temporarily halted shipping and sent *Achilles* to find the raider, supported by the flying boat *Awarua*. However, by this time the HSK *Orion* was near the Kermadecs, where Weyher captured the wheat carrier *Tropic Sea*.

Orion's activities soon became entangled in a political storm that brewed between New Zealand and Britain in June 1940. The fall of France prompted the British to abandon their 'main fleet to Singapore' strategy. A telegram to that effect prompted alarm in Wellington, and Prime Minister Peter Fraser pointed out that while New Zealand 'did not demur', the 'undertaking to despatch an adequate fleet to Singapore, if required, formed the basis of the whole of this Dominion's defensive preparations'.[49] '[A] rapid deterioration . . . in the Far Eastern situation . . . reinforced the view . . . that relations between the British Commonwealth and Japan are most unstable.'[50] The New Zealand government questioned sending the Third Echelon to the Middle East, and decided to retain 3050 further reinforcements in the Pacific, hoping they might be sent to Fiji.

Achilles was very busy during July, narrowly missing *Orion* in Fijian waters, and by mid-August was in Wellington preparing to escort the Third Echelon. Meanwhile the *Orion* entered the Tasman, and on 20 July ran into *Turakina*, owned by the New Zealand Shipping Company. Captain J.B. Laird sounded the alarm and engaged the raider with his single 4.7-inch gun. He stood little chance, and within fifteen minutes *Turakina* was a wreck. The quarterdeck was awash when Laird gave the order to abandon ship, and though the gun was virtually submerged he still wanted to continue the engagement. Moments later a torpedo fired by the *Orion* struck home, and *Turakina* sank with a huge explosion, taking down almost all the crew who remained on board, including Laird.

Achilles sailed at once to search for the raider with the assistance of the flying boat *Awarua*. The light cruiser *Perth* also sortied from the other side of the Tasman, supported by five Hudsons, but the German ship again eluded dominion forces. Weyher had actually sailed around South Australia. At the end of the month *Achilles* resumed Third Echelon convoy work, escorting ships to the assembly point in Wellington and taking the troop convoy to Sydney, where escort was picked up by Australian naval forces.

German raider activities rose to a new pitch towards the end of the year. Ship No. 33, usually called *Pinguin*, was known to be in the Indian Ocean and feared to be making for the Tasman. Meanwhile, *Orion* made contact with Ship No. 45, also known as *Komet*. In company with the supply ship *Kulmerland* they began operations along the east coast of New Zealand, hoping to intercept traffic to the Pacific Islands and fatter cargoes being sent to Panama.

Attention belatedly turned to ways of defending the coasts against German mines and possible Japanese submarines and minelayers. Commodore Parry got the ball rolling in August 1940 — wearing his 'second hat' on the New Zealand Naval Board — suggesting that the small anti-submarine ships building in Scotland should be swapped for others under construction in Australia. This was turned down by the Admiralty in November; the Australian vessels were needed in the Middle East. However, Parry had discussed the issue with Australian officials in September, and settled on an alternative scheme involving fast launches. He thought a dozen would do. Although limited to good weather and likely to cost £1,000,000, the launches were within New Zealand's ability to build and support. The War Cabinet approved the scheme in mid-October, and despite favouring trawlers, the Admiralty agreed to provide a dozen Fairmiles.

Some of the pressure in New Zealand waters was relieved by the arrival of the armed merchant *Monowai*. She had been commissioned in 1925 as the P & O liner *Razmak*, and was renamed *Monowai* when she joined the Union Steamship line in 1930. She was a sister of the *Rawalpindi*, sunk by the battlecruisers *Scharnhorst* and *Gniesenau* during their early 1941 cruise into the Atlantic. Shortly after war broke out she was chartered by the New Zealand government and, over the next ten months, converted to an armed merchant cruiser with six- and three-inch guns. S.W. Hicks recalled that when *Monowai* was recommissioned with the New Zealand Division in August 1940, there were rumours that:

> ... she would never clear a path through the mountain of beer bottles discarded by the Dockyard Maties. However, apart from building the magazines ashore and then finding they wouldn't fit through the hatches, they did a splendid job and we proudly sailed out under the White Ensign...[51]

On 25 November *Komet* sank *Holmwood*, bound for Lyttelton from the Chathams, and two days later the two raiders intercepted *Rangitane*, whose 111 passengers and crew were taken off and the ship sunk. *Achilles* sailed from Lyttelton at once, but no aircraft were available for some time. The flying boat *Awarua* eventually took off in support. *Achilles* would have had her work cut out had she encountered the three raiders. Weyher intended to engage any lone warship with *Orion* while the other two escaped. Next day a worried Fraser sent an urgent message to Churchill:

> *Yesterday a New Zealand ship, the* Rangitane, *with a valuable cargo and precious lives, was attacked and presumably sunk some 400 miles from the New Zealand coast. The only aircraft available for reconnaissance at such a distance are the two flying boats, and as it happened one of these boats was on the slip and the other on passage from Sydney. As a result it was not until eight hours after the warning was received that the first [flying] boat was despatched . . . what chances there were of destroying the raider were accordingly lost before the search commenced. We should be most grateful if you could personally look into this matter and . . . arrange for us to receive at any rate a limited number of Hudsons or other suitable aircraft in order to remedy our helplessness in such circumstances.*[52]

Achilles' search for the raiders was transmuted to a hunt for the *Holmwood*. There were concerns that the raiders had found the merchants with the help of a 'leak', but in fact they were chance encounters. The experience also highlighted the difficulties of relying on a single cruiser and one or two flying boats to defend the coasts. The Germans had no idea that New Zealand defences were so poor — their plans were apparently based on the assumption that Auckland, Wellington and Lyttelton each had four long-range aircraft that would be deployed in fan-wise patterns.[53] This was reasonable: just before war broke out, the RNZAF had been due to take delivery of thirty long-range Wellington bombers. These, however, had been handed to the RAF for the duration. The result was that New Zealand had very few long-range aircraft available for maritime patrol work, and much of the load fell on the two TEAL flying boats that had been operating on the Sydney run. To Fraser, a few aircraft seemed more practical to ask for than another cruiser, but Churchill promised only to 'meet your needs as soon as possible'. Fraser was 'keenly disappointed', reminding Churchill that New Zealand had given away the Wellington bombers:

> ... we wonder if it is fully realised in the United Kingdom how helpless this Dominion is against attacks from seaward ... the whole of our defence measures were built on the assurance that in time of potential trouble in these waters adequate naval forces would be available. They are not ... at present local naval forces are far from adequate to protect New Zealand shores and shipping against attack, and it is plain fact that at present the New Zealand Air Force [sic] possesses not one single aircraft suitable either for reconnaissance or for attack against a raider ... We believe we are the only Dominion in this situation ...[54]

Even half a dozen aircraft, he continued, would 'enable us to relieve the disheartening effect upon our people of our present obvious helplessness in this matter, which is potentially a most mischievous effect upon the whole of the Dominion's war effort'.[55] Churchill again promised to send forces when available. Meanwhile the German raiders went unmolested, supported by a steady supply line from Japan. *Monowai* had a narrow escape; she had regularly escorted *Rangitane* and subsequently:

> [run a] routine patrol between Nauru and Ocean Island while the ships like Triadic *and the like were loading phosphate ... we were doing that when the* Rangitane *was sunk ... by these three raiders. We came back to ... Suva to refuel; dear old* Monowai *... was very, very thirsty for fuel oil. We refuelled in Suva and came back to Auckland. By the time that we got to Auckland the three raiders had hopped into Nauru and Ocean Island and completely smashed up all the gear for loading the phosphate. We reckoned when we saw the tracks later we must have crossed their tracks, somewhere around the Kermadecs. We had a look in there and also at Minerva reef.*[56]

The Nauru raid was devastating. *Orion* and *Komet* turned up off the island early on 8 December, wearing a Japanese flag, in company with the German-manned but Japanese-owned and flagged merchants *Manu Maru* and *Tokyo*

Maru. They quickly snapped up local shipping, including the phosphate carriers *Triadic* and *Triaster*. G.W. Dillon was a passenger on board *Triadic*, which was attacked about ten miles from Nauru. The first he knew of the attack came around 5 a.m. when 'the scream and burst of a shell . . . brought down the derrick on No. 2 forward hatch', and he watched aghast as a second hit 'passed through the chief engineer's cabin and burst in the saloon'. As fire rippled through the devastated compartment:

> [I] sprang out on the starboard side of the boat deck with my wife and found all the other passengers assembled there. Everything was pitch dark and then two more shells arrived, one going right through the wireless cabin from the portside and bursting on the starboard side, and this shell completely wrecked the aft starboard lifeboat.[57]

Dillon went into his cabin and had found his slippers, an overcoat and a travelling rug when smoke and flames drove him to the deck. G.R. Ferguson had a similar experience, finding '[the] lights had failed, the floor was covered with broken metal and fittings; the stairway to the saloon was a mass of smoke with a glow of fire at the bottom . . .' He had only his pyjama pants on and went to his cabin where he collected an overcoat, lifebelts, and his watch. His wife wore only her nightdress and his dressing gown.[58] By this time the Germans had ceased fire and were playing a searchlight on the stricken freighter. The passengers and crew lowered boats as the fire spread and rowed for Nauru. After about two hours they were half-way, in growing daylight, when rockets went up on the island. Dillon and the other survivors 'expected Jimmy Langar to be coming through to us with his launches . . . the swell was fairly high, but our boat was riding well . . . and we were singing and very happy'. Their mood ended when *Komet* put herself between the boats and the island. Dillon saw 'scores of German sailors' looking down, and 'with a dramatic click, down came the German naval ensign completely covering the Japanese colours amidships'. He advised the others to '"Say a prayer to God", for I felt that once again I was to face machine gun fire as I did before in the last war.'[59]

The Germans took them aboard. One of *Triadic*'s officers spotted a German officer and demanded to know why they had been attacked without warning. As Dillon recalled, 'the officer replied, "You were an armed ship and I treat you as a warship, why do you carry passengers on your ship with a gun on?"'[60] He was hustled to crowded compartments in the fore part of the ship. Soon afterwards *Komet* attacked the freighter *Komata* and more survivors were brought on board, some badly injured. The Second Mate died and his clothes were distributed — Ferguson 'was fortunate in securing a pair of pants and a shirt; I had previously cut off one pyjama leg to serve as a face washer and handkerchief and the other leg for use as a towel'.[61]

Orion also snapped up *Triaster*. By this time there were 675 prisoners on board the raiders and their consorts, and Dillon recalled that — on board *Komet* at least — they were 'well fed and humanely treated'. The food was 'wholesome, and of the German type, meaning that we had beans, black bread, bean soup and sausages, raw bacon, but our appetites were not good because of our close confinement'.[62] They were offloaded to one of the Japanese freighters a few days later, after signing an agreement promising to take no further part in hostilities. The captain shook Dillon's hand as he left and wished him luck. Dillon 'could do nothing else but return the compliment', then scrambled aboard the other ship. She turned out to be the 'so-called hell-ship', *Manyo Maru*, though Dillon did not find it too bad. He discovered his wife was on board the *Kulmerland*. Food on the *Manyo Maru* was:

> . . . just a plate of boiled rice for breakfast and beans and macaroni for dinner, and some sandwiches for tea, but the jokes that were exchanged over the table were very good. I made myself handy sweeping and helping generally, in the hopes of getting a little extra food and water for the others who needed it, but I did not succeed very well.[63]

Water was rationed after a while, but Ferguson felt the 'spirit of the men could not have been excelled' — it was so good the Germans commented on it. On *Manyo Maru* they had hammocks, but there was only one 'sanitary basin . . . flushed with [a] saltwater hose which also did duty for washing purposes'. The saltwater:

> . . . seemed to cool us down and make us feel cleaner. Unfortunate was the man who walked into the bathroom in his clothes, took up his position in the sanitary basin to find that the person with the hose could not aim straight — some of the language was inspired! . . . The German

captain in charge of the three ships was full of his own importance — his egotism seemed to pervade the whole of the crews . . . Their treatment of the women and children, their handling of the injured and the attitude towards prisoners generally was of a high standard, although the food supplies were just enough to keep us alive, but . . . they do not forget the possibility of being themselves caught and as prisoners they would expect the same treatment meted out to us — but we were not prisoners of war, we were pursuing a civilian existence.[64]

The prisoners were ordered below as *Manyo Maru* approached the Bismarck Archipelago on 20 December. They reached Emirau next day, where the prisoners were released. 'We were laughing and crying and stuffing ourselves full of pawpaw and coconut,' Dillon recalled. They trudged ten miles to the home of one of the two European families on the island. It was a long walk after their confinement, but 'heaven indeed' when they got there. Dillon 'got a glass of clear water and a tomato and a glass of bread. I then fell in with Captain Callender . . . and we sat and smoked by the roadside, rejoycing that we were free again, but our sorrow was for those we had left behind on the other ships.' Soon afterwards they were picked up by the government launch *Leander* — women, wounded and husbands first — and taken to Kavieng. '[A] flying boat moored close to the wharf gave a sense of security and a feeling of proximity to Australia.'[65] By 28 December they were at Rabaul, and Dillon reached Townsville on 3 January.[66]

Some 514 prisoners were released at Emirau, but Weyher refused to release the Europeans, who were transferred to the *Ermlandt*. The freighter returned to Bordeaux disguised as a Japanese vessel. One of those on board, K.W. Goodridge, recalled that for the whole four-month voyage he had only the clothes he stood up in, and no shoes — he had lost his in the water. There was also 'no soap, [no] water for washing other than salt water, [no] hair brushes and combs, toothbrushes etc.'.[67]

Komet took on the last 1100 tons of fuel from *Kulmerland* at Emirau, and returned to Nauru where she bombarded the British Phosphates plant on 27 December. Initial reports suggested that the ship flew the Japanese flag, a move decried by the *Evening Post* as a 'typical act', and by London newspapers as a 'crude Nazi idea' designed to provoke an international incident.[68] In fact reports of false colours proved mistaken. *Komet* arrived off Nauru around 5.50 a.m. local time and signalled those ashore not to radio for help. This signal 'was complied with to save destruction of human life and property'. The raider opened fire around 6.40 a.m. and 'shelled at close range [the] cantilever, shore storage bin, mooring gear store and other phosphate buildings'. The oil fuel burned for more than a day afterwards, and the Germans used machine gun fire to destroy a mooring buoy. However, they did not fire on private homes, and the wireless station and power station were left intact.[69]

The dent in Nauru's output was a heavy blow. Sir Albert Ellis, a New Zealand member of the British Phosphates Commission, tried to calm fears. Although the damage was a 'grievous loss . . . [there was] no need for farmers to get the wind up . . . This is just a difficulty to be overcome, and we are going to use every available means to overcome it.'[70] However, Japan was also a customer of Nauru Phosphates, and when advised that 'force majeure prevents the shipments'[71] threatened to cut off supplies to the German raiders. The New Zealand government also asked for *Leander* back, but the Admiralty wanted her tour of duty in the Indian Ocean extended by three months, which Fraser's administration accepted. Partly as a result of *Leander*'s absence, *Achilles* was extremely busy during the early part of 1941, escorting convoys and shipping in New Zealand waters and the islands. By July, when she was docked for refit, she had steamed 82,679 miles since mid-1940, 41,937 miles of that since January, averaging 24 days every month at sea. This was an outstanding performance.

Orion returned to Germany and was replaced by Ship No. 16, *Atlantis*, under Captain Bernhard Rogge. She commenced operations in the South Pacific in July. Meanwhile a captured whale chaser, renamed *Adjutant*, laid magnetic mines off Lyttelton and Wellington harbours during June 1941. Incredibly, none went off, regular sweeping failed to locate anything, and the fields were not discovered until German records were inspected after the war.

Leander in the Middle East, 1940–41

While *Achilles* searched for raiders in local waters, *Leander* settled down to operations in the Red Sea, attached to the 4th Cruiser Squadron, part of the East Indies Station. She reached Port Sudan on 4 June, where Rear-Admiral

Murray briefly hoisted his flag in her. Italy declared war six days later. Almost at once *Leander* found and arrested the liner *Umbria*, and subsequently searched without success for an Italian U-boat operating south of Aden. On 26 June she engaged another Italian submarine, straddling it and forcing it down. The sinking could not be confirmed, but an oil patch was seen on the water and survivors found on a raft claimed that the submarine, *Evangelista Torricelli*, had been holed.

Early excitement gave way to monotony as the New Zealand cruiser chopped back and forth in the narrow waterway between Africa and Asia, usually with other destroyers and occasionally cruisers, escorting convoys from Aden waters to Suez. Italian forces in Italian Somalialand initially did not do much to hamper the British. An air attack on 6 September was almost a relief; *Leander* fired 65 four-inch rounds at the Italian planes.

In mid-October, Italian surface forces at Massawa sailed to intercept a northbound convoy which was escorted by *Leander* with the destroyers *Auckland* and HMAS *Yarra*. The first warning of their presence came in the early hours of 21 October, when *Leander* spotted smoke against the night sky to the north, and *Auckland* reported two enemy destroyers. *Leander* engaged one of the Italian vessels at 2.45 a.m., but the target was soon lost in the darkness. Then she ran into the second destroyer, pinned it with searchlights, and opened fire at 4600 yards. However, this target also disappeared into the night. The destroyer *Kimberley* subsequently ran into one of the Italian ships in the lee of Harmil Island, closing in despite fire from a shore battery. She sank the Italian destroyer, but was crippled by the shore battery and limped away. *Leander* rushed to the rescue, achieving more than 28 knots despite not having been docked for seven months. Captain H.E. Horan expected air attacks and was reluctant to tow the crippled destroyer, but finally did so at 10 a.m. The Italians flew in to attack at about the same time, missing both ships.

Action of a different kind came in November, when *Leander* — now under Captain Robert Bevan — led Operation CANNED, an attack on a coastal canning plant at Banda Alula in Italian Somalialand, near the Gulf of Aden. *Leander* was tasked with destroying the factory, canned fish and a radio direction finding station. She attacked on 29 November, initially with her Walrus spotter plane, then with her 6-inch armament at a range of 4000 yards, near point-blank, expending 98 rounds and causing serious damage ashore.

The cruiser made her way to Bombay for overdue docking and a welcome Christmas break for her crew, and spent the early part of 1941 in the Indian Ocean. The HSK's *Pinguin* and *Atlantis* were at large there along with their supply ships, and the *Admiral Scheer* was reportedly also at sea. The Italians, meanwhile, prepared several *Ramb* class fruit-carriers in Italian Somalialand as raiders and sent them into the Indian Ocean. *Leander* found the first on 27 February, partly by chance. Bevan ordered the ship to turn north in the hope of crossing the track of any Italian vessels and *Ramb-1* was spotted 67 minutes later. *Leander* accelerated to 23 knots, but this was not fast enough. Instructor Commander S.F. Hermans was in the plotting office:

> *I had a look and, 'hell's teeth' she was doing 22 knots according to my estimate. When the Navigator, Commander Vereker at that time called down 'what speed is she doing Plot?', I thought 'oh 22 knots is a bit fast', and so I said '18 knots Sir.' He said, 'don't be so bloody wet, a merchant ship doing that speed!', and I thought gee! Johnny Kirk was then the Assistant Navigator so I called up to him and I said: 'what is it John?' ... he said 'Oh, I think it's one of ours, she is flying a very small flag though.' We gradually closed ... she was still battling along, and it took a while.*[72]

Twenty-two knots was very fast for a merchant, but it was not until a gun became visible on the stranger's forecastle that 'suspicions were aroused'.[73] Bevan called the crew to action stations at 11.15 a.m., at a range of 5½ miles. The turrets remained fore and aft. By 11.25 a.m. the range had dropped to 10,000 yards and Bevan signalled the strange merchant to hoist her colours. After four minutes she raised the Red Ensign. Bevan then asked the stranger to hoist her signal letters. A further five minutes passed before 'GJYD' rose on the halyards, suggesting the ship was *Grosmont Castle*. Bevan had the secret challenge made by light, and at 11.45 a.m. ordered the stranger to 'stop instantly'. There was no acknowledgement. By this time the range was down to about 3000 yards. Hermans heard:

> *... the Chief Yeoman through the voice pipe yelling out ... 'It's an Italian raider' to the Captain. He said 'oh you know we have got to make sure', and we were making sure all right, we closed to well within a mile or so, and just as I opened up the dead lights I heard the Yeoman say 'she is*

*hauling down her flag Sir.' At that very moment I saw flashes of gunfire coming from the for'ard guns.*⁷⁴

Bevan was apparently about to have a warning round fired when the Italian flag went up and the shells 'went hurtling over the bridge'. Thirty seconds later *Leander* returned the fire:

*Pop Harvey who was the Gunner in charge of the four inch guns on that side opened up and put a four inch shell right through her W/T office. Immediately 'Guns' swung the six inch round and we were so close that the shells were going clean through her and exploding some distance away on the other side.*⁷⁵

Leander fired five salvoes, setting *Ramb-1* alight; by the time she checked fire the Italian flag was down and there were signs of the crew abandoning ship. Two lifeboats pulled clear and 'stragglers were jumping overboard or climbing down the sides'. Bevan had *Leander*'s cutter lowered and a boarding party sent away, but they were warned off by an Italian officer who advised that the blazing ship was loaded with ammunition. The fires continued to rage, sending debris spiralling high into the air. Some crashed on *Leander*. By this time the fruit-carrier was down by the bows, lying head to wind. The fire passed under the bridge and 'caught hold aft where, at 12.43 p.m., there was a very heavy explosion, evidently of the magazine and ready use cartridges'. The ship sank five minutes later, 'leaving quantities of oil fuel still burning on the surface'.⁷⁶

The cruiser picked up ten officers, the captain, and 92 men. One man was seriously injured and ten slightly wounded, and it turned out that another had been killed on board by shell fire. The injured prisoner died later that afternoon and was buried at sunset with full honours. Interrogation revealed that no scuttling charges had been set or fired, and gave Hermans a moment of triumph:

I was still smarting because when the Commander called out and asked me the speed and I said 22 knots, he didn't believe me. I turned around, and asked . . . the Italian Captain, who spoke quite good English. I said 'what speed were you doing Captain?' He grinned and said 'oh, she had twin Fiat 4-cylinder diesels fitted onboard.' He was so proud as he said '. . . she had a designed speed of 18 and a half knots, but we were doing well over 20.' I just looked at the Commander and grinned.[77]

Leander headed for Addu Atoll, where she met the tanker *Pearleaf*. The prisoners were transferred under guard of three petty officers and sixteen ratings led by Commander B.E.W. Logan. Some of the prisoners apparently got a glimpse of the port and realised they were in Addu, but Bevan believed that anybody who knew those waters could have deduced this from their transit time.[78]

Afterwards there were recriminations — Bevan had put his ship alongside an enemy that could have done them serious mischief. Hermans was under no illusions that they had been 'pretty lucky . . . there is no doubt about it, the ship was endangered . . . Instead of keeping astern of her, we pulled in broadside on just a mile or so off.'[79]

None of this was revealed to Kiwis hungry for news. On 28 February the New Zealand Naval Board requested copies of photographs taken by an RAF officer on board the cruiser,[80] and these arrived at the beginning of April. Meanwhile, however, a storm erupted over the story. On 8 March the Admiralty confirmed that the news could be released, but wanted *Leander*'s subsequent involvement with *Canberra* against the German supply ships *Kitty Brovig* and *Coburg* withheld. By this time news of the *Ramb* had escaped in an *Auckland Star* report. The War Cabinet were 'shocked' to learn of an apparent leak, and it transpired that the story had come via a press telegram from Australia. The problem with news of the *Kitty Brovig* and *Coburg* was that *Admiral Scheer* was known to be in the vicinity, and the Admiralty were determined this information should 'not repetition not be published for the present . . .'[81] The argument burbled on into June, when the New Zealand Naval Board finally told the Prime Minister's staff that 'it does not require much intelligence to appreciate that to keep the enemy in ignorance of the loss of one of his ships may be very inconvenient for him and very convenient for our forces'.[82]

The rendezvous with *Canberra* raised the spirits of *Leander*'s crew 'because *Canberra* had eight-inch guns' — vital against a German armoured ship.[83] However, a report on 5 March that the *Admiral Scheer* was in the vicinity proved a false alarm. Politics now played a part in *Leander*'s fortunes. On 4 March the First Sea Lord, A.V. Alexander, met New Zealand's High Commissioner W.J. Jordan in London and asked permission to retain *Leander* on the East Indies Station. This was softening up for a formal message the following day, revealing that *Australia* or *Canberra* were returning to Australia, bolstering forces there to one 8-inch and three 6-inch cruisers. The Admiralty advised that '. . . if position necessitates HMS *Leander* will return',[84] but they really wanted her in the Indian Ocean, although they admitted next day that 'the possibility of . . . [*Scheer*] appearing in Tasman Sea cannot be ruled out'.[85] From New Zealand's perspective *Leander*'s return would have been justified, but the War Council reached a qualified agreement to leave her in the Indian Ocean, and asked Jordan to pass the message on to Alexander:

Though we are . . . not without apprehension as to position that might develop in local waters in certain contingencies we are always happy to feel that New Zealand naval vessels are being used to best advantage. In present circumstances we make no objection to the retention of HMS Leander *abroad always provided of course that the matter can be raised for immediate reconsideration should the local situation deteriorate.*[86]

There was excitement late on 23 March when *Leander* located a merchant, initially thought to be the HSK *Atlantis*. The ship turned out to be the French merchant *Charles L.D.*, sailing under Vichy colours. She would not stop until *Leander* fired several 4-inch shells across her bows. There was a brief signal exchange by light, during which the Kiwis also saw 'weak and somewhat irregular signals . . . coming from aft, such as "Help!", "Help!", and "Please hurry.". . . There was also a signal about "Dynamite on board", but this was read as "Dynamite off board", and we did not jump to it.'[87]

A boarding party found that the *Charles L.D.* was en route to Reunion to pick up coffee, cocoa and sugar, which would almost certainly have wound up in Germany. The captain and second officer refused to co-operate, explaining that they had been instructed to sink the ship rather than allow her to be taken — some of the crew were actually wearing lifejackets when the boarding party arrived. Third officer la Coley then told the New Zealanders that there was dynamite on board, and showed the boarding party 'a box of explosives in the store room under the saloon'. Lieutenant P.C. Sanders 'cut the electric leads, and after reporting to Lt. Thompson, had the box thrown overboard'.

There were also reports of dynamite in the shafts. The boarding party finally talked the crew and engineers into heading for Mauritius, and the ship went on her way with a small armed guard of New Zealanders. Everything was done by the book, as Sanders later reported:

> *It was found that the armed guard had left certain stores behind, and some food was supplied by la Coley. A tally was kept of all stores from the ship, and the bill was duly paid to the Captain, who gave a receipt. Also wine ordered by the officers willing to help was paid for by Lt. Stevens, Lt. Lee-Richards and myself.*[88]

Some of *Leander*'s crew were drafted to HMS *Neptune*. The New Zealand government wanted two cruisers in local waters. Britain wanted the Kiwi contribution elsewhere, and by late 1940 looked to New Zealand to help make up the crew of a third cruiser. Fraser's government agreed, apparently in the hope that *Leander* might then be able to come home. Finding the men was another matter; New Zealand's manpower situation was critical, and trained naval ratings in particularly short supply. However, some 150 New Zealanders were assembled in Britain, including 'quite a number' from *Leander*, 'all of my cobbers', as W.M. Gibbs recalled. He had 'put in to go with that draft' himself, but 'the Commander . . . decided that I couldn't'.[89] *Neptune* sailed for the Mediterranean in May.

The Mediterranean Fleet took a hammering during early 1941, and despite a spectacular victory off Cape Matapan remained hard-pressed. Efforts to support the army on Crete stretched Admiral Sir Andrew Cunningham's force to the limits. The military situation on Crete was approaching crisis, and Fraser went to Cairo. When the Admiralty approached him on 23 May with a request to despatch *Leander* there he was happy to agree, telling Nash the ship was 'essential to support our men in Crete'.[90] *Leander* was at Trincomalee, and her passage to Egypt was slowed by mines:

> *. . . even at that stage we were still not completely prepared for war. The ship still wasn't camouflaged and until our refit in Bombay in December we hadn't been degaussed. We had no protection against magnetic mines, but the ship was degaussed and had the degaussing coils put around it in Bombay. When we got to Aden, the ship was held up because*

> the Germans had dropped . . . acoustic mines in the canal, together with magnetic mines . . . they still hadn't had the answer to the acoustic mines. Until they could be certain that the canal was fairly clear we were held up in Aden awaiting orders. During that time every man and his dog was employed camouflaging the ship and the Shipwrights were ripping out all the inflammable lining in the officers cabins and all that sort of thing . . . When we did eventually go through, it was a pretty slow passage because positions where they knew the acoustic mines had been dropped were buoyed . . . we would get up a head of steam and drift over those areas . . . we actually got through to Alexandria when the last of the ships were coming back, some of them pretty damaged from dive bombing attacks . . . from the evacuation in Crete.[91]

The cruiser reached Alexandria on 29 May, while New Zealand soldiers still awaited evacuation from Sphakia, on the south coast of Crete. However, the General Staff decided that day not to send ships beyond those already committed. Fraser argued the point with Cunningham, who agreed to send an additional cruiser with the last planned sea-lift on the night of 30 May, and selected *Phoebe*. One of the New Zealanders on board her, Able Seaman A.D. Beck, received the DSM for his actions during the campaign.

Leander was welcome reinforcement for the Mediterranean Fleet, which was down to two battleships, three cruisers, a minelayer and nine destroyers as a result of losses around Greece and Crete.[92] She was fitted with additional anti-aircraft guns and joined a squadron under Vice-Admiral E.L.S. King, supporting ground forces in the campaign against the Free French in Syria. 'Every time we poked our head outside Alex [sic] we were getting dive bombed,' Hermans recalled.[93] On 12 June *Leander* sailed to relieve *Ajax*, and the squadron briefly came under Bevan's command when King's flagship *Phoebe* left to refuel. Action was sporadic but intense when it occurred. On one occasion an Australian brigade was halted by Vichy French tanks on a bridge. *Leander* was called on to provide supporting fire.

> As the Aussies tried to poke their head around the corner the tanks would open up on them. We got a signal giving the tanks as target, to see if we could knock them out, [which] also said 'for God's sake don't hit the bridge.' Well, you know good old Army have no idea of the limitations

of Naval gunnery and our first salvo didn't straddle the bridge, it hit the bridge completely, but it also knocked the tanks out. It also meant that the Aussies couldn't advance as quickly as they expected...[94]

The Luftwaffe had command of the air, and S.J.F. Hermans recalled that to avoid air attack the naval forces would 'leave Haifa in the late evening and steam up the coast like hell and get there around about dawn in time to do a bombardment and then sneak back again. Otherwise in daylight hours we were getting stonked by dive bombers.'[95] Later they attacked Beirut, an assault that involved close action with Vichy French destroyers:

... we chased after them, they were faster than us and for some unknown reason we didn't fire on them. You had to be careful that you didn't upset the Vichy French too much I suppose. However they fired torpedoes at us. I heard the Captain calling out: 'comb the tracks', you could see the torpedoes coming and we steamed between them. At any rate to stop that operations [the] C in C decided that we should go in and knock these destroyers out, actually go into Beirut. We went up there one night, got into the harbour itself, steamed around firing torpedoes, with all hell let loose. The Naiad went in ahead and broke through the boom. They had some shore batteries, and so we had to stonk them too. It was quite an exciting evening.[96]

Chief Petty Officer W.M. Gibbs did not think their efforts were particularly productive, recalling that they 'got around 20 torpedo hits on the coast of Syria'. He felt the French were 'sound asleep' because there was no serious opposition until 'we were getting away', when:

... the shore batteries, which I was told were 9.2's, opened fire on us. Y turret, my turret, was actually out of action because of a jammed training ring, but we were all closed up. I can remember somebody saying, 'oh look at all the pretty lights', and somebody else said 'you so and so fool, they're not pretty lights, that's what the French use for spotting at night time...'[97]

There were several other actions with Vichy French vessels, mostly desultory, which ended on the night of 22 June when *Leander* and three destroyers ran into two Vichy French ships while running inshore north of Beirut. There was a brief battle; *Leander* fired 'blind' and launched four torpedoes which apparently hit the coast. She remained in Syrian waters until mid-July when the Vichy French surrendered, and after briefly escorting a troop convoy to Cyprus, was ordered back to New Zealand waters. She returned home in early September 1941 and was docked for refit.

War politics and the genesis of a navy

The Royal New Zealand Navy became an independent service in late 1941. Superficially, the change had no apparent implication beyond bringing New Zealand into line with Australia, Canada and India — all of which had separate navies. However, the move needs to be seen in the context of New Zealand's broader strategy. It was a political manoeuvre that, in a broader sense, reflected Labour government imperatives that had been bubbling along since before the war; but it was particularly spurred by the early war experiences with marauding HSK's, by official British withdrawal from the 'main fleet to Singapore' strategy, and particularly by the outcome of the campaigns in Greece and Crete. Fraser sought new ties with the United States during 1941 in direct response to the Singapore issue, appointing a minister in Washington despite British objections.[98] His naval initiative was another expression of the same thinking — a step towards establishing forces under full New Zealand control, able to work with a strong ally.

Fraser's timing appears to have been prompted by the experiences in Greece and Crete, which to his thinking risked the loss of virtually the whole New Zealand Division, and appears to have brought the whole issue of the defence relationship with Britain to a head.[99] He rushed to Egypt to intervene, and in June told Nash that 'unless the necessary adequate air protection is available . . . in no case must we again allow our New Zealand troops to . . . meet a highly developed mechanised attack armed solely with their rifles and their courage'. He explained this to the British 'as forcibly as possible',[100] and went on to press the issue in London, delivering 25 questions prepared by Carl Berendsen to discover why Kiwi forces had been so poorly treated. Churchill was reluctant to see him, and in any case had nothing concrete to offer. However, he was eager to oil the waters if he could, particularly as Australia was threatening to withdraw from North Africa in response to the Japanese threat and what the Australians perceived as their own poor treatment. Consequently, when Fraser asked at the same time to have the New Zealand Naval Division converted into a separate service, Churchill was willing to agree.

While Fraser was making a political point by asking to have an independent navy, it was by any practical measure simply an administrative shift. The Order in Council making the change on 1 October 1941 substituted the term 'Royal New Zealand Navy' for 'New Zealand Division of the Royal Navy'.[101] The ships gained the prefix RNZN. Nothing else altered. New Zealand ships continued to operate with a proportion of Royal Navy personnel and to be subject to requests for use outside New Zealand waters. The country continued to rely on Britain for ships and support. Fraser knew this when he made the request — the gesture was symbolic at a time when he was unhappy with the way New Zealand servicemen had been treated. However, and again probably as Fraser intended, the change laid the foundation for development as a truly independent service after the war, and the service always celebrated its birthday on 1 October. Not everybody liked the idea of a New Zealand Navy at first. S.W. Hicks recalled:

> . . . *[I was] still in* Monowai *when we got a signal that old Fraser, he was so proud of himself, he had created the Royal New Zealand Navy. Well we were horrified, and the whole Navy was. Up to then we had been a rather proud Unit of the Royal Navy. Now we were little wee fish in a little wee pond, you know.*[102]

While these political issues were played out, *Neptune* fought on in the Mediterranean. Shortages of destroyers forced the British battleships to remain in Alexandria during December, and on 15 December Cunningham despatched cruisers under Rear-Admiral Philip Vian to escort the tanker *Breconshire* to Malta. *Neptune* left Alexandria with Vian's flagship *Ajax* and the destroyers *Kimberley* and *Kingston*, intending to take *Breconshire* to rendezvous with 'Force K', which was coming to meet them from Malta. The Italians sortied a battle fleet to intercept, and Vian encountered the Italians alone on the night of the 17th. He sent *Breconshire* south, and after an exchange of fire the two Italian battleships and their escorting force disengaged.

Vian left *Neptune* in Malta and returned to Alexandria. New information suggested that the Italian battle fleet had turned to escort a convoy to North Africa, and *Neptune*, *Aurora* and *Penelope* with the destroyers *Kandahar*, *Lance*, *Lively* and *Havock* sortied from Malta to intercept, under Captain R. O'Conor of the *Neptune*. Wary of mines, the warships streamed paravanes as they left harbour and worked up to 30 knots. Heavy weather forced them to slow during the night. By about 1 a.m. they were just north of Tripoli and making around 24 knots when *Neptune*'s paravane hit a mine. The force had run into a field laid by the Germans some time earlier to prevent the British bombarding Tripoli. O'Conor ordered full speed astern, but it took time to bring the cruiser to a standstill. *Aurora* — next astern — sheered out of line in an effort to avoid other mines, and immediately hit one. As *Neptune* slowed she hit a second mine which smashed her propellers and rudder. She slid to a stop and drifted into a third mine that tore a hole in the shell plating and left her listing to port. *Penelope* also set a mine off with her paravane.

Aurora was still able to make 10 knots, and was detached back to Malta with two destroyers. *Kandahar* then tried to get a line to *Neptune*, but was warned off by O'Conor. About 3 a.m., as *Lively* manoeuvred to get the disabled cruiser under tow, a mine blew the stern off *Kandahar*, and at around 4 a.m. *Neptune* drifted onto another mine. She sank rapidly in the heavy seas, leaving most of her complement of 750 bobbing on Carley floats. Some tried to swim to the immobilised *Kandahar*, without success.

German airfields in Tripoli were twenty miles distant, and as dawn approached Captain Nicholl of the *Penelope* could see no option but to abandon the position. Lieutenant-Commander W.F.E. Hussey of the *Lively* wanted to pick up the men, but after a brief exchange bowed to Nicholl's orders and left the area; Nicholl himself was reluctant to go but could see no option. *Penelope* was the last available cruiser in Malta. He radioed for a flying boat or submarine to pick up survivors. *Kandahar*'s crew were rescued by the destroyer *Jaguar* on 20 December, but *Neptune*'s complement of 750 gradually succumbed to exposure and thirst. By the time an Italian torpedo boat found the one surviving raft late on Christmas Eve, only one man remained alive, Leading Seaman J. Walters. All one hundred and fifty New Zealanders on board died.[103]

Royal Navy Kiwis

Although *Neptune* was New Zealand's largest single contribution to the Royal Navy outside the New Zealand Division, about seven thousand Kiwis served in Royal Navy ships, with a peak contribution of more than 4900 men in 1944. Organisationally they were always considered part of the Naval Division and later the Royal New Zealand Navy, and they were present at virtually all the major naval battles from the Arctic to the Pacific. Sub-Lieutenant Stanley Watkinson went down with *Hood* when she was sunk by the *Bismarck* in May 1941. Ordinary Seaman A.F.R. O'Connor of Auckland was on board *Ark Royal*, whose aircraft played a critical role in disabling the German battleship. Wellingtonian Max Richmond was in command of *Bulldog* when she drove off persistent attacks on one Arctic convoy in April 1942, and eight months later Lieutenant Lewis King led damage control parties that put devastating fires out in *Onslow*, after she and four other destroyers drove off the armoured ship *Lutzow* which was attacking another convoy. New Zealanders were also on board ships of the Home Fleet which sank *Scharnhorst* off North Cape on the stormy New Year's Eve of 1943.

New Zealanders fought prominently in the Battle of the Atlantic, the crucial struggle for British sea lanes. Lieutenant-Commander John Holm, of Wellington, was appointed to command the 'Flower' class corvette *Crocus* in January 1942, based in Freetown and covering the convoys coming up from the South Atlantic. He took this small ship into combat with U-333 on the night of 5 October that year. The German boat, under Peter Cremer, was lying on the surface when *Crocus*' radar picked it up. Holm attacked at once, closing to ram and opening fire with his 4-inch guns. He did considerable damage to the submarine and was awarded the DSM.

The war in the Atlantic reached its peak in March 1943 when German 'wolf packs' converged on two huge convoys, one inbound and one outbound. A massive battle raged for three days, during which 22 merchants were sunk. Freighters belonging to the New Zealand Shipping Company were among those lost, while the *Tekoa* under Captain Albert Hocken rushed to rescue survivors of the *Irene du Pont* and *Southern Princess* from the freezing waters. Kiwis battled on for the rest of the war in the Atlantic. In January 1944 Lieutenant-Commander Leo Bourke, commanding HMS *Bayntun*, attacked a surfaced U-boat and with HMCS *Camrose* forced it down.

More than a thousand Kiwis flew with the Fleet Air Arm, at one stage making up ten percent of the officer cadre, and serving from the Atlantic to the Mediterranean. Some operated over the African desert. Some 152 Kiwis were killed flying for the service during the war. Lieutenant (A) V.H.G. Cowper of Havelock and Lieutenant M.S. Latter served on *Avenger*, the first escort carrier, and went down with her when she was sunk in late 1942.

Perhaps the most difficult and spectacular action by Kiwi naval pilots came in April 1944 when they joined a series of air attacks on the *Tirpitz*. The German battleship posed a serious threat to the Arctic convoys taking supplies to Murmansk and the Eastern Front, forcing the British to maintain a significant battleship force in home waters. Stopping her was remarkably difficult; she was anchored in well-defended narrow fjords, essentially out of range of British land-based bomber forces, and surrounded by anti-torpedo netting. She had been seriously damaged in late 1943 by British midget submarines, but by early 1944 there were indications that she was ready for sea again.

This time the British had opportunity to deploy the Fleet Air Arm. Six carriers were despatched to attack the 'lone queen of the north' in her remote anchorage at Altenfjord on 3 April. The attack came in two groups, the first catching the Germans by surprise at 5.29 a.m. Not all the anti-aircraft batteries were manned, and although the bombs did not have enough momentum to penetrate the armoured deck, significant damage was done to the upperworks. The second attack at 6.35 a.m. met stiffer resistance and one Barracuda was shot down. There were fifteen hits and one near-miss. The battleship was not closed up to action stations and damage was compounded by lack of integrity; flames and blast poured through open hatchways, water gushed through splinter-riddled shell plating and the upper decks were torn up. Some 122 Germans died and 316 were injured. Shock responses undid some of the repairs made after the midget submarine attack.

Grand Admiral Karl Donitz was determined to keep the ship operational, and the British tried to sink her again on 17 July. *Formidable*, *Indefatigable* and *Furious* sortied 45 Barracudas that day, without hitting the German battleship. New Zealand aviator Lieutenant-Commander (A) Archibald Richardson was nonetheless recommended for the 'highest posthumous award' after he pressed the attack home in the face of heavy fire, at the cost of his own life. Three further carrier-borne air attacks were made in August without success. Part of the problem was that the carrier-based aircraft could not carry bombs heavy enough to seriously damage the battleship, and the confined spaces of the fijords made it difficult to launch effective attacks. In the end the British were able to make arrangements with the Soviets to operate land-based aircraft from Yagodnik. This allowed them to deploy the Lancaster heavy bombers of the RAF's 9 and 617 Squadrons, carrying 6-ton 'Tallboy' weapons, each armed with more than 2.5 tons of torpex. These weapons were dramatically larger than anything the battleship's protection scheme had been designed to handle. An initial attack blew *Tirpitz*' bows apart. The battleship limped to Tromso, where she was sunk on 29 October after another raid that scored two direct hits and several near misses.[104]

CHAPTER FIVE
Pacific Crisis 1941–45

War between Japan and the United States seemed inevitable by late 1941. Japan's main problem was oil, which was wholly imported. An American embargo brought the Japanese to crisis point — forcing them to either capitulate or engage in a risky military venture through South East Asia to get Dutch East Indies supplies.

War in Malaya threatened to bring in Britain. In June 1941 the British asked New Zealand to bolster the defences at Singapore, and with difficulty a fighter squadron and construction crew was supplied.[1] Tensions did not diminish as the year wore on. Despite other war pressures, Admiralty staff intended to assemble a fleet at Ceylon by early 1942, based around *Nelson*, *Rodney*, *Renown* and an aircraft carrier, while the four old 'R' class battleships were slated for convoy escort in the Indian Ocean. Churchill disagreed and persuaded the Admiralty to despatch the modern *Prince of Wales* and the elderly battlecruiser *Repulse* to the Far East in advance of a larger planned fleet. He advised Fraser in late October.[2] They were intended to act as a diplomatic show of force, a deterrent to Japan declaring war, and were going to be joined by other ships over the next weeks and months. Churchill thought they might ultimately join the United States' Pacific Fleet, which had been deployed to Pearl Harbour in the face of the growing crisis.

Nobody anticipated that war was imminent. However, War Minister Hideki Tojo took control of the Japanese government that month amid spiralling tensions. Japanese advances in Indo-China undermined diplomatic efforts and threatened British Far Eastern interests. Churchill asked Roosevelt for a 'deterrent of the most general and formidable character'. The latter demurred. However, on 26 November the United States issued a 'Ten Point Note' which, as Churchill put it, 'not only met our wishes . . . but indeed went beyond anything for which we had ventured to ask'.[3]

On 1 December, Tojo resolved to attack the United States, Dutch East Indies and British Far Eastern possessions. The British did not know this, but reconnaissance around the Malaysian peninsula revealed Japanese preparations, and the attack came on 8 December — timed to match the attack on Pearl Harbor, on the other side of the date line. New Zealanders were in the front line — airmen equipped with Brewster Buffaloes, and sailors on board the capital ships *Prince of Wales*, *Repulse*, and a handful of other Royal Navy ships in harbour. Half a dozen New Zealanders were on board the two capital ships, including 21-year-old Lieutenant (A) G.M. Holden — pilot of *Repulse*'s Walrus amphibian — Chaplain the Reverend W.G. Parker, and Joiner K.H.W. Morgan. Commodore Parry was also in Singapore when the Japanese attack began, and signalled the New Zealand Naval Board to send *Achilles*. The cruiser was escorting *Wahine* to Suva and short of men after sending nearly a hundred on leave in anticipation of a period in dock. Nevertheless the Board had no hesitation in changing her orders.

Phillips decided to launch a hit-and-run raid on the invasion force, which was landing up the peninsula at Singora. The two heavy ships, now dubbed 'Force Z', sailed at 5.35 p.m. on 8 December. Five hours later Phillips was told there would be no air cover; Singora was in Japanese hands. The Japanese were aware of the British and Vice-Admiral Kondo hoped to engage the British with his two *Kongo* class battlecruisers, but was unable to find them, and aircraft despatched from Saigon in filthy weather failed to locate anything. Next day Phillips decided to abandon his mission, but at midnight heard that the Japanese were landing at Kuantan and changed course to investigate. Reconnaissance early on the 10th revealed that the harbour was empty, so Phillips set course for Singapore. At 11.10 a.m. the force was attacked by eighty Mitsubishi G4M1 'Betty' and Nakjima G3M3 'Nell' torpedo bombers, 170 miles northeast of Singapore. These were part of the 22nd Air Force based at Saigon, and were on their way back to bases after searching for the British towards Singapore.

The initial attack was conducted by eight high-altitude bombers, which were engaged by *Prince of Wales* with her 5.25-inch DP guns. Five aircraft were damaged, but the squadron pressed the attack and scored one hit on *Repulse*. Half an hour later, 25 torpedo-carrying aircraft arrived, and nine launched torpedoes at *Prince of Wales* in the face of intense anti-aircraft fire. A single Type 91 torpedo with 330-lb charge struck the port side aft, adjacent to the outboard port propellor shaft and bent the strut. The shaft continued to rotate, out of line, with the result that the stuffing glands lost integrity and the ship began flooding. Within ten minutes the battleship had a list of 11.5 degrees to port, a stern trim of three feet, and was reduced to 16 knots. Damage control parties had established flooding boundaries by 12.20 p.m., but as a result of the flooding, five of the eight turbo-generators failed, preventing the aft 5.25-inch guns firing and immobilising the prodigious pumping system. This could handle up to 8900 tons of water an hour and was a serious loss.

Repulse now came under torpedo attack. Captain William Tennant turned bow-on to 'comb' the tracks, then closed with the crippled *Prince of Wales*. At 12.19 p.m., 26 torpedo bombers attacked both ships and scored one hit on *Repulse*. She might have survived, but nine torpedo bombers then came in from several directions, scoring four hits. The old battlecruiser listed to port and sank at 12.32 p.m. During the same attack *Prince of Wales* was hit once amidships, then twice more aft on the starboard side. Eight aircraft bombed her at 12.41 p.m., scoring one hit despite fire from the remaining 5.25-inch guns. By this time the battleship had 18,000 tons of water on board, some of it from counterflooding. Free-surface effects threatened stability, and *Electra* came alongside to take off her surplus crew. There were still hopes that the battleship might be saved, but at 1.15 p.m. she began listing rapidly. She capsized at 1.20 p.m., almost taking down *Electra*, which was still alongside. Some 870 men were lost on both ships, including Morgan and Parker, Captain John Leach, and Admiral Phillips.[4] Holden was airborne when the attack occurred and landed the Walrus in open ocean, where he was rescued by an RNZAF-manned Catalina.[5]

The ships were within range of the Singapore-based fighters, but Phillips kept radio silence and the first hint of trouble did not come until *Repulse* signalled that the squadron was under attack. Buffaloes immediately sortied from Sembawang. However, by the time the first pair flown by Flight Lieutenant MacKenzie and Sergeant W.J.N. MacIntosh arrived, the ships had been sunk.[6]

Achilles had been ordered to join Force Z: she was in Suva, and at first steamed for Port Moresby at nearly 28 knots — a respectable speed for a ship so long out of dock. The loss of the heavy ships, however, changed the picture. She reached New Guinea on 11 December and was instead told to concentrate with Australian forces at Brisbane, helping escort a convoy taking more than four thousand Australian troops to Port Moresby. 'Things were getting grimmer,' R.W. Kirkwood recalled. 'Included in the group was a big team of nurses, and I still grieve, I still wonder, and think . . . The *Aquitania* couldn't go alongside and so we acted as a ferry boat taking the troops and nurses ashore, they were all up on the HA gun deck and on the waist deck. We . . . put them alongside the wharf in Moresby and I think most . . . of those nurses were raped and murdered by the Japanese when they went over the Kodaka trail.'[7]

Singapore did not last long. New Zealand-born Able Seaman L.C. Hurndell, on board the gunboat *Grasshopper*, realised something was up when the Japanese raided the city on the night of 8 December. Soon afterwards:

> . . . [the gunboat was sent to] round up Japanese fishing boats . . . they were spying. We . . . deposited them at Changi Wharf where the local police took charge. It was a matter of keeping ships off minefields. We had two submarine alarms and on Boxing morning 1941 we engaged in a submarine attack. I had just come off watch . . . had just got down to the mess deck when action stations sounded. Apparently the chappy who relieved me on the top watch on lookout duty had spotted two torpedoes on our starboard bow. The First Lieutenant . . . immediately turned the ship towards the torpedoes and they disappeared down the side. All hell was let loose when the skipper decided that he was going to make a submarine attack . . . at slow speed, and when the depth charges went off they lifted the ships stern about 6 feet out of the water. My action station was the Transmitting Station . . . I was knocked completely over with the movement of the ship . . . I remember coming to and there was dead

> silence and I heard tinkle, tinkle, tinkle of little nuts and bolts falling off bulkheads. The ship was in darkness because the generator had been damaged... The Captain said 'Standby machine gunners'... he said 'We are not taking any prisoners.' He was a tough old boy Commander Hoffman...[8]

They found only clothing. Soon afterwards *Grasshopper* joined two troopships evacuating survivors from the city.

> We were standing off... about 5–6 miles out and we could see the dive bombers just machine gunning and dive bombing around the city... all the oil tanks were burning and Singapore was just a massive glow at night... we finally went in about 11 p.m. on the night of the 12th to Clifford Pier to take out the last of the survivors. The Japanese by that time were just down the road about half a mile away... We were subjected to a mortar attack and mortar shells were exploding all around us, but funnily enough not one hit us. Whether it was our good luck or poor aiming by the Japs, I'll never know.[9]

Singapore fell that night. *Grasshopper* picked up a mixed batch of civilians, servicemen and a handful of Japanese prisoners, and sailed at midnight for Java with her sister ship *Dragonfly* and a motor launch. They did not get far; late next morning they were bombed by Japanese aircraft which sank *Dragonfly* and 'blew the middle' out of *Grasshopper*, a bomb exploding on Hurndell's mess deck. The survivors jumped into the water to swim ashore, but:

> ... the Japs came down machine gunning us and as they went away the rear gunner would have a go and they killed a hell of a lot of people in the water. That was an awesome day, a terrible day... We lost most of the civilians and we lost most of the children, they were killed on the mess deck... and the bomb exploded... I managed to get ashore somehow on an uninhabited island... I don't remember a hell of a lot because I floated in and out of consciousness.[10]

Hurndell was badly injured and taken to a Malaysian hospital, where he was treated by a British doctor. He was still recovering when the Japanese arrived:

> ... The Jap officer walked in, he spoke to me first and held a pistol at my temple, and asked me what was wrong with me and I told him. I thought this is it, 'Goodbye Mum and Dad', [but] nothing happened. I opened my eyes and he was doing the same to the next guy and he did it to everybody and finally walked out and said: 'You are prisoners of war from now on'. I suppose in some ways we were lucky, but that was mental torture....[11]

Dramatic action — early 1942

First blood of the war in the South Pacific went to *Monowai*. Amid rumours of a Japanese thrust south, she spent some time near the Marshall Islands at the beginning of 1942, listening to morse transmissions, and then escorted *Taroona* to Fiji. She left Suva at around 3.30 p.m. on 16 January and was about to commence zig-zagging half an hour later when two 'heavy explosions' sent water and black smoke rocketing into the air nearby. Captain George Deverell initially thought he was under air attack. The crew were at cruising stations; one 6-inch gun was manned, and the anti-aircraft armament was closed up. He ordered action stations and began snaking at full helm. S.W. Hicks recalled how the explosion '... took us all by surprise ... *Monowai* wasn't used to this sort of caper. We looked up in the skies ... Nothing up there ... Suddenly a noise from down aft. We had taught our lookouts very well ... Sir it's a blankety-blank submarine ...'[12]

By the time Able Seaman Malcolm J. Mackay's report reached the bridge, a conning tower was clearly visible about 7500 yards away. Deverell ordered the 6- and 3-inch guns to open fire, then altered course to comb any torpedo tracks. However, this also prevented the guns bearing on the submarine, which as Hicks recalled:

> ... was a whopper. Then we saw orange tongues, which we realised were tongues of flame from ... a 4-inch gun ... he started to fire bricks at us. Fortunately they fell short. I can hear old Paddy Bourke [who] was the Gunnery Officer, screaming his head off from the Gunnery Control Tower

above us, for the Captain to open the A-arcs. In the meantime Johnny Watson an RNR Lieutenant who had charge of the two 12-pounders on the poop deck aft . . . didn't wait to be told and let fly.[13]

Before the guns swung away, *Monowai* straddled the submarine and Deverell saw 'two shorts that appeared to be very close'. The submarine lobbed five rounds at the converted merchant before crash-diving. Hicks thought the shooting was 'absolutely superb . . . I think Leading Seaman Holmstrom was the Range Finder and he was jolly good. The Japs thought better of it then and submerged but I think we straddled them alright.'[14] By this time Deverell had 'heeded old Paddy's screaming' and swung his command back into action. *Monowai* fired eleven rounds of 6-inch and twelve of 3-inch at the submarine as it disappeared.

Deverell then ordered *Taroona* to 'return through the Mbennga passage', and led the way with *Monowai*. It was a risky manoeuvre; the tide was right up and the 'dangerous Caesar rocks' were invisible. Navigating officer Lt G.H. 'Bronc' Edwards was dismayed when Deverell ordered him through. 'I have never seen a jaw drop so far as "old Broncs" that morning,' Hicks recalled. 'He was a splendid Navigator.' Edwards brought *Monowai* through safely at 16 knots. Deverell later remarked on Edwards' efforts and added that the engines also 'rose to the occasion excellently and in spite of leaky boilers and condensers, and defective turbo-generators, a speed of 95 revolutions (nominally 18.1 knots) was quickly reached'. Once clear of the passage Deverell shaped course for Auckland.[15]

The only casualty was Ordinary Seaman Leslie Coombes, whose arm was burned by flash when a gun misfired. Deverell was later quite critical of his guns. They were manually trained, and the training crank needed a force of some 110 lb (55 kg) to turn it. This was not possible in seaway or if *Monowai* was listing under helm. Nor did the guns train to all bearings. But he felt the 3-inch armament 'if properly used' could be a 'valuable anti-submarine weapon because of its high rate of fire'.[16]

The event had a sequel. Deverell had signalled to *Taroona* in plain language, which drew heavy criticism from the Board back in New Zealand. 'I understand the full story was generally known in Auckland last week, and now it appears to be common knowledge in Wellington,' the Naval Intelligence Officer minuted. 'As the original sighting was signalled in plain language so that ships and w/t stations would hear and understand it, this seems almost inevitable.'[17] Deverell was hauled over the coals for not following procedure. 'HMNZS *Monowai* being a man of war,' the Board wrote acidly, 'should adhere to the codes and cyphers used in enemy reporting . . . Warning to merchant ships in the immediate vicinity should be by Mersigs, by w/t flashing or flag signal as appropriate. A general warning or diversion to merchant ships is the responsibility of the appropriate shore authority.'[18]

The submarine was the I-20, which had been despatched to the South Pacific in November. However, although Japan had nearly seventy submarines, their underwater effort remained erratic. I-25 cruised into the Tasman early in 1942 and reached Cook Strait on 25 March, where it surfaced and launched its onboard reconnaissance floatplane. This overflew Wellington, apparently without being detected.

Desperate defence

The prospects for New Zealand seemed grim in early 1942. Singapore had fallen, and the attack on Pearl Harbor had disabled the United States' Pacific Fleet. From New Zealand's perspective there was nothing to stop the Japanese sweeping into Australasia, or to stop them when they got there. An attack on Darwin by carrier aircraft in February seemed a precursor. The depth of the crisis was officially admitted two years later:

> . . . *anti-submarine defences and booms and gate vessels at the main ports were non-existent, anti-submarine craft were deficient in numbers, and facilities for servicing these craft were inadequate . . . The state of Devonport Dockyard at Auckland, in many respects, left much to be desired, and there was still much to be done with regard to the development of the Naval Base and the completion of the Naval Barrack . . . Ammunition supply and Naval Store depots had to be constructed and developed . . . existing shore tankage capacity was insufficient to meet probable needs . . .*[19]

Churchill rushed to Washington in mid-December 1941 to discuss war strategies with Roosevelt. The conference that followed put Europe ahead of the Pacific, though Churchill thought it would be 'wrong to speak of our standing on the defensive' and wanted to regain the initiative 'albeit on a minor scale'.[20] Joint command in the Far East was controlled from Washington. The British had direct representation on the Joint Chiefs of Staff, but Australia and New Zealand were represented via British intermediaries. Both Fraser and Australian Prime Minister Curtin argued the point, and Roosevelt's staff concluded that 'all political and governmental matters' relating to the South Pacific dominions should be handled in London while 'military matters' would be resolved in Washington. The President promised Churchill a 'close and intimate working relationship' with Australia and New Zealand to ensure their advice was 'in no sense perfunctory but will be considered important and essential'.[21]

A new ANZAC area that included Australia, the Gilbert and Ellice Islands, Fiji, Tongatapu and New Zealand came under Vice-Admiral H.F. Leary, who flew to Wellington in early February. He reported to the Commander in Chief of the Pacific Fleet (CINCPAC), Admiral Chester W. Nimitz. This administrative shift also produced the ANZAC Force, a naval group that included both Kiwi cruisers, the entire Australian fleet, and a small American contingent. These ships came under Rear-Admiral J.G. Grace of HMAS *Australia*. The obsolescent British carrier HMS *Hermes* was also due to join, but was delayed in the Indian Ocean and subsequently sunk by Japanese air attack. There were several crisis points in the Pacific by this stage. Australia was concerned about the imminent capture of Port Moresby, which threatened to close Torres Strait, and there was every likelihood that chrome and nickel from New Caledonia would also be cut off. Japanese forces were already at Rabaul.

Both Kiwi cruisers were extraordinarily busy during the early part of 1942. *Leander* was at sea for 24 days in February, steaming 7546 miles, while *Achilles* spent 21 days at sea and steamed 6703 miles. Both cruisers and *Monowai* concentrated off Suva in early February with the Australian forces to patrol the Fiji-New Caledonia waters. A powerful American task force based around the carrier *Lexington*, and four heavy cruisers arrived in support. March was no less hectic. At the beginning of the month the two Kiwi cruisers took over a convoy from USS *Portland* and ran the ships to Brisbane, before moving rapidly to Noumea and Vila to cover American troop movements. They were both back in Suva by the end of the month.

Leander hastened to meet a convoy coming from Panama, while *Achilles* went to meet a San Francisco convoy. *Monowai* escorted *Rangatira* from Napier to Fiji with Kiwi troops on board.

There were more political ructions in March, when Curtin, the Australian Prime Minister, approached Churchill with a proposal to create a united ANZAC Council in Washington. To resolve this and other issues, Roosevelt suggested that the 'whole of the . . . responsibility for the Pacific Area will rest on the United States', and that Australia, New Zealand and other local powers would be represented in Washington. He added to Churchill that 'the Pacific Council now sitting in London might well be moved here'.[22] Fraser thought this was well worthwhile.[23]

The ANZAC area was disestablished in favour of a new South-West Pacific area that included Australia, New Guinea, the East Indies and the Philippines, but excluded New Caledonia, Fiji and New Zealand. Nimitz deputed Vice-Admiral Robert L. Ghormley to run the South Pacific area. There was a further shift in May when Nimitz became Supreme Commander of the Pacific campaign, with the exception of land forces in New Zealand. These political gyrations did little to alter the practical naval situation, however, and Kiwi ships continued to work closely with Australian vessels under American direction.

Into the Solomons

By March 1942 the Japanese had reached the Solomon Islands. Ahead lay New Caledonia and Fiji. Japanese planners envisaged a perimeter extending to Samoa. However, the Battle of the Coral Sea in May lost both Japan and the United States an aircraft carrier. Admiral Yamamoto hoped to destroy what remained of American sea power in a decisive battle off Midway. Failure there was one of the factors that prompted them to abandon their advance at the Solomons, which became the front line. Japanese forces consolidated there in early July, landing marines at Lunga on the large southeastern island of Guadalcanal, and building an airfield.

The Joint Chiefs of Staff planned a limited offensive, intending to seize the Santa Cruz Islands and Tulagi by way of stepping stones to attacks further into the Solomons and an eventual drive to Rabaul and New Guinea. Ghormley did most of the detailed planning in Auckland. He had nearly 20,000 marines under Major-General A.A. Vandegrift, and naval forces that included three carriers, the new battleship *North Carolina*, six cruisers and supporting destroyers. The assault force included 23 transports, but was screened only by cruisers and destroyers. The force accumulated in Wellington Harbour and sailed on 22 July. Another group of marines were carried to Fiji by *Monowai*.

By September the battle for Guadalcanal hung in the balance. *Achilles* docked at Devonport for refit that month, while *Leander* joined Task Force 64. Japan had command of the seas at night, running forces and supplies to the island on destroyers and cruisers. This 'Tokyo Express' had put nearly a division into Guadalcanal, threatening the tenuous American hold on the airfield. The only immediate American reinforcements were 5000 troops coming across from Nuku'alofa, escorted by USS *McCawley*, the flagship of Rear-Admiral Turner. Task Force 64 sailed from Espiritu Santo on 14 September to stiffen the escort. In the face of possible air and sea opposition, Turner declined to land the force until 18 September. *Leander*, *Minneapolis* and *Boise* stood guard while the transports went in.

There were a number of sharp night battles in the waters around Guadalcanal during October which cost both Americans and Japanese heavily — the Japanese more so because they could not easily replace losses, whereas the Americans were rushing increasing quantities of men and *matériel* into the war zone. The naval struggle reached its climax in mid-November when the Japanese tried to bring large-scale reinforcements to the island. During two ferocious night actions less than 48 hours apart the Japanese lost two capital ships, and though Guadalcanal did not fall for another three months, the Japanese focus shifted to New Georgia. Neither Kiwi cruiser was directly involved. *Leander* was sent to join Task Force 16.6 at the end of the month, but had to be withdrawn for urgent repairs at Devonport when cracks were discovered in shell plating adjacent to her oil tanks. The Kiwi naval presence in the islands was kept up by *Achilles* and the 600-ton anti-submarine minesweepers *Kiwi* and *Moa*, which were joined by *Matai* and reached the Solomons on 15 December as the 27th Minesweeping Flotilla.

Achilles was assigned to Task Force 67, and at the beginning of January 1943 helped escort transports to Guadalcanal. The task force split into two divisions overnight — the first division went to bombard Munda — and rejoined around 9 a.m. on 5 January in fine weather. The division was in line ahead, steaming at 15 knots to the north of the first division. *Achilles* was at standard air defence stations; the 4-inch guns, Oerlikons and control systems were manned, there were skeleton crews in B and X turrets ready for barrage fire, and lookouts were posted. There was about 5/10 detached cloud at around 8–10,000 feet, and a surface wind of force 3.

The Japanese sortied fifteen bombers and ten fighters to hit the force. They were whittled down to four Type 99 dive bombers by Allied fighters, but these pressed on and at 9.25 a.m. erupted from the clouds towards the second division, coming from dead ahead. *Honolulu*'s crew mistook them for Grumman Avengers, as did the Officer of the Watch on *Achilles*. He was corrected by the signal boy, but — as Sergeant P.H. Stapleton recalled — dismissed him with the remark '... don't be silly boy, with all these American ships here they would know whether they were their planes or Japanese planes'.[24] He was not the only one to make that mistake. R.W. Kirkwood recalled that:

> [I] was on the focsle that morning ... with a book and lifejacket and was lying back in the sun reading when I looked up and saw three or four planes overhead and thought, 'don't worry they are Americans,' and joyfully went back to reading. We were only doing about four knots, the Yanks were picking up a seaplane ... we were just keeping station and there was a bit of a flurry and excitement and someone said, 'They are not ours, they are bloody Japs.' I looked up and you could see two red balls of fire coming towards us, about that far from the ship's side, you could see the bullets striking the water ... on the port side of the focsle.[25]

The alarm rattlers sounded and men rushed for their action stations. Kirkwood was stranded on the foredeck — he had to get to the forward air compressor compartment and 'it was a question of how many men can go through that little hatch up on the focsle'. He hid behind a 'piece of rope, the only shelter just near A-turret'.[26] Oerlikons 1, 2 and 3 opened fire. The first three Japanese bombers went for *Honolulu* and the fourth for *Achilles*, releasing a bomb from around 1500 feet at a dive angle estimated at 40 degrees.[27] Captain Cecil Mansergh had already ordered a turn to starboard, and the cruiser was swinging when the bomb, 'visually estimated to be the Japanese equivalent of a 250 pounder', struck and penetrated X-turret.

The blast appeared 'relatively slight' from outside the turret — though there was a 'considerable flash estimated at 30 feet high and 50 feet across' followed by 'a quantity of white smoke'.[28] Inside the gun-house was a different story; the explosion killed or injured everybody in the turret and blew the right-hand wall of the gun-house over the side. The left and rear walls were bent and buckled. Stapleton, in charge of the midships 4-inch HA gun, watched the left half of the roof sail 'over our heads' and crash down into the starboard quarter-deck passage, complete with the turret-top Oerlikon pedestal, which was still precariously attached by a single bolt.[29] The Oerlikon itself was subsequently located, but unserviceable. The right-hand half of the roof was 'blown straight up into the air and arrived back on the gunhouse upside down'.[30]

Eleven men died at once, at least ten were wounded, and two of the seriously injured died later. Four New Zealanders lost their lives, including Leading Seaman W.J.A. Rogers and Boy 1st Class H.J. Honeyfield. Able Seaman B.F. Grice and Ordinary Seaman R.J. Halcrow were missing.[31] For Chief Mechanical Engineer M. Seyb the horrifying part was 'seeing . . . my friend's head looking at me from under the officer's table, his body was nowhere to be found'.[32] Smoke poured into X-turret lobby below the wrecked gun-house. Temporary Corporal Roy Ormond Osment took charge immediately and rallied the crew to hurl cordite, shells and gun tubes overboard, then 'rigged hoses and assisted the wounded in a most cool and exemplary manner'. Acting Stoker Petty Officer James P. Watson, in charge of the No. 3 fire fighting party, rushed fire-fighting gear into the damaged area. Temporary Surgeon R.J. Walton RNZNVR took charge of the casualties. Signalman William D. Kennedy, though knocked down by the explosion, 'recovered immediately, and while the action was still in progress, with great coolness went aloft to re-hoist the ensign . . .'[33]

The attacking aircraft was shot down, and the pilot took to a rubber raft not far from *Achilles*. Mansergh went to pick him up, but — as Stapleton recalled — 'this chap just took a revolver out of his pocket and started firing at the ship, so the Captain said, "right, sink him".'[34] Two other bombers were shot down by gunfire from the first division, and the task force steamed off to the southeast.

Damage to *Achilles* was so minimal apart from the gun-house that there was an argument over the size of the bomb and whether it had completely detonated. It was thought to be a 250-lb device, but one 'experienced observer' thought it might have been a 500-lb weapon. The largest fragment *Achilles*' crew could find measured 14 inches by 8, but was 'so distorted as to give no indication of the diameter of the bomb'.[35] There had been no need to flood X-turret magazine, for which Kirkwood was relieved. It would have been his responsibility, and 'having seen the magazine crew go down the hatch I don't think I could have lived with it if I had to flood the compartment. It would have been an awful decision had one had to do it . . .'[36]

Temporary repairs were made with the help of the maintenance ship USS *Vestal* at Santos — though not before *Achilles* collided with the American vessel as she was coming alongside. The gun-house was temporarily boxed in with 5-pound plating 'on a framework of angle-irons', making the mounting watertight, and the cruiser sailed for Devonport. Mansergh was of the opinion that the attack had been a 'very partial and fleeting test of the damage control organisation' but was admiring of the crew, remarking that 'everything that should have been done was done, promptly and well'.[37]

News of the attack on the cruiser was not immediately made public back in New Zealand. This prompted official alarm in mid-January when rumours began circulating through Auckland that *Achilles* had been damaged and several crew killed: 'If there is any truth in these rumours it would appear that a leakage of information has occurred.'[38]

The gun-house was unrepairable at Devonport, but by coincidence the blow fell on the eve of a planned trip to England for general repair and modernisation. *Achilles* was 'completely outdated' by this time, as Kirkwood recalled. 'We did have ASDIC, we had a very, very basic radar . . . we had a few Oerlikons, we were just sitting ducks really. They decided to do it all in one foul sweep and they sent us home.'[39] *Achilles* sailed for Portsmouth on 19 February:

> . . . with all despatch, I think we had about 50 tons of oil left when we got to Panama . . . fuelled up and then straight to England as fast as we could, and by the grace of God as we got near the English Coast the cloud came down and Jerry didn't see us . . . It would have been a feather in their caps I think if they had got *Achilles*, they never lived down the fact that the pride of their Navy had been sunk by *Achilles* and they were always after her.[40]

The minesweepers *Kiwi* and *Moa* now took centre stage in the islands. *Kiwi* was inadvertently attacked by an American motorboat on the night of 14 January. Later they patrolled 'up and down Guadalcanal beach', and towards the end of the month, as Leading Seaman E.C. McVinnie recalled:

> We eventually noticed a ship on the beach, an American ship ... and we went alongside and stripped it of what we could. One of the things we got off it was this Oerlikon, and ... the only place we thought of putting it was right on the peak of the bow. One of our crew was a very good chippy and he went ashore to the Seabees. The Americans ... supplied him with all the tools he wanted and he chipped out [a] ... great big chunk of ... some native wood, mahogany or something ... They even made us the bolts for us to bolt this right on the peak of the bow.[41]

Kiwi's Oerlikon stood her in good stead on the night of 29 January. *Kiwi* and *Moa* were working their way in pitch darkness along Kamimbo Bay, on the northwestern corner of Guadalcanal, when McVinnie heard a Japanese submarine on his hydrophones. The ship went to action stations and he switched the ASDIC to transmit. The target was the 2000-ton Japanese submarine I-1, carrying troops and rice to Guadalcanal. McVinnie 'got a constant echo ... and I kept repeating the ranges until the instantaneous echoes indicated that the thing was pretty close. I took the earphones off and waited for everybody to throw things at her.'[42]

Kiwi dropped a pattern of six depth charges. 'Somebody said they saw the phosphorus wake as we went over it,' McVinnie recalled. 'We kept steaming ahead to clear the water and turned about and came back and lost it and picked it up again and did another attack.' One of the depth charges went off very close to the stern, popping several rivets and setting the 'old steam whistle on the funnel' going.[43]

ASDIC contact could not be made on the second run, but on the third the submarine boiled up to the surface, apparently disabled, and attempted to engage the approaching minesweepers with her deck gun. The shells passed over *Moa* with a 'noise like an express going through a tunnel'.[44] Then the Japanese sprayed *Kiwi* with accurate .303 fire, wounding Acting Leading Signalman C.H. Buchanan of Port Chalmers. Although fatally injured he stayed at his post and continued to operate a searchlight, illuminating the

Japanese boat for the gunners. *Kiwi*'s 'liberated' 20-mm Oerlikon swept the submarine's deck, stifling the Japanese gun fire.

Signalling *Moa* to hold fire, Commander Gordon Bridson closed to ram, crashing into I-1 abaft the conning tower. For a moment the two vessels were locked. *Kiwi* continued firing at point-blank range, raking the landing craft strapped to the submarine's deck, while Bridson called for full astern. Foam boiled around the propellers, and with a shriek of metal *Kiwi* pulled clear. Moments later Bridson ran his ship in again, colliding with I-1's stern. Again the minesweeper pulled away in a welter of foam and a howl of tortured metal, and Bridson circled for a third attempt. This time *Kiwi* ran right up on the submarine's deck and canted over, rupturing the Japanese boat's oil tanks and starting a small fire. Pulling clear was not so easy, but finally the minesweeper drew back. Unknown to the New Zealanders she had an extra passenger — a Japanese officer who was hoping to board. He had gripped the deck edge of *Kiwi* while the ships were locked, but could not make his way up and evidently fell into the water, where he drowned.

By this time *Kiwi*'s 4-inch gun had overheated, so Bridson drew back to give *Moa* a clear field of fire. I-1 continued to move at about 12 knots, but was well down by the stern. The engagement became a chase punctuated by intermittent gunfire and frequent changes of course. At around 11.20 p.m. the submarine ran onto a reef in Kamimbo Bay, where she stuck fast. *Moa* waited until dawn and as the light grew reopened fire with her machine guns, killing one man on the wreck. Another was rescued. 'I think he was a gunnery officer,' J.L.W. Salter of *Moa* recalled later:

> *He had a hole in his leg from a bullet, but he was a big powerful bloke and he could speak English well. He had been in the water for a long while, he was just sinking and then popping up for a breath of air and going down again, he was very near the end of his tether. He didn't want to be taken prisoner. We said: 'At the end of the war you will be able to go home.' He said, 'No, I can't go back, it's a disgrace to be taken prisoner.*[45]

Japanese artillery ashore opened fire and the New Zealand ship had to depart. Some 66 men escaped from I-1. *Kiwi* withdrew first to Noumea and then Auckland for repairs; her place on the patrol line was taken by *Tui*. The next night there was more action when *Moa* and *Tui* found Japanese landing craft inshore near Cape Esperance. The Japanese opened fire and the shell passed through the sighting aperture of *Moa*'s 4-inch gun shield, firing a cordite charge. The injured gun crew were tended by British sailor Ernest Barton, who worked for 90 minutes before collapsing from his own wounds. *Tui* returned the fire, sinking one of the Japanese landing craft and ending the engagement.

The Japanese pulled out of Guadalcanal during January 1943, falling back to prepared positions on New Georgia, the next island up the chain. Continued Kiwi naval involvement was difficult. *Achilles* was in a long refit, *Kiwi* under repair, *Leander* refitting at Devonport, and the British wanted *Monowai* transferred to the Atlantic. There was a sharp exchange of messages before the New Zealand government bent to this demand. In mid-February, *Moa* took an advance party of American, Fijian and Malaitan scouts to New Georgia. *Leander* returned to the fray in early March and was sent on convoy escort duties deep into the Pacific.

Moa was the next ship in the firing line. She was detached from the 25th Minesweepng Flotilla on 6 April and sent to nearby Tulagi to refuel and resupply. The next day, an American task force under Rear-Admiral Ainsworth had just left Tulagi to bombard Munda and Vila when reports came of an impending air raid. Ainsworth took his ships west into heavy rain, the 25th Minesweeping Flotilla retired to Purvis Bay, and the convoy they were escorting dispersed. Around 2.45 p.m. the Japanese attacked Tulagi, where *Moa* was fuelling from the oil barge *Erskine M. Phelps* — a task that would have been finished if she had not allowed an American destroyer in ahead. Neither *Moa* nor the oiler were advised of the coming raid. Both ships fired back — *Moa* managed a short burst from her after Oerlikon before she was hit, while *Phelps* kept up heavier fire. The Japanese scored two near-misses on the minesweeper, and a hit that crashed through the captain's cabin and burst below with catastrophic effect.

Moa immediately took on a list towards the tanker, which was quickly compounded by a heavy bow trim. Men hastened to lower the boat and abandon the sinking minesweeper, but Leading Signalman J.L.W. Salter and Ordinary Telegraphist W.G.T. Bright:

> . . . *refused to leave Signalman F. Thomas who was unconscious and severely injured on Moa['s] bridge. These ratings realised that Thomas*

> *could not be thrown into the water and therefore in the short time available fitted him with a life jacket, and when Moa disappeared, floated off supporting the signalman . . . The coolness and courage of Salter and Bright undoubtedly saved the life of Signalman Thomas and is considered particularly praiseworthy in view of the fact that they had no knowledge of the side towards which Moa would list or capsize and sink.*[46]

Salter and Bright were recommended for the George Medal. *Moa* sank by the head four minutes after the hit. There was time to lower the boat, but most of the men were left floating in the water. Lieutenant C. Belgrave 'dived for and sustained Assistant Steward W. Molloy who was unconscious from semi-drowning and oil poisoning'. Flotilla commanding officer Commander A.D. Holden was very admiring. 'This rating's life was undoubtedly saved by this officer.' Higgins boats sent by *LCT No. 5* from Makambo, Florida Island, joined *Moa*'s own boat to pluck the men from the water. They assembled on Tulagi wharf. Commander Holden later reported that the 'subsequent treatment of officers and ratings at Makambo base [was] magnificent' and thought it 'extremely fortunate that casualties were not more severe'.[47]

Five men died as *Moa* went down and fifteen were injured, including *Moa*'s commander, Lieutenant-Commander Peter Phipps. Most of the injured were taken to the base hospital at Espiritu Santo, except for Thomas, who stayed on the critical list in Makambo Hospital for a week. Before the survivors left Tulagi they attended a short memorial service on board *Matai*, over the position, led by the United States Fleet Chaplain.[48] Initial hopes that the five missing men might turn up were quickly dashed; they had been in places from which there was little hope of escape, and were declared 'presumed dead' at the beginning of July.[49] Meanwhile the salvage ship USS *Ortolan* tried to locate *Moa* to retrieve secret equipment, a task all the more hazardous because the minesweeper lay in 22–23 fathoms of water.[50]

The battle of Kolombangara

Leander reached the Solomons in mid-1943 as action developed around New Georgia, sailing from New Zealand under Mansergh's command, with a load of 6-inch ammunition in the starboard galley flat — this last somewhat to the concern of the crew. 'I can remember the morning we arrived at Tulagi,' Chief Electrician R.B. Harvey recalled; 'We had prickly heat and there was a foreboding, something wrong . . .'[51] *Leander* was soon in the front line. Admiral W.L. Ainsworth's task group, TG 36.1, had taken a hammering on 5 July when it intercepted a 'Tokyo Express' bringing supplies from Buin. The cruiser *Helena* was sunk by 'Long Lance' torpedoes, and *Leander* was called in to replace her, operating off Kula Gulf during the night of 11 July.

Next morning they returned to Tulagi to refuel, sailing again for Kula at 5 p.m., accompanied by five destroyers. At this point *Leander*'s 'very strong and fairly ruthless Commander',[52] Stephen Wentworth Roskill, 'gave the order to prepare for battle'. He was not popular with the New Zealanders aboard; he had 'set to work with a big stick' when he joined the ship, 'and stirred the damage control situation up'.[53] He gained the nickname 'The Black Mamba' in the process, but his zeal paid off. 'When the ship was eventually hit,' Commander G. Mitchell recalled, 'we closed the ship up very, very quickly and very, very thoroughly because we knew exactly where every valve, and every door and every hatch was.'[54] On the night of 12 July:

> *Everything inflammable had to be put away. Any loose gear had to be put away. The mess tables were tied to the deck head . . . All the lockers had to have . . . little metal clips on them . . . All woodwork was taken down and stowed . . . even to the extent of wood framed mirrors . . . The night before he had come around when we went up . . . looked around and he spotted me you see, Leading Seaman, and so I took the can for anything loafing. There was a green bunch of bananas and a sailor's hat up on the fan trunking and so I had to get that removed . . . he had eagle eyes, he could spot anything old Stephen.*[55]

These preparations did little to calm the nerves of men facing battle. Harvey recalled:

> *We just sat around and waited and that's the worst time that I spent in the following 24 hours, waiting more than a couple of hours. Knowing where you were going . . . gave you time to think and to be a bit fearful you might say. You think 'What's going to come of this' . . .*[56]

Around 12.30 a.m. the following morning, the task force encountered half a dozen Japanese ships coming south at speed. The Allied cruisers worked up to 28 knots while the destroyers deployed ahead of and behind them. The Japanese force comprised five destroyers and the light cruiser *Jintsu*, and the Allied force swung in a sharp S-turn to close the range at 1.08 p.m. Four minutes later *Jintsu*:

> ... *did the worst thing she could do, opened her searchlights* ... *the two American cruisers and Leander all fired at her and they virtually blew her out of the water* ... *According to two survivors later* ... *she had been hit by a couple of torpedoes and received ten shells in the boiler room or engine room and she had virtually broken in two.*[57]

Leander was hampered by a faulty radar target bearing indicator, and when the searchlight went out had to use 'radar ranges and hits on enemy ships and his gunflashes as points of aim'. Visual spotting 'proved impossible throughout, due to the heavy smoke from *Honolulu*'s guns'.[58] 'We were firing for a full quarter of an hour,' Harvey recalled, 'and we fired I think about twenty one broadsides, which didn't seem an excessive number, but the amount of muck they brought down was amazing.'[59]

At 1.14 a.m. *Leander* fired a spread of 'tin fish' from her starboard mounting, but the course was 'based on erroneous data and the torpedoes probably all passed south of the enemy'. About the same time the destroyers *Yugure*, *Kiyonami*, *Hamakaze* and *Yukikaze* responded by loosing their own salvo of 29 'Long Lance' torpedoes. These were on their way by 1.16 a.m., when Ainsworth signalled a simultaneous 180-degree turn to port. *Leander* did not receive the signal, nor did most of the rear destroyers. One minute later her lookouts and bridge crew saw 'through a gap in the smoke that *Honolulu* had started to turn to port ... drastic avoiding action had to be taken and fire was checked after 21 broadsides'.

As *Leander* straightened to follow *St Louis*, sharp-eyed lookouts saw a torpedo approaching about 100 yards away. It came from abeam on a bearing of 335 degrees and 'appeared to be running slowly', taking a 'distinct turn towards the stern' before striking the port side around Frame 87, abaft 'A' boiler room. Those on deck saw a slight flash and a 'heavy column of water was thrown up, much of which descended upon the after part of the ship'.[60]

Below decks, Harvey felt '... this almighty thump ... just as though another ship had hit you right in the middle. We went over to starboard and then she slowly recovered back to port ... We didn't know exactly what had happened. The last thing I thought was a torpedo hitting, I thought gee, we've hit another ship.'[61]

Leander had no torpedo protection, and the effects of the hit were devastating. Every sailor in 'A' boiler room died as the blast ripped a hole in the shell plating and roared through the compartment. The blast vented through a boiler room fan duct, blowing eight men from the No.1 four-inch gun overboard. Their fate was not realised for some time, and as the ship still had way on they were quickly lost in the darkness.[62] Over-pressure from the blast distorted the hull fifty feet fore and aft of the impact point and damaged the bottom plating down to the turn of the bilge, a dozen feet from the keel. The side above the hole was cracked. The stoker's mess deck above was smashed and the deckhead split. Most of the bulkheads in 'A' boiler room were strained or cracked. Oil fuel tanks B1, B2, B7, B8 and A10 were wrecked, and A8 and A9 were contaminated with salt water.

Water gushed into 'A' boiler room, spreading quickly to the main switchboard and No. 4 breaker spaces, the forward dynamo room, the 6-inch transmitting station and the No. 1 Low Power Room. Men from these compartments thrashed their way through rising water in the darkness and escaped. Most of those in the transmitting station were saved by Walter H. Quick, a temporary officer with the Royal Navy. Others were trapped behind an armoured hatchway. A bandsman tried to shift it but, as Harvey recalled:

> ... it wouldn't budge and appeared jammed. When the bandsman couldn't move it Gerry Knox, a torpedoman, who fortunately was a very strong individual, pulled him away and put his shoulder to the manhole. A couple of good heaves and the manhole opened enabling the 6-inch TS crew and the repair parties to escape up the trunking to the stoker's mess deck ... The marvel of this escape was that although the torpedo had caused so much damage in the area and flood water surrounded the trunking the thin sheet metal was still relatively intact and had not fractured enough to let any quantity of water in. Had it done so it would have been impossible for them to get out and another 15 or 16 men would have died.[63]

Shock response compounded the chaos. The port torpedo tube mounting, fifty feet abaft the explosion, was 'lifted bodily aft several feet, leaving the torpedoes lolling over the side'. A circuit breaker snapped shut on the after searchlight and the lamp flared out over the sea. The light could have acted as an aiming point for the Japanese; a sailor slammed his hand through the searchlight hatch and broke the circuit internally, burning his arm but extinguishing the lamp. 'B' boiler room fans were damaged by the shock and quickly failed, forcing the crew to evacuate. Steam failed to the after engines, and electrical power was cut off 'everywhere forwards of "C" boiler rooms'.[64] 'Down in our mess deck,' Harvey recalled, 'it was a frightening experience when all the lights went out . . .' Someone leaned up and turned on the emergency light. The phone system was inoperative, so:

> . . . Harry volunteered to go down . . . He came back about five minutes later and . . . said, 'Gooh! It is in a hell of a mess down there.' He had to dig Ian McDonald out of the water . . . He had been sitting . . . at his desk and when the explosion came the deck went right up about three feet, killed these other two guys who were standing there and shattered Ian McDonald's leg so much that it put him in hospital for nine months . . . I said I would go up and see what goes on . . . we had a little manhole open on the top of the hatch and I poked my head out . . . Just at that time along came Stephen Wentworth Roskill and his retinue of a couple of people. All he was doing was moving around the ship to tell everybody what was happening. In his slow deliberate way of talking he said, 'We have received a torpedo in A boiler room, we have stopped for a few minutes and we will be getting underway in five minutes time,' and then he went off into the next compartment, the same procedure . . .[65]

Roskill had received leg injuries in the blast — he was almost blown off the ship and saved by a rugby tackle. He worked on until he collapsed. Petty Officer Charles Patchett rallied the starboard torpedo tube crews to join the repair parties. Chief Electrical Artificer W.R.J. Jones rushed to help the injured. Fifteen men were treated within fifteen minutes, though some did not report their wounds for hours — among them 17-year-old Mervyn Kelly who 'carried many verbal messages with speed and efficiency . . . [and] neither mentioned nor reported his injuries until long after daylight'.[66] One man had lost part of a finger when the shock response whipped the hull, lifting a depth charge up while he was holding the launching rail. He went down to the sick bay where 'they were very, very busy' and had it wrapped.[67]

Establishing flooding boundaries proved difficult. The torpedo had struck the armoured bulkhead between boiler and engine rooms, and the cruiser quickly took on a ten-degree list. Water leaked through the bulkhead between 'A' and 'B' boiler rooms, the electrical failure cut off all internal communications 'except for a very limited number of sound-powered telephones', all fire-control and radio equipment failed, and the telephone battery also failed 'due to a dead short circuit on its leads in the No.1 Low Power Room'.[68]

Chief Shipwright J.W. Stewart, in charge of the No. 1 Damage Control Party, discovered that the No. 2 Party had suffered casualties, detached men to reinforce it and then brought extra shipwrights to the damaged compartments, where they immediately 'set about the establishment of the flooding boundary'.[69] Stoker Petty Officer A. Fickling and Acting Leading Stoker (Temporary) John R. Halliday led a small party into 'B' boiler room and struggled through darkness, heat and waist-deep water to plug the holes in the bulkhead. Rifts in other bulkheads were plugged and shored by a party under Chief Shipwright A. Stewart, while Acting Chief Engine-Room Artificer Morris Buckley closed the main steam pipes in the partly flooded 'B' boiler room. 'They had to shut all sorts of feeds down,' Harvey recalled. 'They had to close off feed water and all sorts of steam inlets and outlets . . .'[70] Two portable pumps were brought into the boiler room to dewater it, though water continued to leak into the ship and by 1.53 a.m. the radio room was abandoned with 18 inches of water on the floor.

While this went on the ship lay wallowing in the Pacific; fortunately the battle had moved away to the north, because 'it really would have been impossible to fight the ship at that stage'.[71] There was no electricity — one side of the ring main had been knocked out when 'B' boiler room breakers opened. Emergency cables had been rigged before the action 'because of this Damage Control initiative of the Mamba's', which helped. Men hastened to take the place of the dead and wounded; Harvey recalled that 'The chief TI had been killed, the warrant electrical officer had been killed down [by] the switch board as well. Bill Jones took over the Warrant Electrical Officer's job and Alan Patchett worked in with him.'[72]

Getting under way was not easy. *Leander*'s machinery was in a dismal condition. 'A' and 'B' boiler rooms were out of action; the main suction line to 'A' boiler room was broken, 'B' boiler room fans and the outward feet and bearers of B2 boiler had been damaged by shock, and both B1 and B2 boiler furnaces were flooded with oil and water. The lower drain systems in 'A' boiler room had been wrecked, the main feed discharge line from 'A' boiler room was broken, and there were fears that all three high pressure air compressors had been damaged. All auxiliary machinery in 'B' boiler room had been damaged. The two boilers in 'C' boiler room were undamaged, but the feed water had been contaminated with salt water and oil fuel via the lower drainage system, and the boilers suffered 'almost continuous priming' — the contaminants caused the pressurised water to foam like boiling milk. This meant that the dry steam was likely to become 'wet', which could damage the turbines, but after about ten minutes the engineers cautiously fed steam to the engines and *Leander* began to slip through the water, initially at seven knots and later twelve. The evaporators were switched on and although density rose to three degrees at one point — a critical level — the boilers were blown down every ten minutes, changing the feed water and gradually reducing the salting. Meanwhile, damage control parties shored up the bulkheads in 'B' boiler room and the stokers' mess deck. 'We worked all night,' Harvey recalled:

> *The torpedo tubes . . . had been disabled and [were] hanging over the ship's side with the torpedoes virtually hanging out of them . . . The chief TI had been killed and Alan Patchett was a PO TI . . . he immediately left the tubes, came up forward and mustered all the torpedomen for the repair party . . .*[73]

The galleys were also out of action, but Roskill had ordered the galley hands to make sandwiches before the battle. Destroyers operated in relays to escort the crippled Kiwi ship during her eighteen-hour passage back to Tulagi, and — as Harvey recalled — 'we had a fighter escort from Russell Island, supposedly RNZAF, over us patrolling and looking after us . . .'[74] In fact the aircraft were American.

Mansergh could not make a complete examination at Tulagi because of the flooding and residual six-degree list,[75] but thought the ship might be good for a 15-knot ocean passage 'in about ten days' time', using 'C' boiler room and the after engine room to power the inner shafts. The boilers were in very poor shape — inspection revealed that the 'fire row tubes were so badly coated internally with oil that burning out must have been imminent'.[76]

Temporary repairs took seven days. Eight officers volunteered to run a cement mixer, pouring concrete into boxing built against the strained bulkhead of 'B' boiler room. 'It was a make and mend,' Harvey recalled; '... this was the general spirit of the ship, it was great, they considered they could put something more practical into it because all the matelots had been working at night and the stokers had been working particularly hard. They just volunteered as a group ... All the supply people and odds and sods and seaman officers too, they all got stuck in ... It still leaked of course but it cut down the intake of water.'[77] A call went out for volunteers to recover bodies. The Americans also pitched in. Mitchell was 'interested to see the competence of the Americans ... the co-operation that they gave us. They supplied us with all the equipment that we had lost during the action. Their Chief Petty Officers ... were in every case I saw, very very competent indeed.'[78]

Leander sailed with a destroyer escort for Santos on 21 July, passing *Perth* which had almost lost her stern to a torpedo. 'We were there for a couple of days,' Harvey recalled, 'while the American repair people started marking off where the decks were ... so that all plates damaged could be assessed.'[79] Mansergh thought the damage and consequent curtailment of *Leander*'s operations was a 'bitter disappointment to me and to everyone on board; there was but a fleeting opportunity for the ship to demonstrate her weapon efficiency ...' However, he was deeply admiring of the crew, adding '... the conduct and bearing of all hands during the action and during the trying passage back to harbour was a source of extreme pride and gratification to me. All behaved like veterans, in particular ... the Engine Room, Damage Control and Medical Personnel...'[80]

Thirty-seven men were recommended for awards, among them Arthur Barlow, a commissioned electrician who was posthumously commended. Casualties were heavy. Six men died at once and one died later of injuries. Eleven were missing 'presumed killed', and a further ten were simply missing. One man was 'dangerously injured', two 'seriously injured', and a further twelve wounded.[81] There was no trace of the men swept overboard when the torpedo hit, but it took months to confirm their deaths. A raft had been blown overboard at the same time, and other rafts dropped when their fate was realised. As the ship had been near occupied islands there were hopes that the men might have made it ashore and been captured. It was September 1944 before the decision was taken to declare the men officially dead, and even then the NZNB were of the opinion that it was 'possible, but highly improbable, that some of them at least may have reached land and been made prisoners of war'.[82]

Water began rising in 'B' boiler room during the trip south, but the pumps got on top of it and *Leander* reached Auckland at night, entering Calliope dock next morning. Repair was 'definitely beyond the scope of Devonport dockyard'. Even temporarily making *Leander* fit for sea and a speed of at least 15 knots was thought likely to take three months — boilermakers, fitters and 'certain other tradesmen' were needed, and all were in short supply.[83] Devonport administration thought the job could be accelerated if they had authority to buy what they needed without waiting for Defence Purchasing Board approval. They considered that 'urgent demands will have to be made on Australia for super heater tubes and possibly saturated tubes and steam pipes'.[84] The Admiralty, meanwhile, advised that they could not repair the ship in England because of the 'heavy load of refit and repair work in hand and in prospect', and suggested that the United States should be approached, 'certain modernisation work being carried out concurrently'.[85]

Cruiser crisis and a submarine hunt

Achilles' refit at Portsmouth was well in hand by mid-1943, and her damaged turret was removed. Kirkwood recalled that they 'were going to get a new turret but they abandoned that idea eventually and put ack-ack in lieu of the turret'.[86] For the skeleton crew it was a dull period — the log was filled with bland entries, 'hands to breakfast', 'colours', 'Captain on board', 'up spirits' and the like.[87]

The cruiser was due to return to service in September 1943, but in late June there was a catastrophic explosion in a fuel tank, caused by acetylene that had trickled undetected into the bottom of the space from an incorrectly secured welder's lead. Fourteen dockyard hands were killed and many injured. A dozen were hospitalised. The blast wrecked the tank and displaced the deckhead above it by nearly seven feet. Frames were bent and the shell plating adjacent to the explosion bulged outwards. Watertight doors were blown out of their mountings and a fire quickly followed, compounding the damage and filling the ship with smoke. Some of the crew who had remained with the ship during the refit period rushed to the rescue, including Stoker First Class W.D. Dale of Timaru and Stoker First Class E. Valentine of Ohakune.

Repairs were thought likely to delay recommissioning until May 1944. This posed problems for New Zealand, which now had no cruisers, and from a political perspective both government and navy regarded participation in allied activities as essential. Only then could New Zealand expect to be included favourably in any post-war settlement — including trade deals, cancellation of wartime debt, a voice on any post-war international forum, and inclusion in any division of Japan's former Pacific territories. Soon after the explosion, New Zealand's High Commissioner in London, William Jordan, discovered that *Gambia* was about to recommission and suggested swapping *Achilles* for her. Fraser was lukewarm, though he liked the idea of finding work for *Achilles*' crew. The damage to *Leander* changed the calculation, and a scheme to give New Zealand at least one cruiser was hatched on 2 August during a conference on board *Leander* in Calliope dock. After being advised that *Leander* would be out of action for months, the committee suggested that her crew should man *Achilles*, while *Achilles*' crew went on to man *Gambia*, on the basis that 'both *Achilles* and *Leander* are out of action and stressing the desirability of R.N.Z.N. playing an active part in operations in South Pacific Area'.[88]

The Board formally suggested the swap on 17 August, again on the basis that the RNZN needed to play an 'active part in operations in SOUTH PACIFIC'.[89] The Admiralty were reluctant to release *Gambia* into New Zealand service, preferring a *Neptune*-style manning arrangement. However, New Zealand did not have the trained ratings to man three cruisers and an agreement was thrashed out over the next month by which *Gambia* would commission into the Royal New Zealand Navy, but remain under Royal Navy control. This meant she could not join RNZN operations in the South Pacific, but did mean employment for *Achilles*' crew. The financial implications posed other problems — though the principles were agreed to within weeks, it was December before a settlement was reached by which the Admiralty agreed to assume 'complete financial responsibility' for her maintenance, while 'Personnel will receive pay and allowances at the rates and under the conditions laid down in the New Zealand Naval Regulations...'[90]

The New Zealand Naval Board considered these arrangements to be 'satisfactory'.[91] *Leander*'s last voyage for the Royal New Zealand Navy began in late November 1943, when she sailed for Boston via the Panama Canal. Chief Petty Officer W.M. Gibbs recalled:

> ... we could make 20 odd knots from the one boiler room, and I think we waited a few days for the submarine reports to see if there were any wolf packs lurking... Steaming up to Boston we were in the Gulf Stream ... The last day out of Boston we were just wearing blue trousers and a white shirt. During the middle watch we turned from the Gulf stream into the Labrador current and the temperature went down about 40 odd degrees in the middle watch, it was rather a shock to the young Kiwis. When we got into Boston there was snow all over the place... all over the upper deck. A lot of the blokes on the ships... had never actually had their hooks on it, and they went mad. Blokes used to come off shore and bring a handful of snow to dump in their cobber's hammock when they got on board... You would see a bloke walking around on a clean patch of snow, writing his name...[92]

Leander reached the eastern United States two days before Christmas 1943 and her crew went on to England, some manning the American-built frigate HMS *Tyler* for the Atlantic passage. As it happened, *Leander* did not leave Boston until September 1945.

The loss of both cruisers reduced New Zealand's naval presence in the Solomons to the minesweepers, reinforced by the similar *Breeze* which arrived in April to replace *Moa*. In mid-August, *Tui* discovered the Japanese submarine I-17 near Noumea, while escorting a small convoy, and made three depth-charge runs. Despite assistance from a seaplane the submarine did not appear and *Tui* abandoned the hunt. However, the pilot signalled *Tui* to try again, and soon afterwards the aircraft spotted a column of smoke over the horizon. *Tui* made for the sighting and discovered a surfaced submarine, apparently ablaze. She opened fire at 8000 yards at around 5.15 p.m., and although the range opened to over 10,000 yards within half an hour, the minesweeper scored a hit at 5.50 p.m. and another at 5.57 — creditable efforts for such an extreme range with her 4-inch gun. American aircraft attacked the submarine with depth charges and sank it, and *Tui* went in to pick up survivors, plucking six ratings from the water. The 'kill' was shared. Later investigation suggested that the initial depth-charge runs had been ineffective because there was doubt on board *Tui* as to whether the contact was a submarine, and only two charges were lobbed in each run.

A few months later it was *Tui*'s turn to be in the firing line, when three Japanese torpedo bombers flew in under cover of darkness to attack American transports unloading at Lunga Point on Guadalcanal. *Tui* was patrolling in the channel outside and became the first target — though the Japanese aviators missed because they apparently overestimated the speed of the tiny minesweeper. By this time operations on New Georgia were well advanced, and preparations were in hand to advance the campaign further up the chain, prelude to attacks on the main Japanese base at Rabaul. The third New Zealand Division was tasked with capturing the Treasury Islands, essential as air bases for the forward assault. All three New Zealand minesweepers worked hard during the last quarter of 1943 to escort supply convoys to these islands. They were reinforced in early 1944 by the Fairmile launches that had been providing anti-submarine protection to New Zealand's harbours; the tide of war had turned so far against Japan by this stage that the risk of attack so far south was low, and the boats had better employment in the Solomons.

Indeed, the Fairmiles had not had a particularly adventurous war in New Zealand waters, though there was a flurry of activity around Wellington on the evening of 3 November 1943 when a watch station overlooking Cape Campbell reported a radar contact and sighting that could have been a submarine. Four Fairmiles of the 81st ML Flotilla under Lieutenant-Commander W.E. Waylen put to sea to intercept. The effort was dogged with problems. Some of the crews, including commanders, were sick or on leave. Men had to be gathered at short notice to fill the gaps. When the boats did get going at around 9.50 p.m. there were radio problems — the engines threw interference into the usual transmission bands and there was a confused effort to change frequencies.[93] Only ML 409's ASDIC worked properly. The unit on ML 400 was 'completely inoperative . . . owing to our inability to obtain replacements from NSO, Devonport'. The ASDIC on ML 402 worked until the battery ran down — the crew failed to start the charging generator thanks to a 'general misunderstanding' through the Fairmile fleet that

ASDIC should only be run from battery power. The ASDIC on ML 405 was inoperative from the outset. Not only was the battery flat, but the 108-volt generator had been flooded the previous week, the Stewart-Turner petrol engine had failed, and there were no spares in Wellington.[94]

The four boats nevertheless motored for Cape Campbell at 18 knots — the maximum speed available from their twin Hall-Scott 'Defender' petrol engines — intending to join the inter-island ferry *Maori* after the search and escort her into Wellington. By 2 a.m. the boats were in the search area and — though hampered by the ASDIC failures — began sweeping for the submarine. At 3.30 they spotted the smoke of the approaching ferry, and around 4.19 a.m. ML 405's crew sighted an object on the surface to port. The object submerged as the boat approached, and ML 405 dropped two depth charges. In the next four minutes ML 400 and ML 405 made four further attacks, also dropping one 'between ferry and sighted object'.[95] These were not full patterns, but Waylen wanted to conserve the charges 'in case further visual and more definite contacts were obtained'.[96]

There was a good deal of recrimination afterwards. Delays getting away, the incomplete depth-charge patterns, and the radio mix-up prompted a telling-off from the Naval Board.[97] The OC Wellington argued that the experience 'appears to show that until adequate engine and ASDIC spares are available the troubles referred to will always be experienced'.[98] The Board rejected this as far as the radios were concerned — the gear was locally made and had been standard for three years. In any case, the 'question of spares is reviewed monthly by a Committee on which the Naval Board is represented'.[99] However, the Board agreed that the object could have been a 'whale submerging . . . or possibly a large fish'.[100] The event had its sequel a few weeks later; by way of practice the Board sent the Fairmiles out on a 'day's exercises . . . in the Cook Strait area'.[101]

Pacific politics

By early 1944 the main focus of the Pacific war had swung beyond the Solomons, but New Zealand's forces were not able to follow. Churchill, Roosevelt and Chiang Kai Shek agreed in late 1943 to strip Japan of its Pacific Island territories after the war. Neither Australia nor New Zealand was included in the arrangement, setting the tone for bilateral talks in Canberra during January 1944, which culminated in the 'Australia and New Zealand Agreement', also known as the Canberra Pact.[102] This did not go down well with United States officials, who interpreted three of the clauses as an effort to reduce their post-war influence in the Pacific. The Joint Chiefs of Staff responded by limiting New Zealand's military involvement in the Pacific war.

Fraser went to Washington to argue the point, talking to the Senate Foreign Relations Committee and arguing the case with Admiral Ernest King, Chief of Naval Operations. This proved fruitless; the RNZAF was excluded from action 'west of longitude 159 east or north of equator'.[103] The New Zealand War Cabinet decided to accept this as 'necessary in interests of British prestige in Pacific'. Nash reported that 'King's views . . . are personal to him and are due to his strong resentment to the clause 26 in the Canberra Agreement',[104] but after a final meeting on 23 May had to admit that 'King . . . has a complete case on the disposition of our forces'.[105] In July, Halsey's successor Admiral J.H. Newton asked for residual units of the New Zealand Army's Third Division on New Caledonia to go, citing logistics problems in the face of an arriving American division.[106]

Naval fortunes were better. *Gambia* was already part of the Royal Navy's Eastern fleet, and British Pacific operations looked likely to develop as the naval war in Europe wound down. By this time Japan had effectively lost the Pacific war. However, although the Tojo cabinet fell on 18 July, the new government of General Kuniaki Koiso and Admiral Mitsumasa Yonai was not prepared to accept the unconditional surrender demanded by the Allies.

By this time the Japanese threat was minimal in New Zealand waters. Blackout restrictions were lifted 'in the main ports' and 'certain coastal navigation lights' were relit.[107] Local forces refocused on submarine defence. Germany was desperate for chrome and molybdenum, and Admiral Karl Doenitz sent his largest submarines to get it from the Japanese. U-862, a Type IX-D2 boat under *Korvettenkapitän* Heinrich Timm, left Narvik in May 1944, broke through the blockade and reached Penang — headquarters of the small Far Eastern U-boat fleet — on 9 September. A few days later U-862 moved to Singapore to remove her keel-mounted cargo of mercury and replace it with another of molybdenum and tungsten. Timm sailed from Jakarta on 18 November and drove east along Australia's south coast, sinking a Liberty ship off Sydney. To avoid the hunt that followed, he turned for New Zealand and passed North Cape on 7 January 1945, loitering off Cape Brett in the hope of intercepting shipping. He had little luck, so he crossed the Bay of Plenty and moved around East Cape, groping his way inshore at Gisborne on 15 January to find nothing worth attacking. He had actually missed the 177-ton coaster *Koutunui*, under Captain E. Flavel, by one day.

Still searching for merchantmen, Timm turned south. He was probably equipped with pre-war maps of Hawke's Bay and thought there was a 'coaling wharf' in the north of the bay, but ran the gauntlet of unexpected shallows in heavy seas only to find nothing to attack. As night fell on 16 January, Timm surfaced and motored towards Napier. The moment went down in legend; stories even circulated in the 1990s that the Germans had landed and milked cows. This appears to have originated in a tall tale spun by Timm during the 1950s, while he was serving with NATO. In fact, events were far less dramatic. The only ship in Napier's breakwater harbour was *Pukeko*, which had arrived that morning. *Koutunui* had arrived two days earlier from Gisborne, but left the same night for Akitio. Harbour authorities were also awaiting the 1433-ton *Wainui* from Wellington, which was due on the 18th. Timm was unaware of these details, but knew to look for the Bay View beacons marking the route into the harbour. They were not burning, so he lay off the coast amid phosphorescent water to reconnoitre. From half a mile offshore the Germans saw what they thought were street cafes and watched couples moving 'to the old tunes played by the dance music'.[108]

They were wrong about the cafes, though if Timm had brought the boat in off the Westshore spit he might have seen dancers at the Joylands cabaret.[109] As the night wore on the Germans saw a steamer leave harbour with peacetime lights burning. She was the *Pukeko*, bound for Auckland. Timm overestimated her displacement at 1000 tons — a worthy target for a precious torpedo. At dawn on 17 January he dived to attack. The torpedo missed, seen only by a lone sailor on deck who thought he must have been mistaken. Soon afterwards the ship began signalling the Portland Island signal station. Timm feared he had been seen and set course south. Captain Petley and crew never knew they had come within a whisker of death.[110]

Next day Timm received a message recalling all U-boats. He abandoned the cruise, and U-862 was still being refitted in Singapore for return to Germany when the war in Europe ended.

PACIFIC CRISIS 1941-45

The British Eastern and Pacific Fleets

Discussions between the Admiralty, the New Zealand Naval Board and the New Zealand High Commissioner in London concluded in early September 1943 with the decision to take *Gambia* into the RNZN, though under full Admiralty control. The cruiser was commissioned with her Kiwi crew on 22 September under Captain N.J.W. William-Powlett, and put to sea in early October for trials. She spent six weeks 'working up' and subsequently worked with other cruisers in the Bay of Biscay, intercepting blockade runners. At the end of January 1944 she was ordered to join the Far Eastern Fleet based on Ceylon, under Admiral Sir James Somerville.

King asked the British to attack the Japanese forces around Singapore to divert attention from the American assault on Dutch New Guinea. The British decided to hammer the major Japanese base at Sabang, northwest of Sumatra. The fleet that sailed on 16 April consisted of a battleship and a carrier force; *Gambia* initially sailed with the battleships, was detailed en route to join the carriers, and took no direct part in the attack. In May she was detailed to join Operation Transom, a carrier attack on a major Japanese naval concentration at Surabaya. *Gambia*'s chance to hit Sabang finally came in June. Operation CRIMSON deployed four battleships, two carriers, seven cruisers and ten destroyers, and brought *Gambia* into direct action against the Japanese for the first time. With her sister ship *Kenya* she was tasked with smashing a series of shore batteries. The attack reached its peak when the Dutch light cruiser *Tromp* entered the harbour, firing on shipping anchored inside.

Politics re-entered *Gambia*'s destiny during the year. The Admiralty had agreed to pay for the cruiser on the basis that she would remain under Admiralty control even though she was in the Royal New Zealand Navy. However, as far as the Admiralty was concerned the New Zealand government remained liable for *Leander*, including the cost of repairs to battle damage and her refit in Boston. The New Zealand Naval Board outlined the problem to Minister of Defence Frederick Jones in September 1944, and recommended that instead *Gambia* should be acquired on a full financial basis. From New Zealand's perspective *Gambia* had a similar manning commitment to *Leander* — 728 crew versus 747 for the refitted *Leander* — and running costs were thought likely to be similar.[111] The Board also looked into the issue of

143

running two classes of cruiser. It turned out that there were few differences; *Achilles* had the Mk I High Angle Control System whereas *Gambia* had the Mk IV version, but guns, propulsion, torpedo tubes, paravanes and electrical equipment were the same in both ships, as were their ASDIC and echo sounder fittings.[112] The transfer was formally made in October.

Gambia was refitted at Ceylon in September, and during early October was joined by *Achilles*, fresh from Britain under Captain F.J. Butler. There was a crew exchange, designed to put ratings due for leave into *Gambia*, which sailed for Wellington and arrived on 24 November to a tumultuous welcome.

Achilles took *Gambia*'s place in the Eastern Fleet, and at the beginning of December 1944 was reassigned, along with the rest of the Fourth Cruiser Squadron, to the British Pacific Fleet. This assembled in Sydney despite the opposition of Admiral Ernest King in Washington, who — as Admiral Sir Andrew Cunningham noted — 'seemed quite determined to keep the Royal Navy out of the Pacific'.[113] In the end King grudgingly agreed that the British could join in, conditional on supplying themselves. The Royal Navy prepared for Pacific action during early 1945. Forces detailed to the Pacific included all the armoured fleet carriers, all the surviving battleships of the *King George V* class, and but for maintenance issues would apparently have incorporated the surrendered Italian battleships *Littorio* and *Vittorio Veneto*.[114]

The choice of Sydney as the main base reflected the realities of Australian defence policy since before the First World War. By 1945 this had given Australia the capacity to support not only the 123 warships of the British Pacific Fleet, but also the 'fleet train' following its operations into the Pacific. New Zealand, by contrast, could not — though by mid-1945 a lengthened Calliope dock could handle 'any United States cruiser operating in the Southern Pacific',[115] and the 17,000-ton capacity Jubilee floating dock in Wellington was considered able to take 'the largest British, Allied or United States cruiser'.[116]

The fleet came under the command of Admiral Sir Bruce Fraser, who hoisted his flag in the battleship *Howe*. *Gambia* joined the force on 17 February, and New Zealanders also served on British warships committed to the Pacific, particularly in the Fleet Air Arm. Kiwis were among the pilots who flew to attack oil refineries in Sumatra during January. Five were later 'mentioned in despatches'. The carrier force, strengthened by the battleship *King George V*, joined the Pacific Fleet in February. Admiral Fraser briefly visited New Zealand that month, exercising with his flagship and the two New Zealand cruisers.

King permitted the fleet to join United States forces in the attack on Okinawa in mid-March. This was an enormous operation to which 1213 allied ships were committed. *Achilles* was refitting but *Gambia* went with the British force, which was tasked with keeping down air opposition on Sakishima Gunto, and began launching air attacks from the fleet carriers on 26 March. Japan responded with everything from bombers to one-way suicide missions. The destroyer *Ulster* was damaged by a near-miss on 1 April, and *Gambia* was ordered to tow her to Leyte Gulf. The effort was hampered soon after it began when the tow parted. Then *Ulster* ran short of drinking water and had to be passed a supply in casks from the cruiser. Matters were not helped by a mumps epidemic on the New Zealand ship — at one stage there were 45 men on the sick list, and 37 were transferred to the hospital ship *Oxfordshire*.

Fighting around Okinawa continued into May, with kamikaze attacks causing particular problems. *Gambia* looked likely to be a target during a particularly heavy attack on 8 May, but the screaming aircraft veered at the last minute and crashed into the carrier *Formidable*. The fleet remained at sea around Okinawa for 62 days before returning to Sydney in June to refit. *Achilles* sortied that month with Task Force 111.2 to bombard Truk. This former main anchorage of the Japanese fleet had been bypassed in the 'island hopping' campaign and was one of the mopping up targets. With other cruisers *Achilles* hammered a seaplane base on Dublon Island, expending 180 rounds of 6-inch, and engaging two Japanese aircraft with her 4-inch anti-aircraft armament.

In July 1945 the assault shifted to the Japanese homeland, and that month *Arabis* escorted the Fairmile flotilla back from Guadalcanal. *Gambia* sailed from Sydney with the rest of the British Pacific Fleet — labelled Task Force 37 by the Americans — on 28 June. There was 'all sorts of exercising' on the way to Manus,[117] which they reached on 4 July. By this time Harvey was on board *Gambia*. 'What impressed me about Manus was this huge open harbour,' he recalled:

> It was huge and it was jammed full of ships, big ships. Carriers and goodness knows what and it wasn't all the American Fleet, it was just

a Task Force. The British Fleet was barely as big as an American Task Group, very impressive anyway. Off we went up north and now they started exercising seriously. Then we met the American fleet while they were oiling. We oiled first . . . A lot of ships were still learning to oil at sea and there were a lot of mistakes still being made . . . Our oilers were small relative to the Americans and they didn't really provide enough oil for the British as it turned out towards the end.[118]

They were joined by *Achilles* and moved on to Japan itself. The New Zealand Naval Board also offered *Arbutus* under Lieutenant Nigel Blair for the effort; the sloop had been refitted as a radar maintenance vessel. Kiwis with the Fleet Air Arm were again involved in strikes against targets on the Japanese mainland, notably a huge assault against Japanese naval bases on 24 July, which destroyed what remained of the Imperial Japanese Navy. Harvey recalled that opposition was not strong because of losses at Okinawa, where '. . . so many pilots and aircraft had been used and really thrown away to a big extent, although they damaged a few ships . . . they didn't have too many to spare'.[119]

Gambia and *Achilles* found *Arbutus* in the fleet refuelling area at the end of the month, much to the surprise of the men on the cruisers:

It was such a tin pot little ship, this Arbutus, *you would never think of it being off the coast of Japan, and when you get up close to the coast and find a ship of that size off the enemy coast as it was . . . we were standing there feeling all heroic off the coast of Japan, and we looked around . . . and here was this little thing chugging away, reciprocating engine . . . Of course they came fairly close and you could recognise Les [Niven] and a few aboard . . . Huia Panui and all the rest of the crowd with rude signs and noises and call outs etc, we felt quite proud of them actually.*[120]

On 9 August *Gambia* was part of a small force sent to help the Americans bombard the coastal steel works at Kamaishi. This was 'situated . . . 11 miles up this estuary'; the ships had to close the coast, and *Gambia* had to borrow an aircraft to spot the fall of shot.

We were getting ready for it from about 11 o'clock . . . They gave us an early lunch consisting of Tiddy Oggies [pasties] and they also gave us our tot early . . . We didn't start bombarding until about half past 12 . . . By the time we finished the sky was black. The smoke started to rise out of the town or the city, Kamanishi . . . The wind was blowing it out to sea . . . and by the time we had finished bombardment it was right over the top . . . to the horizon . . . a tremendous lot of smoke, absolutely tremendous . . .[121]

The cannonade continued for 67 minutes before the ships withdrew to retrieve the aircraft. While they were stopped:

. . . all of a sudden we had an air raid warning, two or three aircraft came out and attacked us we seemed to be the target. Anyway they credited our pom-poms on the hangar deck on the starboard side of shooting one down . . . Charlie Young who was on the torpedo tubes with me . . . looked at me and he said, 'gee this is no good' . . . we were under the iron deck between the two HA mountings . . . shocking things to be under . . . when they are firing . . . so we went around the other side and we disguised ourselves as stanchions . . . Then we looked out on that side and it was the most frightening thing I have ever seen . . . The Americans put up that much shell and shot and it was all bursting and it had to come down somewhere . . . so we didn't stay there long and we went back . . . it only lasted about 5 minutes or so, gee what a thrill.[122]

Achilles had problems with her propeller shafts and joined most of the carriers, which were despatched to Manus on 11 August. Meanwhile the rest of the British force, including *Gambia*, helped the Americans cover carrier-borne attacks on industrial targets near Tokyo. At this stage the struggle was expected to continue until late 1946. Although the manpower issue meant that New Zealand could not continue to fight at 1944–45 levels beyond the end of 1945, the government nonetheless planned to join the anticipated land war.[123] Operation Olympic, the Allied invasion of Kyushu, was scheduled for November 1945, and Operation Coronet — the attack on Honshu — for March the following year. However, in the face of the atomic attacks on Hiroshima and Nagasaki, and pressure from the Emperor, the Japanese government agreed to surrender on 15 August.

The war had a final moment of drama. The signal to cease hostilities was flying at 11.23 a.m. that day when a Japanese aircraft appeared over the fleet, apparently bent on attacking *Gambia*. American F-4U Corsairs swarmed to shoot down the interloper. Parts of the aircraft fell on *Gambia*'s quarterdeck, and the bomb splashed harmlessly between the cruiser and *Indefatigable*. 'No further attacks were made,' the Naval Board subsequently reported, 'but several "snoopers" were shot down by patrolling aircraft out of sight of the fleet, which retired to await events.'[124]

Three weeks later *Gambia* was one of 400 Allied ships, covered by 1200 aircraft, that entered Sagami Wan and the approaches to Tokyo Bay. 'Hands went to general quarters ready for any treacherous move on the part of the Japanese, and battle ensigns were flown,' the Naval Board reported, 'but the entry was without incident.'[125] Harvey was impressed. 'We stayed there for a couple of days and it was quite a thrill, it brought an emotional choke to your throat.'[126]

Attack could not be ruled out, and *Gambia*'s crew were on alert even after anchoring. 'Watch remained at defence stations. Steam for slow speed.'[127] As dusk drew on the cruiser's motorboat was hoisted out. Patrols began just after 6 p.m. The crew went to air defence stations at dusk, and partly stood down to the '4th degree' of anti-aircraft readiness afterwards. There was another precautionary alert at 4 a.m., in case of a dawn attack. However, Japan seemed remarkably quiescent.

Gambia represented New Zealand at the surrender ceremonies, leaving for Tokyo Bay on 31 August. These were shallower waters than Sagami Wan, and the cruiser was navigated in by a Japanese pilot who came across from an American destroyer. 'He was a naval guy,' Harvey recalled, 'and they had to get on to our quarter deck by the old loading gear . . . and then he had to walk right the length of the ship and up to the bridge. Well you can imagine, all the Matelots are looking at him, everybody on the ship having a look at this guy, who was the enemy until a few days previously . . .'[128] By 1.15 p.m. the cruiser was anchored with seven shackles of chain in Berth 62.[129] The instrument of surrender was signed for New Zealand by Air Vice-Marshal Leonard M. Isitt, during a short ceremony on board USS *Missouri* on 2 September. Isitt was accompanied by Lieutenant J.D. Allingham of *Gambia*, and the cruiser's band was lent to the British flagship *Duke of York* for a sunset ceremony attended by Admiral Halsey.

The war was over, almost six years after it began. For New Zealand it had been a long and often desperate road littered with shortages, making do, and the often dismaying outcomes of allied politics. The world had changed. New Zealand had gone into the struggle an integral part of the British Empire, reliant on the British defensive umbrella for security. The country emerged a different nation, still harking to Britain but also part of a new western political order that, in the Pacific, was dominated by the United States and the emerging Cold War.

CHAPTER SIX
Korea and the Cold War

> *It cannot be expected that in any future emergency we shall enjoy a long period of immunity from attack.*
>
> — Hon. Frederick Jones, 'New Zealand Defence Policy', 5 April 1948.[1]

The Royal New Zealand Navy came of age in the late 1940s. Although made administratively independent during the war, the navy in practice remained a semi-integral part of the Royal Navy, its senior officers and administrators largely drawn from British ranks. True independence did not occur for years — the shift away from Britain was erratic, essentially mirroring New Zealand's own slow and faltering steps towards full national independence from the mother country.

In the immediate wake of the Second World War the main issues for the RNZN were demobilisation and new pay scales — the latter had been authorised in 1941 but were deferred because of the war. Demobilisation caused acute problems for the navy because there were 8237 'war only' personnel in the RNZN on 1 April 1945, many of whom were demobilised from July that year. Just 38 officers and 1026 ratings were 'permanent staff'.[2] By mid-1946 the total number serving in the RNZN had fallen to 4529.[3] This fell further as the year went on, leaving the service with insufficient ratings. 'With an anti climax at peace and the Navy running down,' one sailor recalled, 'life for me was in the doldrums.'[4]

Halting steps — carriers and cruisers

Demobilisation did not prevent the New Zealand Naval Board developing a solid direction for the service. Their thinking was based on an idea that first emerged in a Board recommendation of July 1945, arguing on the basis of Pacific war experience that the RNZN should acquire a *Smiter* class escort carrier. More than two dozen of these 11,400-ton ships had been built to meet an emergency need for convoy air cover. The ship would have been useful during the 1946 campaign against Japan, and there were plenty of experienced Kiwi pilots with the Fleet Air Arm who could be called on. The Board also thought a carrier task force was a minimum for any post-war fleet, arguing that any modern naval force needed an aircraft element.[5]

The Board continued to explore the concept, and later that year requested a full scale light fleet carrier deploying 40-odd aircraft. Britain had two classes of light carrier on hand. The Australians were committed to buying at least one, and the New Zealand Naval Board hoped to follow suit. The Board outlined the proposal to Minister of Defence Frederick Jones just before Christmas 1945. There were practical difficulties — as the Board noted, a New Zealand carrier 'would depend almost entirely for logistics and largely for training either on the British Pacific Fleet or on Australia if that fleet develops a fleet air arm... Moreover, New Zealand cannot dock a CVL and she would have to be docked in Sydney.' However, these issues were far from compelling. Worried that delays would disperse New Zealand's irreplaceable pool of naval aviators, the Board suggested that a New Zealand squadron should be raised to work with Australian or British forces.[6]

The Board call for new cruisers in late 1945 was a rather unsubtle attempt to pursue the same strategy. According to the Board, *Achilles* was ageing and 'somewhat out of date when considering long-term policy'. *Gambia* was 'too large for a Navy of the size which could be foreseen for New Zealand for some years' and needed modernising to be effective. There were costs to maintaining a two-cruiser navy of two different classes, and the Board suggested acquiring two *Dido* class cruisers. These were odd arguments given that *Achilles* had been modernised less than eighteen months before, while *Gambia* had been acquired only after the Board confirmed her high degree of commonality with *Achilles*. Hinting that the *Didos* could join 'any' planned post-war fleet, the Board sold the idea to the government on the basis of 'considerable economy in man-power' and a lower running cost.[7] These were legitimate reasons — which the government accepted — but they were not, it would seem, the New Zealand Naval Board's main rationale. The *Didos*, unlike *Achilles* and *Gambia*, had been designed for the anti-aircraft escort role.

This function became explicit in March 1946, when the Board formally recommended a post-war navy of a light fleet carrier, two cruisers, two destroyers and a tanker, plus the existing corvettes and anti-submarine minesweepers. This basically meant the RNZN would have a small but otherwise complete task force capable of blue-water operations. Annual carrier running costs were thought likely to top £800,000, and the whole proposal was calculated to add £1,050,000 to naval estimates, more than doubling them to £1,999,000. The Board justified the recommendation on the basis that 'experience of the war in the Pacific has emphasised the importance of air power'.[8] However, the government was lukewarm; the navy had to take its place in the queue for funds. This apparently prompted a rejoinder in May. 'Any long-range plan for the defence of New Zealand must be subject to joint consideration by the three Armed Services and the general Empire Defence Scheme,' the Board argued, 'but the Naval Members are still of the opinion that any such scheme is bound to include an air element in the Royal New Zealand Navy.'[9]

In the end the government squashed the carrier. It was perhaps inevitable in the face of demobilisation and post-war economies. However, this did not prevent the escorts arriving. A request for two Group 2 'improved' *Didos* was put to the British in early December 1945. The Admiralty offered the same terms as for *Gambia*. Actually making the transfer was another matter; the Admiralty initially thought the first cruiser might not be available until late 1946 and could offer no estimate for the second. Nor could they predict whether the Royal Navy's manning position would allow them to make up RNZN deficiencies.[10] They offered *Diadem* early in 1946, ahead of the initial schedule. However, she had been fitted with an electrically powered

5.25-inch mounting, and though the other three were standard, New Zealand's Naval Board balked. Jones couched the issue to reporters as one of 'possible maintenance difficulties'.[11] The Admiralty offered *Bellona* instead; *Diadem* later went to the Pakistani Navy.

Gambia sailed to Britain on 1 July. The Admiralty had wanted some of her crew to stay on during a refit and then transfer to *Diadem*, but when that deal fell through her crew stayed on in England until *Achilles* reached Britain in September, when both crews made up the complement of *Bellona*. She was formally transferred to New Zealand in December.[12] *Achilles* went to the Indian Navy, and although regarded as 'ageing' by the New Zealand Naval Board for political purposes, served a further 23 years as INS *Delhi*. She played herself in a movie about the battle of the River Plate, and when she was scrapped in 1969 some of her equipment was sent to New Zealand.

The second 'improved' *Dido* class cruiser turned up just as the *Diadem* argument reached its peak. *Black Prince* — which had fought alongside *Gambia* in the last months of the war — was part of a task force visiting Australasia in 1946, and in early May the Admiralty suggested she might be transferred to New Zealand and — given the manning situation — placed into Category B reserve. The Board accepted the offer on the proviso that a handful of British officers and ratings would help skeleton man the ship. The cruiser changed hands at the end of May. 'We leave *Black Prince* in your care with regret but confidence,' a message from the crew advised. 'Thank you for your assistance in everything.'[13] De-storing her for reserve posed problems. Her chillers were full of Australian meat, which the Agriculture Department regarded as 'in effect imported from Australia'.[14] The Army agreed to take it, but even that did not go smoothly. 'Army have taken beef only,' the Devonport base commander urgently signalled the Board on 6 June. 'Ox liver still held request directions.'[15]

The cruisers had a variety of teething problems in New Zealand service. Modifications suggested by the Board in November 1946 included grouping the messes, fitting separate boys' accommodation, adding a bathroom for seamen forward, adding scuttles, isolating the heads in the vicinity of both galleys, electrifying the galleys, adding a better laundry, improving ventilation, and adding accommodation ladders and gangway access at the forward end of the waist.[16] There were also arguments over the armoured hatch shackle pins; experience on *Swiftsure* led the Admiralty to conclude they were too soft and liable to fail, which could injure a crewman as the hatch slammed shut. They issued an official warning in 1946, but the New Zealand experience suggested otherwise and it was 1951 before the problem was uncovered in the Kiwi cruisers.[17]

Load limits were a major problem for both cruisers. The original design pre-dated the war, and by the end of it so much equipment had been added that even the four-turret *Dido*s were pushing the limits of what the hull could stand without undue mechanical strain, draught and stability problems. Additions for New Zealand service compounded the issue. The captain of *Bellona* was soundly told off in early 1951 when the Board discovered he had been operating at draught up to 3.5 inches beyond extreme deep, which was forbidden 'owing to the comparatively high stresses to which this type of vessel is subject'.[18]

Mutiny and communism

A dispute brewed during 1946 over pay and conditions, spurred partly by inequities between navy pay rates and those of the other services. Although the system had been due for revision in 1941 when the service was made independent, the task had been put off for the duration of the war, and the old navy rates were lower than those of the RNZAF and the New Zealand Army. Wartime allowances of two shillings and sixpence a day plus a shilling 'overseas bonus' were cut off at the end of the 1945 financial year, but servicemen with the Japanese occupation forces still got it, a point that rankled back in New Zealand. New pay codes were meant to be introduced on 1 April 1946, but it was the start of the 1947 financial year before the government moved, and a dispute erupted over whether the pay would be made retrospective. Rumour that it would not prompted the men to strike on 1 April.

The strike affected HMNZS *Philomel* and the ships in harbour at the time, *Arbutus* and *Black Prince*, though the latter was under refit with only a skeleton crew on board. Some two hundred men — about eighteen percent of the total manpower in the navy — gathered in *Philomel*'s canteen. The base senior officer, Commander Peter Phipps, initially sent Master at Arms C.V. Harris to deal with the problem.

> As I entered the main lounge there was a lot of yelling and screaming, 'throw him out, chuck him through the bloody windows' and other complimentary remarks. The bloke who was at that point addressing the mob restrained them and he said to them, 'now let's hear what the bugger has to say, and then chuck him out.' As near as I can remember . . . I said, 'first I want you to understand that I am more mad about this than you are. I get more pay than you, and I am losing more money over this Government's bloody inefficiency than you are, and I am definitely on your side over not getting this rise in pay . . . Now I haven't come over here to give you the heavy Jaunty stuff, but what I am prepared to do is put my career on the line for you and represent your case for you. I am doing this only if you do it my way.'[19]

The men left the lounge and 'marched through the dockyard to *Black Prince*', before heading for the parade ground, where they were challenged as mutineers by the Devonport dockyard commander, Captain Charles Richard Vernon Pugh. He was on secondment from Britain, a 'real pucker RN officer', as A.V. Kempthorne recalled. His walking stick and dog were 'a bit of red rag to a bull to the mutineers and I thought that both of us were going to be thrown into the drink at one stage'.[20] Kempthorne managed to get Pugh into Phipps' office. Apparently Pugh demanded the arrest of the men, but Phipps declined with the comment 'Don't be a bloody fool!'[21] The striking sailors apparently would have been joined by others from *Arbutus*, but the latter could not get ashore immediately.[22]

Next day the strikers met in the Devonport park near the ferry wharf, and walked 'in orderly fashion' to the gates of the base, where they were met by Phipps and the MP Dr A.M. Findlay. It turned out that the pay rates were not retrospective, and so the strike continued, though normal naval discipline was maintained — officers were saluted, and a rating later told reporters that 'this is not intended as any sort of action against the Navy'.[23] The navy seemed to agree; the men were merely told to return to work by 10 a.m. on 3 April to face punishment, or they would be discharged. Twenty-nine turned up, and around 180 left the service. However, Fraser was dismayed by what, in military terms, was indeed a mutiny. 'The serious acts of indiscipline of a number of ratings,' he explained, 'were very much to be regretted.'[24] Most of the men who returned were bundled on to *Arbutus*, which was sent on a lengthy Pacific Islands tour. There were also signs of government vindictiveness; men discharged from the navy were apparently debarred from work in the public service.[25]

The whole affair re-erupted a few weeks later. *Bellona* was in Australia during the mutiny, and in the face of growing shipboard unrest the government recalled the cruiser to New Zealand. She arrived just before ANZAC weekend, at which point about a hundred of her crew appointed a 'strike committee' and indicated they would not return from weekend leave until ten grievances were aired and discussed.[26] This time the public offered no great support. The *New Zealand Herald* hoped the incident would not involve a 'repetition of the shocking breakdown of discipline' of a few weeks earlier. 'Precipitate action will yield nothing but shame for them and for the land they profess to love and serve.'[27]

Once again the men were asked to return, but by 29 April, 54 sailors had failed to report for duty. The issue was drawn into new opposition between the government and the Federation of Labour (FOL), and on 1 May the local communist party telegraphed Fraser to protest the treatment of the discharged *Philomel* ratings. To Fraser this was indicative of more insidious dealings, a view shared by some within the service. When 'Disgusted Parent' wrote to *Truth* protesting the treatment of the ratings, one officer saltily annotated a clipping sheet with the remark that: 'I bet "Disgusted Parent" has a hammer and sycle tatooed [sic] on his bottom.'[28] There were accusations of phone tapping and undue pressure on the families of striking ratings. On 2 May an FOL representation went to see Minister of Defence Frederick Jones, asking him to place the men on the same standing as those of *Philomel*. Jones rejected the plea. Fraser met the FOL a week later and told them there would be no vindictive punishment if *Bellona*'s men returned to duty, but 'at the same time discipline had to be firmly upheld', and 'government was compelled to take a very grave view of the matter'.[29]

Soon afterwards the government began to take precipitate action. The Navy issued arrest warrants, and by late July all but eight ratings had either returned to *Bellona*, or had 'been arrested by the police under warrants issued by the naval authorities'.[30] Punishments varied but largely revolved around forfeiting annual gratuities, pay and allowances, and loss of any right to 'readjustment of pay from the old rates to the new'.[31] The result was more hardship for the sailors' families, an issue that boiled along in the media for months. The strike had its sequel a year later when the government decided to pay ratings for deferred wartime leave. Naval Secretary G.T. Millett pointed out to Jones that some of the ratings discharged after the strike were eligible and recommended the money to avoid 'what is in effect a further penalty'.[32]

Frigate navy — Cold War response

The real origins of New Zealand's 'frigate navy' can be traced to the turbulent post-war years, as the country struggled to reorient its defence thinking around the needs of the Cold War. Despite New Zealand's wartime shift towards America, and a strident voice in wartime conferences designed to shape the post-war world, the policy that Defence Minister Frederick Jones introduced in early 1948 was framed within the structure of the Commonwealth.[33] This was not surprising. The wartime relationship with America had not been without problems, and once the struggle was over New Zealand looked back to the 'old country', rushing to help when Britain entered a deep financial crisis in 1947. Pro-imperial sentiment remained strong, and Britain was still New Zealand's largest single trading partner.

The next enemy was an old one in a new guise. The uneasy wartime alliance with the Soviets collapsed as Germany fell.[34] Trouble first flared in May 1945 when Yugoslav troops occupied Trieste, contravening agreed demarcation lines. The New Zealand Division was on the spot, and Peter Fraser offered its services.[35] In July the last conference of 'the three' — Churchill, Stalin and United States President Truman — ended with what Churchill called 'frustration'.[36] Within eighteen months the bi-polar orientation of the Cold War became the dominating factor in world politics.[37] The perceived danger for New Zealand — as always — was strangulation. A feared 90-day drive by the Red Army to the Middle East threatened New Zealand's links to Britain as well as oil supplies. Kiwi planning focused on despatching forces there more quickly than before. War experience also suggested that New Zealand would have to rely on its own resources to protect its trade and South Pacific interests. At the same time, whatever ships the Navy operated would have to complement Commonwealth forces.

The Board sought advice from the Admiralty, and by August 1947 discussions focused on a fleet of six or seven 'Loch' or 'Captain' class frigates, or a mix of those and smaller 'Castle' class corvettes. The Board also wanted a similar ship for survey work. The main limiting factors were manning and cost.[38] By 1947 the navy had shrunk to 1580 officers and men, of which 150 were 'loaners' from the Royal Navy; plus 40 Wrens, and there were going to be challenges running the cruisers and an expanded frigate force. The Admiralty suggested that *Bellona* could be laid up while efforts focused on the frigates.[39]

Two options were put to the government in February 1948. Scheme A proposed a force of three 'Loch' class frigates and four 'Castle' class corvettes at £1,304,700. Scheme B comprised seven 'Lochs' at £1,643,000. The Admiralty recommended that if cost and manpower were an issue, then 'rather than obtain a mixed flotilla, a smaller force of six "Lochs" should be acquired'. Either way, *Bellona* would be retained in a training role, *Black Prince* kept in reserve, and *Arbutus* and *Arabis* returned to Britain.[40] The government opted for Scheme B. As implemented it was reduced to six frigates anyway; the Admiralty balked at the idea of converting a 'Loch' for survey work. The New Zealand Naval Board, following Admiralty advice, also recommended a replenishment ship as a priority because neither the frigates nor *Bellona* could operate in the Pacific Islands without refuelling at Suva.

The plan was almost derailed before it could be executed. The Royal Navy had to withdraw its Far Eastern submarine flotilla, preventing exercises with the New Zealand anti-submarine force. Prices also rose above the original estimates. The Admiralty based its offer on depreciated values, with on-board spares but without depot-level parts. By early 1948 the cost of spares needed at Devonport had bloated the price to £2,055,000. The frigates also carried an annual running cost of £560,000 — though the return of the corvettes saved £63,000.[41] The capital was paid out of the Consolidated Fund, and Treasury insisted that the government should accept no liability until the ships were actually transferred.[42] Cabinet approved the programme on 10 March, and it was executed by Jones with a single terse command — 'Proceed.'[43] He announced New Zealand's switch to a 'frigate navy' in a twelve-page policy document that encompassed all the armed forces.[44] Naval defence, he explained:

> . . . must extend to that vital area, including the islands to the north of us. We must at the same time provide that our forces are so organised

and balanced that they can, with other countries of the British Commonwealth, or other nations of the Pacific, if and when regional arrangements are developed, make a useful and effective contribution to combined forces.[45]

Jones added that the 'Loch' type frigates were 'described by the Admiralty as having "the most formidable anti-submarine armament of any ship of the post-war fleet"' and assured the public that 'immediate steps are being taken to receive the first two'.[46] He also announced plans to increase permanent naval manpower to 1820 men and officers by 1948, with a final figure of 2500 by 1950. News that the frigates would be named after lakes prompted the *Dunedin Evening Star* to come up with a list of candidates, suggesting that the navy should employ a Maori linguist 'who can translate and interpret the meanings and legends of the favoured lake name'.[47]

Original delivery plans, based on manning, suggested that the ships could be despatched to New Zealand in pairs at six-month intervals. In fact the first four were handed over as a flotilla. *Arabis* and *Arbutus* sailed for Britain to transfer their crews to the frigates, where the men were supplemented by 330 Royal Navy ratings who were supplied for various terms ranging from three to six years — a strategy designed to prevent all departing in quick succession. *Loch Shin, Loch Achanalt, Loch Achray* and *Loch Eck* were handed over as *Taupo, Pukaki, Kaniere* and *Hawea* in November 1948. Their arrival in Auckland at the beginning of January was inauspicious. *Truth* reported that they reached 'their home port under dull skies, on a flat calm and still flatter, unbroken silence'. Apparently Minister of Defence Frederick Jones wanted to formally welcome the frigates, but their crews were more interested in getting ashore to see their families.[48] The remaining pair, *Loch Katrine* and *Loch Morlech* — renamed *Rotoiti* and *Tutira* — were due to sail from Britain in March 1949,[49] but were delayed until May by problems with the fan impellers in *Tutira*'s No. 1 boiler room.[50]

Servicemen liked the ships — 'they were easy to maintain and our dockyard facilities ... could look after them'.[51] However, the public did not always agree. John McKay of Wellington wrote to the Naval Board in May wondering what use the new frigates would be put to. 'England lives by the sword, and does it follow that we should follow suit?' British loans to the colonies were apparently reaping huge profits, and McKay argued that 'we are expected to take over a portion of the British navy, and police British interests in the Pacific, or fight whatever battles British diplomacy may lead us into . . . As regards the Russian bogy, it is probably not as bad as it is painted.'[52] This was the first protest about Kiwi frigates; it was not the last.

Korean conflict — first phase, 1950–51

The Korean civil war that broke out in mid-1950 derived in many respects from internal opposition that could be traced back for decades. However, the immediate trigger was the Cold War and the settlement that emerged during the last days of the Second World War, when the Soviet Union belatedly advanced through Japan's mainland conquests, notably Manchuria and the Korean peninsula. Stopped on the 38th parallel by a hastily brokered deal, Soviet forces set up a Communist government in North Korea. A Communist government also emerged in the south, but was ignored by the United States in favour of a pro-Western administration. Tensions between the two regimes continued to develop, and North Korea invaded the South in late June 1950.

Rotoiti was 'showing the flag' in the islands when the news came. Navigator Neil Anderson, who was off duty when the news came in, later recalled:

> . . . most of the officers off duty had gathered at the back of the bridge for a quiet 'Shovril' — which was Bovril but somehow the sherry kept getting into it — when the Captain was handed a signal: 'North Korea has invaded South Korea; the South has appealed for help from the UN', he read out . . . The Captain then turned to me and said 'Navigator, which way is Korea?' We were heading east at the time so I gestured over the port side of the bridge to the north-west: 'That way, sir.' Immediately the Captain ordered 'Port thirty' to the startled helmsman. 'Full ahead, and steer north-west. Officer of the watch, sound Action Stations.' And he instructed me to send a signal to the Naval Board in Wellington telling them we were on our way to the war . . . The signal must have taken them by surprise, since it was about 20 hours before we received a reply, telling us to resume our duties . . . our Captain's initiative was not just bravado; a warship at sea is fully operational and if they had chosen us we had a 20-hour and 400 mile head start.[53]

There was a widespread belief that the North Korean attack had been ordered from Moscow. New Zealand's Cabinet Defence Committee met on 26 June to discuss the issue with Field Marshal Slim. Next day the United Nations condemned the invasion — helped by an earlier Soviet boycott of the Security Council. However, it was not until 28 June, when North Korean forces entered the southern capital Seoul, that the United States and Britain offered to support the southern government.[54]

The New Zealand government debated possible responses. Being able to draw on up to six frigates meant New Zealand could make a credible contribution without too heavily denuding other commitments. The Chief of Naval Staff, Commodore F.A. Ballance, outlined a range of options. Speed seemed of the essence — North Korean forces were sweeping down the peninsula and the plight of the South looked grim. However, Holland did not decide to join in until the morning of 29 June when news came that the British had put their Far Eastern Fleet at American disposal. Australia followed suit within hours.

British and American warships were already skirmishing in Korean waters, among them HMS *Jamaica* — a sister ship of *Gambia* — with three New Zealand midshipmen on board: Michael Muschamp, John Burgess and Tom Riddell. Riddell had joined the Royal New Zealand Navy in 1949 and been sent to Britain for training. He and his comrades were 'delighted when we were posted to a ship in the Far East' and 'assumed it would be a bit quiet'. In fact a goodwill visit to Japan was truncated to 24 hours, most of which was spent fusing 6-inch shells. *Jamaica* sailed on 26 June and 'began a series of shore bombardments to disrupt the enemy's coastal supply lines'. The cruiser was involved in the only surface action of the war, an attempt by seven North Korean motor boats to attack *Jamaica* and her consort, the sloop *Black Swan*. 'In a fast moving engagement,' Riddell later recalled, they 'sank five and drove the others off.'[55]

The main issue for New Zealand was what to send. Two of the six frigates were in the Mediterranean, *Kaniere* was in reserve, *Rotoiti* was on tour of the islands with *Bellona* — which needed a refit — *Pukaki* was in dock for refit, and *Tutira* was en route to Auckland from Suva. The latter two seemed the best bet. *Pukaki*'s refit was postponed and *Tutira* was hastily prepared for overseas service when she reached Auckland. Volunteers brought the ships' complements up to war levels, and the two frigates reached Hong Kong where they had to be docked for repairs, a consequence in *Pukaki*'s case of the deferred refit. Dockyard engineers also replaced the 20-mm Oerlikons with 40-mm Bofors. The frigates arrived in Sasebo — the main United Nations naval base — on 1 August, joining the British Far Eastern Fleet's 3rd Frigate Flotilla.

So began a three-year land and sea campaign. All six frigates eventually served in Korean waters, steaming 339,584 miles and expending 71,625 rounds of ammunition.[56] It was not easy for the RNZN. Having six frigates helped, but even so — as the Board reported — the 'Korean commitment... placed an added load... and only with difficulty has it been possible to cope with essential training and normal peacetime routines'.[57] Some work was abandoned, though despite the 'pressure of other commitments' it proved possible to send *Kaniere* to the Cook, Samoa, Fiji, Ellice and Tonga islands. Frigates also visited the meteorological stations on Raoul and Campbell islands. Training needs could only be kept up by recommissioning *Kiwi* and *Tui*. The situation was not helped by a drop in manning levels during 1951, as 'an unusually large number of ratings completed their post-war engagements...'[58]

It had been a significant effort, but the pay-back to New Zealand of its participation in the Korean War was immense. Basic commodity prices soared during 1950 as a result of war demand, panic buying in the United States, and the fact that Second World War stockpiles had almost been exhausted. Wool prices rose threefold in 1950 from the prices of 1949, which were already record-breaking, and wool sales to the United States increased fivefold. While this resulted from rare demand for one of New Zealand's main products, favourable trade arrangements and preferential dealings with Washington did not come in isolation.

The frigates were integrated with the British Far Eastern fleet, initially part of the Third Frigate Squadron under the general command of Captain A.D.H. Jay of the *Black Swan*. They shifted to the Fourth Frigate Squadron on 10 August. Both Kiwi frigates began work at once, joining an escort force known as TE 96.50, designed to keep the supply lines to Pusan open. A daily convoy of up to four ships was despatched from Sasebo. *Pukaki* got the job of directly escorting the convoy on 2 August, while *Tutira* ran anti-submarine patrols. The frigates reached Pusan next day, delivered the ships and were on their way back to Sasebo within the hour.

The return journey was not without incident, and *Pukaki* contacted what Commander L.E. Herrick thought was a submarine. He ordered a pattern of depth charges dropped, but could not relocate the contact. The frigates returned to Sasebo on 5 August. So began six weeks of escort work to Pusan. Wartime blackout, summer heat and what the navy called 'restricted amenities ashore' made life difficult for the crews, and the need to keep the ships ready for action was hard on men and equipment.[59] But it was essential work. The material helped UN forces stabilise the line in the 'Pusan Perimeter' — a pocket of land in the southeastern corner of the peninsula which was all that remained of the South.

Meanwhile HMS *Jamaica* with her Kiwi midshipmen 'continued the vital task of cutting the coastal roads and railway lines behind the North Korean forces'. It was often dangerous work. Riddell recalled:

We went in close one day, attempting with our gunfire to drop a tunnel onto a passing enemy train. But North Korean artillery was sited nearby and they returned fire, hitting the ship. Six men were killed on board, and others were wounded — the first naval casualties of the war.[60]

In September the situation was reversed. General Douglas MacArthur planned to cut off the North Koreans with massive amphibious landings at Inch'on, Seoul's principal harbour. Code-named Operation CHROMITE, these were on a par with some of the massive set-piece landings of the Second World War, made more complex by tidal movements in the landing zone. The forces were ready by mid-September, and embarked on 120 transports escorted by 110 warships. The two Kiwi frigates were attached to Task Group 90.7, screening the armada as it churned towards the western landing zone in rough seas. The landings took place without serious incident on 15 September, and the two New Zealand ships were sent to screen the supply lines back to Sasebo. All aircraft and ships had to be identified, and on 19 September *Tutira* joined two other ships in a hunt for a suspected North Korean submarine.

Jamaica joined the bombardment force. 'One of our targets proved to be an enemy ammunition dump,' Riddell recalled. 'It blew up with a spectacular explosion.' The North Korean air force then made a rare appearance — two North Korean Ilyushin-10 fighter-bombers tried to attack the cruiser. 'Our AA fire drove one off and shot down the other,' Riddell explained, 'but not before one of the guns' crew was hit in the stomach by a machine gun bullet. He needed surgery, and I was ordered to take him in my boat [one of the pinnaces] to the hospital ship anchored off Inchon. Sadly, despite surgery, he later died.'[61]

Soviet mines began appearing in local waters around other North Korean ports during September. Twenty Japanese minesweepers were organised to clear them — a point not widely advertised because it was less than five years since the Japanese had been the enemy. This involved an unprecedented amount of sea time for the Kiwis. Supplies and fuel came from replenishment ships, and brief visits to Inch'on did not relieve the boredom. *Pukaki* finally went to the harbour for three days of maintenance with the US repair ship USS *Hector*. *Tutira* followed in early October.

By this time United Nations forces stood once again on the 38th parallel. Bolstered by a Security Council resolution which seemed to authorise an invasion, MacArthur let his forces loose into North Korea. His plan called for landings at Wonsan to further cut off the North Korean forces, but by the time X Corps could be embarked from the crowded UN-held harbours Wonsan had fallen to South Korean troops. The operation went ahead anyway to get the troops to the front line. *Pukaki* and *Tutira* again joined the screening force, but landings scheduled for 20 October were delayed by the need to deal with North Korean minefields. *Pukaki* destroyed one mine with Bofors fire on 22 October, while *Tutira* destroyed another on 24 October, though the explosion sent debris flying over the frigate which knocked out Petty Officer H.N. Blizzard.

Late in the month *Pukaki* left for refit at Kure. There seemed every chance that the war might end as United Nations forces surged towards the Chinese border. However, Chinese leader Mao Tse Tung had already decided to intervene. By September more than a quarter of a million men had assembled on the Yalu River separating North Korea from China. When North Korean leader Kim Il-Sung called on his neighbour for help in early October, Mao was ready for action. Ostensibly called the Chinese People's Volunteers, his forces were actually elements of the XIIIth Army Group of the People's Liberation Army under General Peng Teh-huai. They were joined by the IX and XIIIth army groups, and essentially reversed the course of the war. By the third week of November, the United Nations forces were falling back on the 38th parallel.

Pukaki was relieved by *Rotoiti* that month, returning to Auckland on 3 December after 153 days and a journey of 27,871 miles. *Rotoiti*, under Commander B.E. Turner, joined *Tutira* in convoy escort duties to Chinnamp'o and Inch'on. Again there were few incidents to break the monotony. In the middle of November *Rotoiti* found some derelict sampans, which were sunk despite hopes on the part of some of the crew to save them for sale. The only other excitement came on 21 November when *Rotoiti* reported a submarine. This was later found to be a false alarm. *Tutira* was on hand when Eighth Army elements had to be evacuated from Chinnamp'o by sea, joining a small multi-national force to cover the withdrawal.

Work for the New Zealand ships was punctuated by brief periods in Japan, leave eagerly snatched by crews hankering for time ashore — and, as Anderson recalled, for an opportunity to come up trumps against other navies:

When in Japan we could play rugby against the other ships, British, French, Australian, Canadians, even the Dutch. Of course the New Zealanders kept beating everybody, but we couldn't play Tutira since we were working on the West Coast in rotation. Eventually both RNZN ships were in port together so we had an opportunity to play each other. There was a huge crowd, in fact as the game progressed and the cheering got louder, even the Yanks stopped playing baseball and came to watch. After a series of particularly tough rucks and mauls there was one of those brief moments of silence and an American voice from the Deep South could be heard saying 'An' they call dese guys humans?'[62]

Tutira's crew won. The New Zealanders on board the British ships in theatre had similar experiences. 'Our constant patrolling and shore bombardments were broken only to re-ammunition at Sasebo . . . or for brief maintenance periods in Singapore and Hong Kong,' Riddell recalled. 'But even in those places the atmosphere was tense — The Malayan emergency was on, while Hong Kong had a tense border with newly communist China.'[63]

In mid-December 1950 the two Kiwi frigates joined three British frigates to form Task Element 95.13, under Captain W.L.M. Brown, employed mainly on screening duties. The northern winter created problems of its own. 'Christ it was cold,' Anderson recalled. 'On the open bridge it was purgatory, you wore everything you owned. But at least after a watch we could go inside the ship.'⁶⁴ The steam heating built into both frigates for their original role in the North Atlantic stood them in good stead, though there were still problems. T.W. Abbott recalled that 'we were all the time dripping with the condensation' until cork lining was added during a refit at Hong Kong.⁶⁵

The Chinese launched a new offensive, and *Rotoiti* was 'sent upriver to assist the evacuation from Pyongyang and Chinnamp'o. We were the last ship out and realising that anything left would soon be in North Korean hands, we shelled the oil tanks as we went, setting off some very satisfying explosions.'⁶⁶ The Chinese were in Seoul by early January. Inch'on was blown up and abandoned. Task Element 95.13 was dismantled about this time and both New Zealand ships classified as 'spare'.

Korean conflict — second phase, 1951–53

The land war settled down to a stalemate roughly along the 38th parallel during early 1951. *Tutira* was relieved in April by HMNZS *Hawea*, under Lieutenant-Commander F.N.F. Johnston, which first saw action in May while patrolling along the coast with orders to attack targets of opportunity. She found a North Korean lookout post, anchored, and loosed 29 rounds from her 4-inch gun. Three direct hits did serious damage to the North Korean installation. Less than two months later a group from *Rotoiti*'s crew went ashore to raid a North Korean observation post high above Chinnamp'o harbour. Covered by 4-inch and 40-mm Bofors fire, the assaulting commando — Able Seaman E.J. Button and Able Seaman N.J. Scoles — scaled the cliff and reached the top to find a North Korean soldier about to hurl a grenade at them. They shot him and captured three other North Koreans who had taken cover in a fox-hole.⁶⁷

At one stage *Rotoiti* was required to patrol off Inch'on. The US authorities were worried that North Korea might take the harbour and, as Anderson recalled:

> . . . issued three different plans, each about 10 cm thick, and we had to know each one, in case any one was put into action. Rotoiti was assigned as Harbour Entry Control Vessel, which meant we had to patrol

continually across the harbour entrance, checking every ship in and out, even the sampans. The North tried to infiltrate guerillas by sea so we had to board each one, and if there was anything suspicious we took off the crew and scuttled it... We realised we would spend Christmas on patrol off Inchon, and the Captain wanted a Christmas tree. We sent a tree cutting party onto one of the many islands nearby, not sure at the time whether it was occupied by the North or South. The party came back with enough trees for every mess deck and a tall one, which we hoisted to the mast head. Later, in fact, that island was occupied by the North.[68]

Armistice talks began towards the middle of 1951. Hoping to keep the pressure up — but reluctant to do anything that might derail the fragile decision to negotiate — chief UN negotiator Vice-Admiral Joy asked Task Force 95 commander Rear-Admiral G.C. Dyer to attack the Han River estuary near the Kaesong neutral zone. This complex waterway was riddled with tidal mudflats, and the only two navigable channels were barely marked. The most likely channel looked to be the Songmo, running between the islands of Songmo-do and Kyongong-do. The hazards were accentuated by the risk of attack either from air or artillery pieces. The two New Zealand frigates were among the ships of Task Element 95.12 despatched to make the attack under Captain W.L.M. Brown.

Brown was uneasy about the whole escapade; just two years earlier HMS *Amethyst* had nearly been lost up the Yangtse. The Han had notorious tides, with a rise and fall of over 40 feet. Kempthorne later recalled that '... as you went up the river you saw the mud banks that looked like cliffs either side at certain stages of the tide'.[69] Brown detailed the New Zealand frigates to secondary duties, though an officer from *Hawea* was on board one of the South Korean patrol boats leading the attack up the river. However, when ordered to extend the operation on 6 August, Brown changed his mind and *Rotoiti* was despatched up the Songmo Channel to bring ammunition to a South Korean force near the eastern edge of Kyongdong-do. She was relieved three days later by *Hawea*, which went upriver in company with HMS *Cardigan Bay*. The main target was the North Korean-held town of Yonan, on the Yonan Peninsula to the west of the neutral zone.

Kiwis on board the British ships in theatre also saw action during 1951. Riddell, now serving with *Black Swan*, was alerted to the reality of war when the sloop was ordered up the Han River, to 'draw fire in an attempt to locate enemy batteries'. Officers were issued with morphine. 'That was when I thought, "Hold on; this is getting serious",' Riddell recalled. 'We were all relieved when the plan was abandoned.'[70] A little later, *Black Swan* was sent up the Yalu River to bombard a power station near the Chinese border. 'The charts were suspect,' Riddell recalled; 'there might have been sea mines, and we had to go in by night and get away before daylight in case of enemy air attack. They issued the morphine again; we went to action stations and did the job.'[71]

A typhoon drove the frigates from the Han estuary back to Sasebo late that month, but a few days later they were able to continue the operation. *Hawea* surveyed the Songmo channel, in company with a South Korean boat, aided only by tattered army charts held together with tape. She was ordered upriver on 28 August, almost stranding on a sandbank. However, *Hawea*'s crew were soon considered experts in river navigation, taking the USS *Weiss* upriver and later 'tagging' a Korean fort with the name of their ship. Sounding parties were sent ahead in the motorboat to feel out a channel. They were fired at on one occasion. A.G. Long, in charge of the boat at the time, recalled that 'all my sounding party rushed like hell to the port side . . . and it took quite a lean on . . . I thought we were going to capsize, but nobody was hurt'.[72]

Opposition to the naval forces grew as time went on. On 28 September HMAS *Murchison* came under artillery and mortar fire while upriver, and was hit 'to such an extent' that Kempthorne, temporarily in command of *Hawea*, 'thought I had to go up and rescue them. Luckily the Australians were able to carry on under their own steam and return to the anchorage lower down the river.'[73] After another sharp engagement on 30 September the two ships went upriver to 'fork' position and engaged the North Koreans, supported by air strikes from the carrier USS *Rendova*. A more systematic effort to reduce the North Korean artillery position followed on 3 October, when *Rotoiti* joined a larger force sent upriver through several channels to attack the North Koreans.

The risks were enormous; apart from the possibility of being caught by artillery or running aground, there was also the chance of sucking mud into the condensers. *Hawea* also developed salting in the boiler feed water while anchored upriver during one patrol.

> [Hawea *was*] *on immediate notice . . . which meant having both boilers and both engines available to move . . . without any delay. This was a bit disconcerting having salinity in the boilers at this stage. I tracked it down to one condenser and I told the Captain that I had a problem, and I said 'could I reduce to say half an hour or an hour's notice?', and he said 'no, we must remain at immediate notice without any doubt whatsoever.' On my own bat, without the Captain's authorisation, I shut down one engine and took the doors of the condenser, tested it, found where the leak was, plugged the leaks, put the doors back on again and tried to reduce the salinity of the water remaining on the ship, and got the ship back in reasonable working order in about three hours, but still with a high salinity, and made no report to the Captain whatsoever.*[74]

The effectiveness of the bombardment was unclear. Years later, D.E.C. Barratt remarked that the frigates were unsuited to making an 'indirect bombardment when underway . . . a hit would be such a fluke . . .'[75] Even shooting from anchor was apparently difficult. 'Whenever we went up Knife or Sickle we were close enough to engage, even with an Oerlikon and God knows what at. Nobody could see the target if in fact there was a target . . . Our shoots were fairly blind shoots.'[76] Shooting with the help of spotting aircraft was easier. It was 'difficult to believe' that the 4-inch gun could achieve much, but 'it was nice to have coming back on the spotters' radio . . . after a few rounds had been fired and a few corrections made to be told it was on the button'.[77]

The river ventures were not the only things the Kiwis were called upon to do. On one occasion, A.G. Long was put ashore on an island to contact a local spy and:

> *. . . give him a change of codes . . . He had all sorts of ways of finding out junk movements. I sat on the top of a hill one day having been put ashore and I thought I was going to be there for a day or more because fog came down, a hell of a lot of fog around at that stage. The ship couldn't come in and pick me up and I had this impression of being alone on an island and looking at* Hawea *two or three miles out, and I thought what a tiny little ship in a great big ocean. When you are aboard of course it is a whole world and you don't realise that you are just a speck on the ocean.*[78]

Rotoiti was relieved in October by *Taupo*. Her voyage back to New Zealand was not without incident. She was in the East China Sea when a distress signal came from the SS *Hupeh*, which had been attacked by pirates operating from the Yangtse. Long recalled that they 'found the *Hupeh* on radar and belted as hard as we could . . . but then had to stand off because the pirate chief threatened bloodshed if we attempted anything . . .' It turned out that *Hupeh* was in the hands of nearly fifty desperadoes who were holding the women and children on board hostage. Commander Brian Turner could have sent away a boarding party, but the risk of carnage seemed high. 'We were never more than a couple of stones' throw away from the *Hupeh* as we circled around it,' Long recalled. After tense negotiation, Turner promised safe passage to the pirates, who wanted to be let off on a nearby island. Long recalled:

> . . . a Chinese gun boat took off the pirates and we didn't know whether he was going to fire at us or we were going to fire at him. The ship was ready for anything at that stage. As we circled one another the guns kept pointing as we went around, every gun on the ship was trained on the Chinese gun boat and all his guns were trained on us too . . . eventually the pirates were taken off and Rotoiti gave them a fairly good supply of rice.[79]

Back at the Han River estuary, *Taupo* put men ashore to help spot the fall of shot from both her own gun and those of Yangtse River veteran HMS *Amethyst*. *Taupo* ran into trouble on 19 October when she hit a mudbank and ended up aground with a ten-degree list. The tide was rising, but she was still in contact with the bottom when the water peaked ninety minutes later. Her captain, RN officer Commander K.A. Cradock-Hartopp, ordered the crew to the quarterdeck where they jumped in unison, and the frigate limped away with clogged condensers. The near-disaster highlighted the risks of operating up the river, but operations were not brought to a close until November when the North Koreans returned to the bargaining table.

In December the Kiwi frigates attempted to cut railway lines with limited success — one bridge was hit by *Hawea* and bombed by F-4U Corsairs, but continued to carry trains. The Kiwi frigates spent the early part of 1952 protecting supply lines to the UN garrison on Songjin Island, frequenting patrol routes with midwestern names such as 'Corn Likker'. Crisis loomed when the island of Yango-do came under heavy shell fire during the early hours of 20 February, apparently the prelude to an invasion. *Taupo* and USS *Endicott* raced to deflect the assault, taking up positions each side of the island by 2.45 a.m. The invasion force comprised fifteen sampans which were engaged by *Taupo* for about twenty minutes until shore batteries joined the fray. A near-miss damaged the shell plating outboard of the engine room. The destroyer USS *Shelton* then arrived, providing covering fire to enable the two other warships to disengage.

Hawea returned to New Zealand in February 1952, stopping in Hong Kong to represent New Zealand at the Royal Proclamation ceremony. She was relieved by *Rotoiti*, which sailed up the Han River on bombardment duty. Late in February she forayed a second time into the icy river. Fifty minutes after anchoring in the bombardment position she came under accurate fire from three North Korean artillery pieces near the Yesong River, which scored five straddles. Lieutenant-Commander George Graham, a British officer, ordered the anchor let go. He returned later that day and attacked the batteries, but North Korean fire prevented them retrieving the anchor after dark.

There was a more serious incident in June when *Rotoiti* collided with *Piet Hien* in fog. The other ship was spotted just in time for Lieutenant-Commander G.O. Graham to order full speed astern, but the frigate smashed a hole in the *Piet Hien*'s hull and buckled her bow. In July there was a report that a small invasion fleet was approaching Paengyong-do. They were engaged in bad light and poor weather by the South Korean tank landing ship LST No. 898. *Taupo* circled the island to deflect a possible pincer attack. The South Koreans sank about eight boats before they were identified as South Korean fishing vessels. A month later, *Rotoiti* rushed to rescue the crew of a junk sunk in another 'friendly fire' incident. The same month she was involved in a raid on Mahap-to. A commando of some 120 soldiers attacked North Korean positions on the tiny island, while *Rotoiti* and HMCS *Crusader* poured heavy fire into a developing counter-attack, supported by an air strike.

Taupo was relieved by *Hawea* in October — the latter returning for her second tour in Korean waters under Commander G.R. Davis-Goff, who had a habit of emerging from his cabin every morning puffing on a 'filthy great' cigar.[80] *Hawea*'s deployment began with rare excitement; she came under artillery fire off Wollae-Do, returned the fire and came back next day to re-engage. The battery was silenced. *Rotoiti* left for Auckland that month, via Hong Kong and Sydney. Meanwhile *Hawea* helped deflect an attempted invasion of Yango-do Island, acting as aircraft director to bring a counter-strike against the North Korean commando. Later that month she had completed a shore bombardment against North Korean artillery positions and was turning to depart when she came under accurate 76-mm fire from an unexpected direction. Her 4-inch gun would not bear to return the fire, which to Barratt:

> . . . didn't really seem fair, we couldn't shoot back because with only a pom pom . . . that faces aft, you can't really do much about batteries when you are a couple of miles away . . . Then the Captain very wisely asked for smoke and to start weaving at maximum speed. I believe on that occasion Roger Simmonds, the engineer, managed to give us more speed than had been done on the original trials of the ship . . . it was very exciting.[81]

T.W. Abbott remembered the incident, recalling that as all steam was required for propulsion Davis-Goff apparently had to 'send a message to the galley . . . to make smoke, so we made smoke to try and camouflage the ship . . .'[82] The closest shell fell just fifteen yards from the frigate. *Kaniere*, under Lieutenant-Commander L.G. Carr, arrived late in April to replace *Hawea*. She supported an evacuation from the mainland and engaged a North Korean mortar battery.

By mid-1953 the end of the war seemed imminent, and a scramble followed to evacuate partisans from north of the expected border. Both Kiwi frigates were heavily involved. The guns fell silent on 28 July, more than two and a half years after fighting had originally been expected to end. It was an uneasy peace — officially the two Koreas were still at war. *Kaniere* returned to New Zealand in March 1954, leaving *Pukaki* on the Far East station. All six frigates had been deployed, steaming 339,584 miles and firing 71,625 rounds of ammunition. Some 1350 service personnel were involved, and one man died.[83]

CHAPTER SEVEN
Frigate Navy

During the 1950s and 1960s the Royal New Zealand Navy developed new independence. The proportion of officers seconded from the Royal Navy fell dramatically, and the service also acquired its first new-built frigates.

The shift to a full frigate navy — achieved in 1965 when *Royalist* was decommissioned — was not the radical change it may have seemed. Frigates had essentially been the core of the navy since the late 1940s, and in any case the capabilities of Cold War-era frigates were considerably greater than those of earlier cruisers. By the 1960s anti-aircraft missiles offered theoretical 'one launch-one kill' capabilities; anti-shipping missiles could give a small ship the punch of a battleship's broadside; and anti-submarine missiles could drop homing torpedoes on enemy submarines at unprecedented distances. Ship-borne helicopters revolutionised anti-submarine warfare. New small-calibre naval guns could develop a volume of fire that would have required three or four guns twenty years earlier.

Yet at the same time, the frigates operated by New Zealand for the last quarter of the twentieth century were less than half the size of the cruisers. The drop in numbers from up to eight major warships in 1950 to four by the early 1970s was also a potential problem. Review after review indicated that New Zealand needed to deploy a minimum of three frigates in order to credibly fulfil the tasks required by the government — and as at least one would always be under refit, four hulls was the minimum needed to keep three at sea.

Peacetime work in the 1950s

One of the navy's biggest priorities at the end of the Second World War was surveying New Zealand's coasts and harbours. The last work had been done in the late 1930s by the Royal Navy steam yacht *Endeavour*, and a resurvey from scratch was really needed. Initial plans to develop a frigate navy had called for a survey ship as part of the deal, but Britain had balked at the idea of converting a 'Loch'. The war-worn survey vessel offered as an alternative did not seem likely to do the job. However, the RAN operated the 'River' class frigate HMAS *Lachlan* as a survey vessel, and in 1948 the New Zealand government asked to borrow her. She was transferred the following year, initially for a three-year loan, and began survey work in November.[1]

Lachlan's crew included several RN and RAN surveyors and two New Zealand officers who intended to learn the role. By 1951 the surveyors had produced new charts covering Cook Strait, Wellington Harbour, Bluff Harbour, Patterson Inlet, and 'two covering the area from Cape Saunders through Foveaux Strait to Centre Island'. The following year, assisted by two 'survey motor launches', *Lachlan* worked on Otago and Lyttelton harbours and Cook Strait, and spent some time in Fijian waters surveying Suva Harbour.[2] This set the pattern for the next few years, during which time the ship was sold outright to New Zealand. Surveying was a slow and exacting task, but the charts were welcomed by the maritime community.[3] G.S. Ritchie recalled that there were no technical problems:

> *We had a very good Marconi radar set . . . A very good chap down in the . . . DSIR . . . invented a ranging panel which was fitted to this machine where you could increase the scale very greatly . . . by putting down floating beacons with radar reflectors made by the Dockyard we could fix ourselves on these beacons . . . we could also use a point of land. For instance on the north side of Hawke's Bay there is a very distinctive little point at the south end of the Mahia Peninsula . . . we would keep a constant range on that . . .*[4]

Lachlan's first New Zealand captain, Commander W.J.L. Smith, took over in 1960, and *Lachlan* remained a familiar sight around New Zealand coasts and harbours until the mid-1970s.

Naval personnel also stepped in to fill some of the gaps during the 1951 waterfront strike. The dispute had been building for some time, and by 1950 a range of issues had boiled down to outright struggle between the newly formed Trade Union Congress — of which the Watersiders Union was a member — and the Federation of Labour, the government and various employers. In January 1951 the arbitration court allowed a fifteen percent general wage increase, but watersiders had received a fifteen percent increase shortly before, and were not included. They felt they should have both and struck on 13 February. The government declared a state of emergency and implemented draconian measures originally developed during the depression.

The military were on the job by 21 February.[5] For the navy this meant joining soldiers on the waterfront and providing crews for coasters and merchant vessels. Some 220 sailors helped man nineteen vessels. *Lachlan* and *Taupo* were sent to the West Coast where their crews helped shift 30,000 tons of coal 'from dumps and bins', mine a further 114,000 tons, and load 95,000 tons of coal into colliers at Westport and Greymouth.[6] The military stayed on the job until July when the strike ended.

Naval staff of the 'stone frigate' HMNZS *Irirangi*, the wireless shore station at Waiouru, were on hand to help after the Tangiwai disaster, when the bridge over the Whangaehu River was destroyed by a massive surge of ice and water shortly after 10 p.m. on 24 December 1953. Motorist A.C. Ellis ran down the track to alert the approaching Wellington–Auckland express, which had 285 people on board. Although driver Charles Parker and fireman Lance Redman threw on the brakes, the locomotive and five carriages plunged into the frothing river, leaving four carriages and the guard's van remaining on the line. Ellis and a guard helped passengers out of a carriage teetering on the brink before the couplings broke and it disappeared into the raging waters. Although most of *Irirangi*'s staff were on leave, 35 men and five officers were on hand, and the first party left Waiouru ten minutes after the news arrived. Leading Cook T.W. Abbott was among them:

> *I can't recall who roused me out of bed, the Skipper Ted Thorne, there was a Sick Berth Tiffy, a Steward, a ship's company cook and myself were all taken by him down to the Tangiwai river ... there had been a train accident, that's all we knew. We must have been the first after the Post*

Office employee Mr Ellis... When we got there, we saw the bridge was all on a kilter, the road bridge that was, we saw there was no rail bridge and I think it was Ted Thorne who organised a rope across this road bridge and we crossed over. I remember the water being very high... There was a great big gap in the bridge and you could see the railway engine on the north bank lying flat on its side.[7]

A second party followed soon afterwards, joining soldiers and civilians at the scene. There seemed little hope for those in the water. The naval party rigged a rope ladder between the road bridge — which had also been destroyed — and the east bank of the river, enabling rescuers to try and locate victims on the far side. Another group from *Irirangi* went to the Waiouru railway station, where they installed a naval public address system and provided tea and sandwiches. Other ratings, with the help of their wives, organised food, clothing and money for the shocked survivors.[8]

One hundred and fifty one men, women and children died.[9] The next day the navy were back on the scene looking for bodies. By this time, Abbott recalled, '... all you could see was just the bogie wheels sticking up, no carriages ... you could still see the engine on the other side and ... you wouldn't get your knees wet crossing the river.' The navy used the facilities at *Irirangi* to accommodate visiting officials, including the Prime Minister and Leader of the Opposition. They were 'both pint-size men ... only about 5 foot 2 or so. I used to cook breakfast for them in the morning, they would just have singlets on.'[10] The navy also set up a temporary studio to relay the Queen's Christmas speech — the bridge had taken the land lines down.[11]

Meanwhile the 'sharp end' of the navy was kept busy. *Bellona* was hit by practice rockets during one exercise with Australian forces in late February 1951. An Australian Sea Fury was flying in formation 'straight and level at 1000 feet' when two of its rockets suddenly flew off in the direction of the cruiser. One 'passed between the funnels', while the other burst through the quarterdeck and into the 'after mess deck of *Bellona*'. There were no casualties. Investigation revealed that the 'Firing button safety device was at safe and accident appears due to electrical defect.'[12] It was New Zealand's turn in March 1955. During a live-fire exercise in Jervis Bay, on the New South Wales coast, *Black Prince* missed the target and sent several rounds screaming into the coastal town of Nowra. Fortunately there were no casualties.

Fire and ice — Cold War

The navy quickly struck the cutting edge of the Cold War. In addition to contributing to the Korean war, the government agreed to forward-deploy two frigates into the Mediterranean for six months in early 1950, 'in exchange for two frigates of the Royal Navy who will serve on the New Zealand Station'. This came on top of an August 1949 agreement to provide up to three frigates for the defence of Hong Kong. *Taupo* and *Hawea* sailed for 'the Med' on 3 April,[13] and HMS *St Austell Bay* and *Veryan Bay* arrived in New Zealand.[14]

The New Zealand government subsequently sent *Pukaki* and *Rotoiti* to join a Commonwealth task force monitoring the first British thermonuclear tests near Christmas Island in March 1957. *Pukaki*, under Commander Richard T. Hale, was given the task of weather watch, launching balloons to monitor high altitude winds. 'We spent most of our time at sea letting off these balloons and tracking them with the old 277 radar,' D.B. Domett recalled. 'We used to easily track the balloon up to about 100,000 feet.'[15] In mid-April they ran a dress-rehearsal. All exposed crew wore heavy goggles and flash gear, and the ship was sealed against blast and fall-out — not a comfortable prospect in the tropics. Other precautions included saltwater drenching to wash the upperworks and decks clear of fall-out.

The first bomb was dropped just after 10.30 a.m. on 15 May by a Vickers Valiant. Domett recalled the moment on *Pukaki*, 45 miles distant:

> *We were all in white overalls, dark glasses and before the bomb went off we were pointing the ship directly towards zero, and all facing aft. The ship's company went down on their hands and knees and hands over their eyes when the bomb went off. Some could still see the flash . . . They counted down to the bomb burst and then I would count up, I think it was 20 seconds before people could stand up and turn around and look at the mushroom cloud . . .*[16]

Some of the men turned to watch the fireball rising over the horizon. It was replaced by a pillar of water and steam that was sucked high into the air and spread by high altitude winds. The blast wave rolled over the frigate, felt even at their distance as a heavy pressure on the eardrums. A few hours later *Pukaki* steamed for a rendezvous with the carrier *Warrior*, passing within six miles of 'ground zero' as she did so. The crew had 'tags and dosimeters', but were unable to detect any contamination. *Warrior* herself, Domett later recalled, had an 'enormous radar on its flight deck just forward of the bridge . . . They were the mine watching radars that they used to have on shore around England during the war . . . [the momentum] used to swing the ship off course when they started it up.'[17] The frigate stayed on duty at Christmas Island until the test series drew to a close in June.

Other work took the navy to the opposite climatic extreme. By the middle of the decade the United States was heavily involved with 'Deep Freeze' scientific operations in Antarctica. This too was partly driven by the demands of the Cold War. Scientific development and exploration, particularly where it harnessed the industrial might of a nation, became a particular focus of activity on both sides of the 'iron curtain'. As the last real frontier on earth, Antarctica swiftly became a venue for rivalry. The British planned their own venture in the form of a huge multi-year programme culminating during the 1957–58 'international geophysical year' with the first motorised crossing of the ice. New Zealand was expected to play a key role, and both the RNZN and the RNZAF were heavily involved.

To facilitate this work the New Zealand government purchased a former net-laying ship built in 1944 for the United States and subsequently transferred to Britain. As *John Biscoe* she had been working for the Falklands Islands Dependencies Survey since 1947. The 1000-ton ship was refitted and renamed *Endeavour* for Kiwi service, reaching New Zealand in October 1956.[18] She made her first voyage south in December, taking an RNZAF Mk 7 Auster as deck cargo. It was an eventful journey. The Auster was strapped to the quarterdeck, and Captain Henry Kirkwood, a Royal Navy officer on loan to the RNZN for the expedition, accidentally rammed the port wing into a freighter as he manoeuvred his ship out of Port Chalmers. 'I've damaged your Auster,' Kirkwood told Squadron Leader J.R. Claydon, heading the RNZAF detachment. Air Force engineers removed the damaged wing for repairs, and *Endeavour* left with her lopsided deck cargo.

Endeavour was escorted south by *Pukaki* and *Hawea*, which turned home on 27 December when the little flotilla reached 67° 27' south, while *Endeavour* forged on into rough southern waters. They encountered the first of a series of storms, in which *Endeavour* 'behaved magnificently'. Strong headwinds and heavy seas on the night of 2–3 January broke up two dog kennels and left many passengers groaning with seasickness, but by next morning Kirkwood was able to report that they were in a 'fine sunny Antarctic day, and all eyes are set for first sight of Ross Island'.[19]

There was more trouble a week later when the ship punched through pack ice for six hours in an attempt to pick up a reconnaissance party at Butter Point, damaging her false stem. Kirkwood assured the Board that the vessel was seaworthy and 'temporary repairs within our capacity'.[20] When these were completed a few weeks later they left *Endeavour* 'not quite as formidable an icebreaker as we were', but 'quite seaworthy and fit to do the job'.[21] These were not the only problems. Domett, who was with her a year later, recalled that the ship 'wasn't designed to . . . go to sea in any sort of rough weather, and it certainly wasn't designed to spend any time in the ice, because all the outlets from the heads and galley, all came out at water level . . . We had to put the boat down and go around and chip the ice off the water line so that the outlets from the heads and galley could drain over the side.'[22]

USS *Curtis* arrived with the repaired Auster wing, and by the end of January the little aircraft was ready for a test flight.[23] The Auster took to the air soon afterwards. *Endeavour* finally sailed for New Zealand on 22 February, with eleven expedition members, 'one seal and one Skua gull'.[24] Storms four days later left her 'hove to in east north easterly gale and doing rolls of 53 degrees'.[25]

Endeavour sailed south again in December 1957 both to support the Trans-Antarctic expedition — due to reach McMurdo in March 1958 — and to conduct a four-month scientific research programme. 'Berwick our Biologist estimates that the collection of biological specimens duiring the last four weeks has now produced one of the biggest and most comprehensive collections ever taken from the Area,' Kirkwood reported.[26] Domett recalled the excitement of the early days:

> *When we got down there . . . the sun was up all the time [and] you didn't feel as though you wanted to actually go to sleep. A lot of us . . . stayed awake for the first couple of days. The scenery was magnificent, so there was plenty to see and do . . . Slowly we adjusted and went to sleep at the usual sort of time and up the next morning . . . We went to Scott's hut at Cape Evans, and we also went to Shackleton's hut at Cape Royds. When we went to Scott's hut it was packed full of ice . . . the windows had been*

> blown in and no one had been there for a long time . . . We started to dig this hut out, one of the officers and three or four guys. We took it in turns to dig, with pick axes and shovels. We finally dug it out and we got down to the table which was still set . . . There was an open jar of marmalade on the table, and although it was something like forty years old, we ate it.[27]

This was not simple curiosity; the sound was filling with ice, and for safety *Endeavour* simply dropped the men off with sleeping bags, primus and supplies. Stocks left by the 1912 and 1913 expeditions came in handy. 'We actually opened tins of cocoa and stuff that had been left down there, and cooked our own meals out of some of the supplies that were at least forty years old,' Domett recalled.[28] The highlight of late January was Fuchs' arrival at the pole. 'His forthright statement on the continuance of his journey scotched all rumours and was heartening to all on board and also enables us to plan for the future.'[29] In March *Endeavour* anchored within sight of Scott Base during a 'week of low temperatures but one of mounting excitement as Dr. Fuchs and his team draw near . . .'[30] Fuchs arrived a few days later and the expedition set out for New Zealand. Their departure came right at the end of the short Antarctic summer, as Domett recalled:

> *I think it was about thirty degrees below. You were breathing out and were slowly forming ice around your face. All of a sudden I opened my mouth and I couldn't close it, because the ice had formed on . . . [my] beard and it just went solid. I had to go up to the cabin and get a basin full of hot water and wash all the ice off my beard before I could go out and move my jaws again and start talking . . . We sailed that night into a gale, and Endeavour used to roll! . . . We were rolling more than 45 degrees one way . . . a total roll of over 90 degrees. In fact when it rolled one way, you could put your foot on a bulkhead and you were more upright than when you were standing on the deck, that's how bad it was. The wheel was on the bridge, the Quartermaster had an hour on and an hour off. When you were an hour off you were the lookout, standing alongside the Officer of the Watch. Brown was on the wheel and Smithy was on the other side of the bridge looking through the clear view screen, and we were rolling all over the place. He asked permission to smoke on the bridge . . . let go his hand hold and tripped and slid across the deck. I let go to . . . grab*

him when the ship rolled the other way. I couldn't take a step to balance myself, because he was at my feet. I went over the top of him, and there was about fifteen feet across the bridge and a sliding teak door on the other side . . . I went head first into this sliding door. I carried the whole door away, out into the wing of the bridge, then it rolled the other way, and I came back in through the door, just as Smithy was getting up off the deck. I hit him as I came back and the two of us were out cold, on deck.[31]

The ship returned to the ice in 1959–60, and again for the 1960–61 season, but by this time was showing signs of wear and tear. The government replaced her with USS *Nakamagon*, an 1850-ton tanker completed at the end of the Second World War. She entered service in 1962 as the RNZN's second *Endeavour*, and worked the Antarctic route until 1971, when the navy ended its Antarctic support role.[32]

Frigate controversies, 1958–66

The 'Loch' class frigates were the backbone of the navy by the 1950s, but were too small to carry some of the equipment being deployed as the decade went on. Plans to replace them were floated as early as 1954, when Captain V.J.H. Van der Byl suggested the service could buy six Type 14 *Blackwood* class frigates. The government was less enthusiastic. Although the 1950s were prosperous, there could be no question of replacing six frigates bought at war surplus rates with an equivalent number of new vessels. And as Chief of Naval Staff Rear-Admiral Peter Phipps argued, six frigates and a dozen maritime surveillance aircraft were the minimum needed to keep the Tasman open in wartime.[33]

By 1956 planning focused on the Type 12 *Whitby* class. They were a considerable improvement over the *Blackwoods* — but also more expensive; and while the navy wanted four, the government was only prepared to buy two. Formal orders were placed in February 1957. One was simply an administrative takeover of HMS *Hastings*, ordered for the Royal Navy in 1956 and yet to be laid down, but the other was entirely new. British names were out; New Zealand's new warships commemorated provinces. *Otago* was laid down at John Thornycroft's Southampton yard in September 1957.

J. Samuel White & Co. won the tender for *Taranaki*, laid down in their East Cowes yard on the Isle of Wight in June 1958. They were completed in 1960 and 1961 respectively.

The government indicated it would buy a third *Whitby* in the 1958 defence review. However, that year — dominated by Finance Minister Arnold Nordmeyer's so-called 'black budget' — was financially difficult. Although things picked up the following year,[34] the price of the first two frigates rocketed from £5.5 to just over £9.5 million per ship. This was traced to a combination of inflation, new equipment and miscalculation, and meant a third ship had to be postponed. There was a storm of protest against this decision, which ran against British opinion that three *Whitbys* were the minimum needed to counter a single nuclear submarine.[35] The issue was still hanging in 1961, when a defence review formally deferred the third frigate and allowed tenders to lapse. The government then decided to buy an existing *Whitby*, but this was unsuccessful and the decision was finally taken to order a new-build Improved Type 12 *Leander* in mid-1963.

This successor to the *Whitby* class added a flight deck which enabled them to operate the Westland Wasp, a small but effective helicopter capable of casualty evacuation, vertical at-sea replenishment and reconnaissance. Its primary task was as a light all-weather anti-submarine platform. The down side was that the government still had to spend more than if a Type 12 had been ordered in 1958.

A further Improved *Dido*-class cruiser, *Royalist*, was delivered in exchange for *Bellona* in 1955. *Black Prince* entered reserve around the same time, was transferred to extended reserve in early 1959, and stripped for disposal the following year, leaving *Royalist* the only cruiser in the RNZN. She had been updated in the early 1950s and served for ten years, achieving high standards of operational efficiency during that time. However, while her electronics and weapons fit had been updated, her engines and boilers had not. 'She was a magnificent ship in many respects,' T.M. O'Brien recalled; 'She had been well modernised in terms of weapons and sensors, but not the accommodation nor the machinery spaces.' By the mid-1960s this plant was over twenty years old, and O'Brien recalled that 'keeping her going was a major challenge. I remember Terry Arthurs was the Double Bottom Engineer at the time and he used to spend his life in a pool of furnace fuel oil as another hole was found in the tank tops underneath the machinery spaces.'[36] The government decided to relinquish the cruiser in 1966. However, in November 1965 — during her final cruise — *Royalist* suffered a catastrophic mid-ocean breakdown.

The trouble began on 1 November, when *Royalist* was on her way from Manus to Suva prior to returning to Auckland. O'Brien, who was Engineer Officer of the Watch, recalled:

> . . . we were steaming on the aft unit, in the forward unit the boiler room was shut down being stripped for a boiler wash. I had just wandered off on my rounds and was returning to the after engine room and had stopped by the office to write out some job cards, which I probably never did finish, when I got a call from the Chief of the Watch in the after engine room . . . to say the salinometers had gone off the clock. I raced down below to try and figure out what was going on. I subsequently discovered the degree of contamination was so great that there was no way of isolating it all or minimizing it. I tried to get hold of Commander (E) . . . told him what was happening, got down below, and by this time we had shut down.[37]

Leaks in the condensers had let sea water into the boiler circuits, and the boilers 'primed', meaning dry steam could not be provided to the turbines, forcing a complete shut-down. The emergency diesels came on line, and engineers under Commander H.R. Simmonds hastened to bring the forward boilers into action. These too began priming, apparently because 'someone opened up the main extraction pump discharge cross connection valve',[38] and the ship wallowed overnight only eighty-odd miles south of Bellona Point. This was a little close for comfort, and Captain Joffre Vallant called for help. HMS *Dampier* arrived the following morning to take the cruiser in tow.

Meanwhile, Simmonds and his crew discovered major leaks in the condensers and resigned themselves to a complete overhaul of the 300 valves and 7000 condenser tubes on board. This was a massive job, even with the help of volunteers. O'Brien recalled:

> I don't think I have ever worked so hard in all my life . . . We literally just worked and worked, took salt tablets, drank water, oatmeal and water, oatmeal and water and salt and limers. There was just no time other than to flash up a boiler, steam it at low power, low pressure, distill

the steam coming off, shut down the boiler, let it cool down as much as you could afford, open the doors, get in there, clean it out, fill it up with slightly less contaminated water and start steaming again. At the same time replacing packing in every valve and almost every joint, certainly in B boiler room. The sight of B boiler room at day two, when we got every person we could lay our hands on to pack valves was hilarious. I mean it was like suddenly the monkey cage at the Auckland Zoo had got liberated, there were people all over, from top to bottom, swinging on spanners, stuffing in packing material and shouting and abusing each other. Those are the people . . . who probably deserve the most credit for getting the ship back. There were Weapon Mechanics, there were Electricians, there was God knows what sort of people. They weren't people who normally worked in machinery spaces, but they worked their guts out and were very instrumental in getting us home.[39]

While this went on *Dampier* dragged the cruiser 110 nautical miles out to sea, but had to slip the tow and head for Port Moresby to refuel, leaving *Royalist* again at the mercy of the seas. This was not the only problem. Without power the magazine chillers no longer worked:

. . . the magazines reached temperatures which were beyond the safe limit for the ammunition . . . they then hoisted out all the ammunition and threw it over the side and we had a final burial ceremony for the last cartridge case that went over the side . . . It was probably the best thing to do under the circumstances, it was getting bloody hot to put it mildly.[40]

On 6 November an RNZAF Sunderland arrived from Fiji, dropping off mail and taking photographs. For the crew of *Royalist* it was a 'real emotional moment when that bloody great big white Sunderland came in and dropped off the mail, it was very welcome'.[41] That evening the ocean-going tug *Carlock* arrived from Brisbane to pick up the tow, and shaped course directly for New Zealand. The pair were visited a little later on by *Lachlan*, which 'arrived with her big "Steptoe" banner' to transfer supplies and just over a hundred tons of fuel oil.[42] The Sunderland returned on subsequent days.

Although *Carlock* was capable of towing the cruiser back to Auckland, *Royalist*'s engineers had enough steam up by 9 November to run one of the turbo-generators. On 11 November the forward engines were brought on line and the cruiser worked up to eight knots. She reached Auckland under her own power on 17 November. Simmonds was courtmartialed for negligence, but after a lengthy trial — one of the longest in New Zealand's naval history — was acquitted. *Royalist* paid off five months early, and remained at Devonport while the British government sold her for scrapping. In December 1967 *Royalist* was towed out of Auckland by the *Fuji Maru* for breaking up in Osaka.

New Zealand was left with three frigates. Four were needed to deploy three simultaneously, and a further defence review in 1966 came down in favour of a fourth. The Naval Board — notably Rear-Admirals R.E. Washbourn and John Ross — pressed for six. They were eventually opposed by Rear-Admiral Peter Phipps when he became Chief of Defence Staff in 1965, on the basis that although the country needed them, six would be too costly.[43] In wake of the review the Improved Type 12 class frigate *Canterbury* was ordered from Yarrow & Co of Glasgow in August 1968 for $21.6 million, around twenty percent of New Zealand's defence budget that year. This was not accomplished without further argument. Defence minister David Thomson came under fire for allowing the navy to be whittled back from two cruisers and six frigates in 1950 to just four frigates.

The Type 12 frigate HMS *Blackpool* was leased to fill the gap until *Canterbury* could join. T.M. O'Brien was among the Kiwi sailors sent to Britain to pick her up. 'The only problem,' he recalled, 'was that the RN crew had completely stripped her, there were no comforts left on board at all, no fridges, no carpets, no nothing. We spent quite some time in Chatham trying to get the place habitable.'[44] The frigate returned to Britain when *Canterbury* joined in October 1971. O'Brien recalled the semi-modular construction method:

> *Yarrow's built the ship in ... sections, which they built inside a building hall. That was steelwork only, no equipment went in ... there were about 25 units from bow to stern. These were shipped out of the building hall or the fabricating shop and assembled on the slipway and then welded one to another. It was from that point that all of the wires and the pipes and the boxes and the other bits and pieces were assembled inside the structure ... I guess in all fairness it was the earliest movement in modular*

> construction. Because it was so early in the game there was not what was known as configuration control . . . there were many things in the ship where the position wasn't precisely defined and therefore you could get things like a distribution box in a passageway, but you couldn't open the door because somebody had run a pipe over it, in front of the door. These were issues that theoretically the UK Ministry of Defence Naval Overseers should have dealt with and detected . . . In Canterbury it was the ship's staff who had to deal with these problems and they caused long and bitter arguments.[45]

During these years the RNZN continued to extend its independence from the Royal Navy. A high proportion of the officer cadre were British in the late 1950s, but numbers dropped steadily during the following decade. The shift was also reflected in New Zealand's changing alliance ties — the links that developed after the 1950s highlighted the point that New Zealand was a true South Pacific nation, with critical interests more in that area and South East Asia than in Europe or even the Middle East. This change was highlighted by New Zealand involvement in various South East Asian conflicts, including the Vietnam war. However, the shift towards practical naval independence did not preclude work with Britain, particularly in the Pacific and Asia.

During 1965 New Zealand contributed to Royal Navy operations in Malaysian waters. The Indonesian Confrontation was at its height, and New Zealand leased two minesweepers, *Hickleton* and *Santon*, to join the Royal Navy's 11th Minesweeping Squadron. They were tasked with anti-insurgency, and each steamed more than 60,000 miles in New Zealand service. When the patrols were discontinued in late 1966 the two ships were sailed to Britain by their New Zealand crews and reverted to British control.[46]

The pragmatic aspects of the shift away from Britain were underlined in 1968 when the RNZN received permission to have its own colours. A white version of the New Zealand flag was hoisted for the first time at Devonport.

Bombs and fish

New Zealand's frigates were used in spectacular fashion during the early 1970s by a Labour government determined to oppose French nuclear testing.

France was not a signatory to the Limited Nuclear Test Ban Treaty of 1963, or the Nuclear Non-Proliferation Treaty of 1968. However, their atmospheric bomb tests at Mururoa Atoll in Polynesia, which began in 1972, ran against the spirit of the agreement and prompted protests to the International Court of Justice from Australia and New Zealand. The New Zealand government under Norman Kirk backed these efforts with a naval presence. Politically this was unprecedented; the deployment of a warship sent a significant message both to the French and to the world about New Zealand's official attitude to nuclear weapons. Although the dangers of nuclear weapons were well recognised, none of the aligned nations or their allies had protested to this level before. However, the move was not co-ordinated with the small flotilla of private protest ships that was also on station near Mururoa.

Otago and the Australian stores ship *Supply* sailed for Mururoa in June 1973 with Cabinet Minister Fraser Coleman and a media contingent on board, after being farewelled by Kirk from the Devonport wharf. Once on station near Mururoa there was little to do. French patrol aircraft kept the frigate under surveillance. *Otago* was relieved after three weeks by *Canterbury*, which remained on station a further fortnight.

One of the biggest tasks the navy undertook during the 1970s and beyond was fisheries patrol. New Zealand's 200-mile 'exclusive economic zone' was vulnerable to illegal predation by foreign fishing vessels. While these could be found by aircraft, they had to be actually intercepted at sea for inspection. The frigates alone could not handle the task even if all had been available. *Waikato* was modernised over a two-year period from 1975, recommissioning in August 1977. Manning shortages left *Taranaki* laid up for an extended period the same year — Chief of Naval Staff Rear-Admiral J.F. McKenzie explained to reporters that the navy had only 48 percent of the technical ratings it needed.[47] *Canterbury* was in refit for the first six months of 1978. The navy wanted to supplement the frigates with six large patrol boats for fisheries protection duties, a number dropped to four when the proposal was accepted by the government. They were ordered from Brooke Marine of Lowestoft and delivered in pairs by the heavy-lift ship *Starman* in January and June 1975.

These boats were named after the recent 'Lochs': *Pukaki*, *Rotoiti*, *Taupo* and *Hawea*. The first two sailed from Auckland to Wellington by way of a trial trip in early March 1975, and by the end of the month were out on their first mission, an attempt to intercept two Taiwanese fishing boats off the Taranaki coast.

Submarines or frigates?

The future of New Zealand's frigate fleet seemed in doubt by the early 1980s. A 1970 defence review emphasised ships that could meet New Zealand's collective security obligations. By the late 1960s these were fairly extensive; New Zealand was party to treaties that included the Canberra Pact, SEATO (South East Asian Treaty Organisation), ANZUK (Australia, New Zealand and the United Kingdom) and ANZUS (Australia, New Zealand and the United States). In 1971 New Zealand also joined the FPDA (Five Power Defence Arrangement), a group comprising New Zealand, Australia, Singapore, Malaysia and Britain. All these arrangements required credible air, land and naval forces. There were regular exercises to which the RNZN was invariably able to send one or two frigates.

This changed in the late 1970s. *Otago* and *Taranaki* were ageing, but inflation and the rising absolute cost of defence hardware made replacing them even more controversial than it had been in the 1960s. A defence review in 1978 reconfirmed the government's commitment to a three-frigate 'blue water' navy, but rejected navy plans for expanding the force to six frigates. As before, maintaining three frigates at sea meant owning four. The navy wanted 3700-ton *Kortenaers*, gas-turbine powered Dutch frigates that were available in two variants. When this proposal was turned down the service decided to completely rebuild *Taranaki*. The $42 million modernisation would have taken place at the Devonport dockyard under the supervision of English shipbuilders Vosper Thornycroft, and virtually gutted the frigate; her steam turbines would have been replaced by gas turbines, larger fuel tanks fitted, a flight deck added, and new 76-mm guns installed. Initial orders for GEC gearboxes and gas turbines, worth $3 million, were placed in mid-1980 in anticipation of work beginning in April 1983.[48]

In the end none of this happened. The scene changed again in 1981 in the wake of a British defence review, which discarded a number of Royal Navy ships ranging from the eighteen-year-old *Leander* to the eight-year-old HMS *Ariadne*. There seemed a good chance New Zealand could obtain two frigates at knock-down prices, although the down-side was that the RNZN would face block obsolescence and a potential replacement bill of up to $1 billion in the early 1990s.[49] These objections carried little weight with the government, and a deal was concluded in October 1981 to buy the Improved Type 12 class frigates *Dido* and *Bacchante*, both dating from the early 1960s. As such they could be no more than stopgaps. However, *Dido* was fitted with Australian-designed Ikara anti-submarine missiles and had a modern ADAWS-5 combat data system. The opportunity to gain experience with this equipment was not something the navy could turn down, and the acquisition of the two ships at second-hand prices also offered the prospect of replacing *Otago* and *Taranaki* on a one-for-one basis.

The total cost, including cancellation fees on the contracts to reconstruct *Taranaki*, was announced as $100 million, although in the event the final bill was $137 million.[50] Defence Minister David Thomson described the opportunity as 'fortuitous', adding that 'in the existing financial circumstances it was plainly necessary to seize any opportunity to acquire effective operational part-life vessels as an alternative to the purchase of a new ship'.[51] Delivery of the ships was delayed by the Falklands war of early 1982. New Zealand did not contribute directly to that war, but in May, Prime Minister Robert Muldoon offered to send a frigate to relieve a British ship somewhere else. *Canterbury* sailed for the Indian Ocean, joining the Armilla patrol. She was relieved by *Waikato* in August, and the two New Zealand ships alternated in these waters until October 1983.

The Falklands war led the Thatcher government to reverse some of the 1981 defence cuts, but the two *Leanders* remained on sale. *Taranaki* paid off in June 1982 — touring New Zealand with a 121-metre paying-off pennant — before being laid up for disposal. Some of her crew went to Britain to pick up *Bacchante*,[52] which was transferred to New Zealand in October 1982. Renamed *Wellington*, the frigate reached Auckland in December and paid off for a 20-month, $27 million refit intended to improve fuel capacity, and add new electrical systems and a chaff launcher. This was delayed by technical difficulties and she did not enter New Zealand service until mid-1986.

Dido was transferred to New Zealand service as *Southland* in December 1983, under Captain Ian Hunter. The ceremony took place at Southampton, where she had been refitted at a cost of $14 million — a six-month exercise that had not been entirely without problems.[53] She steamed into a windswept

Wellington to refuel in July 1984 and went on to briefly visit Bluff before sailing for Auckland. She was due for a further refit costing $50 to $70 million in 1988, but three British and two New Zealand tenders were turned down because of what Defence Minister Robert Tizard called 'pressure on the defence vote'. Instead an 'essential maintenance package' was authorised for 1989.[54] The decision was attacked by the National party as 'slash and burn cost cutting'.[55]

The longer term future of the frigate fleet remained in doubt. In 1983 the navy considered submarines, potentially in conjunction with an Australian programme to build conventional boats. Marlborough MP Doug Kidd explained to reporters that a handful of British submarines had kept the Argentine navy out of the Falklands war.[56] In October, Deputy Chief of Naval Staff Commodore D.B. Domett told the New Zealand Navy League that four new submarines provided a 'cost-effective alternative to frigates', on the basis that projected budgets would make it difficult to maintain and replace the existing frigate force.[57] Superficially there were cost advantages, not least being that a submarine needed fifty-odd men in comparison with around 250 for a frigate. Initial investigations suggested that submarines might cost only $140 million each to buy, instead of the $280 million needed for a new frigate. In 1984 an officer was sent to Australia to examine the prospect, but the plan was cancelled in February 1985 by the Labour government.[58]

CHAPTER EIGHT
Age of Reform

The environment changed dramatically for the Royal New Zealand Navy during the last years of the twentieth century. A Labour government elected in mid-1984 introduced a period of radical change that reformed the entire public service. These were particularly difficult times for the military, which had also had to face new constraints in the wake of the so-called 'ANZUS row'. Defence expenditure dropped 30 percent in real terms between 1988 and 1997. This tended to mirror the general run-down of the whole public sector. However, while most of these changes spurred protests, the post-Vietnam, post-Cold War generation popularly viewed the military as an outdated dinosaur. Public defence perceptions still tended to focus on war as large-scale conflict between nations, and on the threat of direct invasion of New Zealand. By the 1990s the former was unlikely, and the latter had never been plausible. However, there was little media effort to encourage an informed public debate on the real defence issues New Zealand faced into the 21st century, still less to discuss the position, role and function of the military in the post-Cold War world.

The end of the Cold War did not bring peace — instead, the world became more dangerous than ever. This was no paradox. The threat of instant Armageddon had suppressed long-standing internal opposition from Africa to Asia, the Middle East and the South West Pacific. These conflicts re-emerged in the early 1990s, transforming warfare from an international event to the national arena. Efforts to keep the peace relied on military intervention

— frequently under the aegis of United Nations administration. Because of the way the international system worked, New Zealand had to join in or lose credibility as a nation, potentially facing disadvantages in apparently unrelated areas such as trade access. This meant having an effective military — a position at odds with the apparent ideals of successive New Zealand government policymakers after 1984, whose philosophies evidently included visions of a stateless market-driven future.[1] There was also an apparent belief that the end of the Cold War had ended any need for the military. New Zealand was out of line with world trends in this regard, and successive Australian administrations — on which New Zealand relied for defence ties — were concerned at the apparent lack of commitment across the Tasman. The result — predictably — was that the New Zealand military came under huge pressure to perform despite cutbacks.

The threat for New Zealand — as always — was not invasion but damage to trade routes and economic interests well away from local waters, including oil supplies. War did not have to break out for these to be affected, as the late 1980s experiences in the Persian Gulf demonstrated — the spot price of oil soared in the face of potential attacks on gulf shipping. There were also plenty of potential flashpoints closer to home. One of the most serious arguments was over the Spratly Islands. The archipelago was claimed by six nations — China, Vietnam, the Philippines, Malaysia, Brunei and Taiwan — each wanting oil reserves thought to lie beneath it. The Straits of Malacca, between Singapore and Indonesia, where much of New Zealand's trade was routed, suffered from piracy.

By the 1990s some forty percent of New Zealand's trade was with East Asian nations. Ethnically complex and rich in resources, South East Asia contained some of the world's fastest growing markets and economies during the early part of the decade. The area was also one of the world's most rapidly militarising regions, a fact that did not slow with the Asian economies as the 'Asian Tiger' stalled during the late 1990s. Thailand deployed the region's first aircraft carrier in 1997, and the number of submarines in the region rose from 89 to 220 around the end of the decade. New Zealand's ties with the Five Power Defence Arrangement (FPDA) were important under these circumstances, as was an ability to contribute to any joint military activity the FPDA might become involved in. Credible anti-submarine capability was particularly important.

The importance of adequate defence forces was recognised in Australia, which embarked on modest but steady military development during the 1990s, introducing airborne tankers, over-the-horizon radar, new frigates, and AWACS aircraft. New Zealand's dwindling defence spending was a significant worry in Canberra, where there was criticism that New Zealand was not pulling its weight in the special defence relationship. The contrasts at sea were clear; by 2001 Australia fielded six submarines to New Zealand's none, and ten major warships to New Zealand's three.[2] The ratio looked likely to shift even further in Australia's favour by 2005; by then the RAN was scheduled to deploy six submarines, eight ANZAC class patrol frigates, six *Perry* class frigates, two LST's and a heavy lift ship, with one or more multi-role aircraft carrier projected to follow. Major RNZN warships, by contrast, were projected to comprise a tanker, a sealift ship, two ANZAC-class patrol frigates and a 70-metre patrol ship.

The New Zealand forces also had an unusual legislative framework. They came under the Defence Act 1990 and the State Sector Act 1989. The latter applied private sector ideals and terms to the public sector as a whole, including the military. Despite following overseas developments this seemed somehow incongruous. Legislation identified 'national security outcomes' and even a 'purchase agreement' by which the New Zealand government contracted the Defence Forces to supply 'services' and 'outputs'. It was not a good fit. A 1991 White Paper on defence admitted that when considered 'simply as a business', defence had 'some complex features'[3] — mostly in relation to asset valuation and erratic large capital purchases.

In fact there was a more basic tension between this kind of thinking and the realities of military service. Despite the profusion of glib new-speak terms such as 'empowerment' and 'knowledge economy', the private enterprise model ultimately treated people as merely another cost, a 'human resource' that could be corporatised, quantitied and then minimised. This stood at odds with the realities of the New Zealand military. The services had been an an integral part of national identity, arguably since the First World War. Furthermore, they were not simply a cost; the bottom line was that, when the crunch came, service personnel were going to risk and perhaps sacrifice their lives to protect their country. The human values associated with this activity could not simply be assigned dollar figures, or reduced to bland figures on a balance sheet.

ANZAC frigates

The difficulties faced by the defence forces during the 1990s were epitomised by the ANZAC frigate programme. Public arguments associated with these ships dominated the politics of naval defence funding for most of the decade. Plans to replace the two frigates bought in the early 1980s were spurred in the middle of that decade when an Australian defence review identified a need for a class of patrol frigates, deploying the latest technology and able to fight alone if necessary. The possibility that the same ships might meet New Zealand requirements could not be ignored, and in December that year the New Zealand and Australian governments released a joint request for proposals. The idea was endorsed during a defence review in 1987, and formalised in March that year by a joint Memorandum of Understanding which confirmed that both nations would buy new frigates of the same class.[4]

The request for proposals prompted 22 responses ranging from the Unisys Corporation FFG-7 *Perry* class to an updated *Leander* offered by Vosper Thornycroft, and private ventures such as the Yarrow Shipbuilding Light Patrol Frigate. Public submissions also highlighted ships such as the Castle class patrol boat or the Irish P-31 offshore patrol vessel, but these were rejected for various reasons, mostly to do with seaworthiness in the blue-water role.[5] By 1987 the list had been whittled down to the Type 23 'Duke' offered by Swan-Hunter; the Dutch M-class of Royal Schelde, and the German MEKO 200p. It took a further year to reduce this to two — the 'Duke' was eliminated. One of the key requirements was joint construction in Australia, and selection boiled down to a battle between two consortiums: Australian Marine Engineering Consolidated (AMECON) and Blohm and Voss on one hand, offering the MEKO; and Australian Warship Systems and Royal Schelde on the other. AMECON — renamed Transfield Defence Systems — won the $5 billion programme to build eight to twelve MEKO 200P frigates under licence at their shipyard in Williamstown, near Melbourne.

New Zealand did not take the decision to participate lightly. At government level, some $3.4 million was spent on the so-called 'Quigley Review' of defence in 1987, and on consultants' fees associated with examining the ANZAC frigate project and new tanker. However, there was massive public opposition. In hindsight this was not too surprising. At a time when the Cold War was ending and so-called 'new right' reforms harked towards a stateless dystopia where the arbiter was wealth, there was a popular belief that military forces were obsolete. The same reforms were retracting the government sector, and anti-frigate sentiment offered successive governments a relatively easy way of earning political Brownie points in the face of public opposition to health and welfare cuts. This certainly had an effect on the ANZAC programme as it finally developed. Precedent dating to the 1950s suggested that six frigates were required for peacetime operations. Four was a compromise, yet by the late 1980s there seemed some doubt that any new frigates would be procured at all. Indeed, the term 'frigate' was so unacceptable by this time that the 1987 Defence White Paper did not actually use it.

To some extent this semantic aspect was facile. The term 'frigate' had a specific meaning in the post-war years, but by the 1980s the boundaries were blurred. Britain classified the Type 22 'Broadsword', which displaced around 5200 tons fully laden, as a frigate; Japan called their 3700-ton *Hatsuyuki* a destroyer; and for the United States — whose missile-armed *Perry* class frigates were as capable as the early missile-armed cruisers — the defining factor was the number of screws. The real argument in New Zealand was whether the government was prepared to buy ships that could meet national 'blue water' needs, and the issue ultimately at stake was the defence relationship with Australia. In the end the government decided to buy two, with options for two more, announcing the decision in November 1989. However, the apparent lack of New Zealand commitment to defence had its effect on the deal — which at Australian insistence included advance components for the third and fourth frigates, whether they were ordered or not.

The Australian decision was unsurprising; the ANZAC frigate controversy had become a political football in New Zealand, undermining the credibility of the New Zealand commitment. As the election approached in 1990, public opposition to the reforms of the day made defeat of the Labour government seem inevitable. There were three changes of Prime Minister in less than twelve months, and a promise to cancel the ANZAC frigate deal was one of the titbits thrown to curry public favour in the lead-up to the election. However, Labour was soundly defeated at the polls. By this time, the cost of cancelling would have been in the vicinity of $500 million, and the incoming National administration — though continuing the unpopular reform programme — kept the ANZAC arrangement.

Ongoing cut-backs to all government services gave critics ammunition to suggest that the new ships were being bought at the expense of health and welfare spending. 'Given that the cost of this heavy metal would provide free, and immediate, healthcare for all New Zealanders for life, it makes you wonder about national priorities,' one correspondent wrote to the *Dominion* in March 1997.[6] Criticism of this kind was poorly informed. The $1262 million frigate deal signed in November 1989 was a sixteen-year arrangement costing an average of around $80 million per annum between 1989 and 2005, about half of one percent of what government was spending on health, welfare and education. It included protection against exchange rate fluctuations and inflation, and was budgeted within the existing defence vote. At operational level, in constant-dollar terms, an ANZAC frigate was cheaper than *Canterbury* both to buy and operate.[7]

Put another way, health expenditure in 1994 alone was more than four times the lifetime cost of the whole ANZAC frigate programme.[8]

The deal was further offset by a guaranteed $800 million worth of work for local companies over the 1989–2005 period. This eventually drew in some 417 businesses, ranging from the largest industries down to one-person concerns. More than half of this had come in by 1997, by which time local industries had benefited from the ANZAC programme to the tune of $470 million. Around $80 million of this had been received that year.[9] This work generated further opportunities for the companies involved — Cambridge-based Papworth Engineering, for instance, won contracts to supply filter systems for ships as far afield as Hong Kong, Kuwait and England.

This engineering windfall was facilitated by the modular design — the MEKO 200 included six hull and five superstructure modules, each completed separately before integration into the ship. The modules themselves contained various large and small sub-assemblies which could also be independently put together. The lion's share of the local work went to the Transfield Industries subsidiary in Whangarei, which received the contract to manufacture the five superstructure modules for each frigate. Hamilton-based MacArthur Group was contracted in 1992 to make control panels, then asked to provide electrical switches and motor controllers. They did so with technical assistance from the Siemens company.

Junction boxes, plugs and electrical equipment were manufactured by Auckland-based Electropar. Steelfort Engineering of Palmerston North got the job of making stainless steel kitchen and laundry fittings. James Hardie Engineering gained an ISO 9000 quality standard ratification and went into partnership with CPD Engineering of Wellington to win the contract for the air conditioning and refrigeration systems. Blenheim-based Safe Air won the contract to build the cabinets into which this equipment was mounted. James Hardie later won contracts to supply similar equipment for new Australian mine-sweepers. Other companies, including Air New Zealand Engineering, Alco Products Ltd, Banner International Ltd, Bostik New Zealand, Interlock Industries, Para Rubber, IST Engineering, Gerrard Springs, Firepro Safety, Fletcher Challenge, Hydraulink Fluid Connectors and Northern Metal Testing Labs also received work or subsidiary contracts for the ten ANZAC frigates.

Final assembly took place at the Transfield Shipbuilding yard in Williamstown, near Melbourne. This former state shipyard had been established nearly ninety years before in Port Philip Bay, and had built ships up to destroyer size during the Second World War. Later it built the Royal Australian Navy's Type 12 frigates under licence. It was privatised in 1988, by which time its facilities included a two-ship building berth, a graving dock, heavy lift cranes, and extensive workshops. The first ANZAC, HMAS *Anzac* herself, was launched in 1995. New Zealand's first, *Te Kaha*, was the second. Transfield Shipbuilding was renamed the Tenix Group in 1997.

Debate during the 1990s focused on whether New Zealand's third and fourth ANZAC's would be ordered. A decision had to be made by 1997, but the military remained an easy target for a public jaded by more than a decade of reforms. The looming deadline for ordering a third frigate prompted further protest. At one point in March 1997 a banner decrying 'useless frigates' was swathed over the cenotaph outside Parliament buildings in Wellington as part of a protest about the vessels. This drew comment from former Defence Minister and Crete veteran Allan McCready: 'It is quite obvious that the spokesman ... had little respect for the men of the Navy who did so much and made the sacrifices that enabled people to enjoy the freedom of a democracy that ... his organisation [has].'[10]

In the end the government decided not to act, and the option on the third ANZAC lapsed. Although there was talk of buying a second-hand ANZAC, or an old FFG-7 *Perry* type frigate, the decision cut New Zealand down to two frigates plus the ageing *Canterbury*. She was not in the best condition

— her machinery could not be pressed to more than 90 percent, limiting her speed to 25 knots.

Frigates were not the only items of navy equipment that needed replacing by the end of the twentieth century. The Westland Wasp HAS.1's purchased for the *Leanders* had served well, but were worn out by the 1990s. They were also obsolete, and attrition had reduced their numbers — NZ3901 crashed into the Hauraki Gulf, and NZ3904 crashed near Taupo when it tangled with an inadequately secured tarpaulin during landing. Six helicopters were needed to keep one operational on each of the four frigates, so a British attrition airframe was acquired as the basis of a rebuild, and the Wasp, reserialled NZ3909, entered service in July 1994. With the help of this airframe, Wasps continued to operate from RNZN vessels until 1997, when those of HMNZS *Wellington* made the final service flight.

The new helicopter had to fulfil tasks that included anti-surface warfare (ASuW), over-the-horizon targeting (OTHT), anti-submarine warfare (ASW), rescue, reconnaissance and utility functions such as personnel and cargo transport. By 1997 candidates had been whittled down to the Westland Super Lynx; the Eurocopter Panther AS 565SA; the Sikorsky S-76C and the Kaman Aerospace SH-2G Seasprite.

The latter won. It was the oldest of the designs — the prototype Seasprite flew in 1959 and deliveries began in 1962 — but it had a proven track record and was still in production. The deal reached by the government provided the navy with four new-build SH-2G aircraft, and to fill the gap until they arrived the navy took delivery of four second-hand SH-2F models — three for operational service and one for spares. They entered service in 1998. Two SH-2F's were deployed on board *Te Kaha* and *Canterbury* during 1999, and saw service both on East Timor and in the Persian Gulf. A fifth SH-2G was ordered for delivery in 2003 as an 'attrition' airframe.

Navy in action, 1986–2001

Women went to sea with the navy for the first time in 1986, on board HMNZS *Monowai*. This was in many respects an extension of the role women had played since the Second World War. The Women's Royal New Zealand Naval Service played an important role during the war, and after reformation in

1951 women continued to serve with the navy ashore. In 1977 the WRNZNS was disbanded and women became an integral part of the RNZN.

Sea service followed twelve years later, and after the successful trial on *Monowai*, women were integrated into the frigate crews. *Wellington* had 225 men and 24 women on board when she left for the Persian Gulf in 1995. There were problems. Complaints of sexual harassment were laid in 1996, and eleven sailors were charged in October 1997 with a variety of offences under the Armed Forces Discipline Act.[11] The same month there were media reports of sexual misconduct in the Solomons by male and female ratings from *Canterbury*.[12] Between 1992 and 1997 there were 39 complaints, of which 26 were made in 1996.[13] Defence Force Chief Lieutenant General Tony Birks told reporters in June 1997 that discrimination and harassment 'of any sort' was 'unacceptable and not tolerated'.[14]

This publicity tended to draw attention away from the other work the navy was doing. One priority remained the ongoing survey of New Zealand's ever-changing harbours and coastline. *Lachlan* retired in February 1975, and the island trader *Moana Roa* was purchased for conversion in mid-1974. Renamed *Monowai*, the rebuilt ship was fitted with up-to-date surveying equipment and continued the task with the help of two auxiliary boats, *Takapu* and *Tarapunga*. Both could work in shallow waters, and were later replaced with 92-ton boats, built by WECO of Whangarei, and given the same names as their predecessors.

Both *Monowai* and the oceanographic ship *Tui* were ageing by the mid-1990s. New-build replacements looked likely to cost up to $114 million, but the navy concluded that hydrographic and oceanographic tasks could be accomplished with a single hull. The American survey ship USS *Tenacious*, which had a bargain-basement price tag of $12 million, was inspected by an RNZN team in August 1995. Cabinet approval was given in September 1996, and the ship became HMNZS *Resolution* in February 1997. *Tui* went to Mururoa atoll to monitor French underground nuclear tests in 1995, and was paid off for disposal when she returned to New Zealand. *Monowai* paid off in mid-1998.

Policy changes made a sealift ship a requirement during the mid-1980s, essential to provide logistic support for the army as well as bringing relief supplies to South Pacific islands after hurricanes. Initial discussion revolved around a new-build vessel able to carry the entire Ready Reaction Force. A stiff price tag of $200 million killed that, and thinking turned to a second-hand military vessel or converted merchant. Studies suggested that a specialist landing craft carrier would not have the capabilities needed for other tasks, and cost was an issue. A defence policy review in 1987 gave the concept official status. Impetus was given by the 1991 Defence White Paper, which identified a 'significant shortfall' in capabilities and predicted that any response to crisis would be governed by 'available transport'.

The Australian government initially offered to sell HMAS *Tobruk*. However, the NZDF wanted a ship with at least 25 years' life, assuming minimum annual usage of 4850 hours at sea and 2100 in harbour, and a purchase team decided that a civilian ship able to meet 80 percent of the army's needs offered the best deal. The *Mercandian Queen 2* — one of a class of five roll-on/roll-off freighters — was for sale in Denmark and was given a preliminary inspection at Gotenburg by British Maritime Technology. A team from the Ministry of Defence — the body responsible for procuring capital equipment for the NZDF — then inspected the ship, and began negotiations to buy her in October 1994. The final price was $14.5 million. The Ministry of Defence also sought a paying cargo to offset the costs of bringing the ship from Denmark to New Zealand, which brought complications of its own. The ship was not due to be commissioned into the navy until it reached New Zealand, but it had to be registered for the journey. Eventually the Ministry went to Lloyds and gave the ship the temporary name *Sealift*.

The ship reached Devonport in February 1995 and was commissioned into the RNZN as the *Charles Upham*, commemorating the country's most decorated soldier. However, a partial conversion to the logistics role proved troublesome. The ship could not be loaded enough to sit well in heavy seas; even container-loads of gravel on the upper deck did not settle her. While waiting for funding to complete the conversion the ship was leased to commercial ship-owners, and the navy sought approval for a full conversion that would add landing craft, a helicopter flight deck, and stabilisation tanks. This was never approved, and in the end the *Charles Upham* was sold and a purpose-built sea-lift ship procured instead, commissioned as HMNZS *Canterbury* (L421) in 2007.

New Zealand's naval activities during the last years of the twentieth century underlined the fact that the country's interests were global, and that armed forces remained a vital part of any credible national initiative.

Wellington was on hand in Suva when the first Fiji coup took place in May 1987. The crisis was complicated for New Zealand when an Air New Zealand aircraft was hijacked on the ground at Nandi. *Wellington* was asked to leave the harbour, but was shortly joined at sea by *Monowai* — which made a 67-hour dash from Auckland — *Canterbury*, and an Australian task force. The navy also contributed personnel to United Nations operations during the early 1990s. With RNZAF and New Zealand Army personnel, the RNZN joined UN observer missions in the Balkans, East Timor, Cambodia, the Arabian Gulf, and the Sinai. This included work with the first observer team in Bosnia in 1992, and with UNTAC in Cambodia in 1993 — when two 30-man units were deployed.

Monowai worked with the air force to rescue crews caught by violent storms during the 1994 Tonga yacht race. In a series of sorties that involved the entire P-3K Orion force and some of the C-130 Hercules, the air force located the missing boats, and dropped rafts, while *Monowai* provided search and rescue facilities at sea level — though she was thrown about violently by the high seas and winds. She picked up three crews and spent some time trying to find another.

Naval vessels were deployed on a variety of diplomatic tasks, including peacemaking in Bougainville. Dissent brewed there during the 1980s over use of the Panguna copper mine on the island by the Papua New Guinea government. This erupted into civil war at the end of the decade. In 1990 the New Zealand government despatched *Waikato*, *Wellington* and *Endeavour* to the island for peace talks. Diplomatically, *Waikato* took the Bougainville Revolutionary Army and Bougainville Interim Government representatives on board; *Wellington* housed the government negotiators, and *Endeavour* was the neutral location of the actual talks. Initial discussions appeared fruitful. An agreement was reached, but fighting broke out again after the navy departed. A further truce was negotiated in 1997, monitored by unarmed New Zealand service personnel brought to the island by *Canterbury*, *Endeavour* and *Manawanui*. *Canterbury*'s crew also contributed to the effort. The force, initially known as the Truce Monitoring Group and later dubbed the Peace Monitoring Group, were supported by the RAN and RNZN over the next three years; *Manawanui* was deployed to Bougainville in 1998 and 1999.

Frigates were sent to the Persian Gulf from the mid-1990s to work with the Multi National Interception Force. *Wellington* was on station between

October 1995 and January 1996; *Canterbury* followed between September and November 1996, and *Te Kaha* spent three months in the gulf between October and December 1999. It was a busy year for the new frigate. She had come from work in East Timor, where violence had erupted in August 1999 after a popular referendum favoured independence. *Te Kaha* was on exercise with FPDA forces, and diverted to join an international task force gathered under Australian control to intervene. HMNZS *Endeavour* joined the group to provide logistic support. *Te Kaha* was relieved by *Canterbury*, which covered the deployment of a New Zealand army battalion on the island. This was one of the largest New Zealand army deployments since the Korean war.

Antarctic poachers drew attention in 1999. Northern hemisphere fishing concerns, sometimes running under 'flags of convenience', were pillaging toothfish stocks in the frigid southern waters. As a member of the Convention for the Conservation of Antarctic Marine Living Resources (CCAMLR), New Zealand was obliged to act, and *Te Kaha* was plucked from a planned Australian exercise, heading south into the Ross Sea at short notice to intercept the summer fishing fleets. The southern waters were among the roughest in the world, and for one anxious night the frigate hammered into 70-knot gales and 14-metre swells, keeping head to wind and hove-to in the teeth of the storm. Next morning the seas surged higher. A series of 20-metre rogue waves tore past, slamming over the bow and ripping off the port capstan controller, railings and external lights. Seawater surged through the hole into a storeroom, and damage-control parties in orange immersion suits hastened to plug the leak. Even simple acts such as feeding the crew became almost impossible under these conditions. Petty Officer Chef John Wright, with his galley staff of eight, shut down the deep-fryers, had pots tied down to the stove tops, and reorganised the menu to suit.[15]

Intercepting fishing vessels operating in these waters was considerably less dramatic. Rules for dealing with suspected poachers were specific, and boarding could only be done with the approval of the fishing vessel concerned. Otherwise the frigate was restricted to observing and recording, collecting data for protest through diplomatic channels. In the event, no illegal ships were located, and *Te Kaha* turned north to inspect waters closer to New Zealand, where she checked fifteen fishing vessels.[16]

There was a fresh Pacific crisis in June 2000 when anarchy erupted on Guadalcanal. The new frigate *Te Mana* was diverted to the island in support of an airlift to take Australian and New Zealand nationals out of the crisis zone. She was relieved by *Te Kaha*, which also provided a neutral venue for peace talks in September that year.

Exercises continued. In early 2001 *Te Kaha* joined French warships for Exercise Ocean Protector in Australian waters. More than a dozen New Zealand, Australian and French warships converged in New Zealand waters during March for 'Tasmanex 2001', which postulated a dispute between 'Strineland' and 'Zenaland' over an exclusive economic zone northeast of the Bay of Plenty. The exercise ran the full gamut of air, surface and underwater warfare.[17]

Into the 21st century

By the end of the twentieth century it was clear that — despite the hopes of the post- Vietnam generation — the end of the Cold War had not made the world a more peaceful place. In many respects the reality of New Zealand's strategic position as a small trading nation entirely surrounded by sea was little different from what it had been 120 years before. Regardless of the idealism of the post-Vietnam generation, the military remained an essential element of credible national identity and an integral part of the international diplomatic system. New Zealand had to join in or lose out. This did not mean having large forces, but it did mean having credible capability where it counted. Government claims in early 2001 that there was no local threat, hence no need for airborne anti-submarine capability among other things, in fact betrayed a lack of appreciation about the way the international system continued to work.[18]

These developments were unfortunate. As always, New Zealand's vital interests lay only partly in local waters. While any overseas crisis involving New Zealand trade routes or interests was bound to draw in other nations, New Zealand had to be able to contribute to any multi-national peacekeeping effort — the risk being that if the country did not, then it would not be taken seriously in other areas such as trade negotiations and access, or persuade other nations to intervene in such areas on New Zealand's behalf. Credible contribution meant being able to deploy a full range of military capabilities if required — even on a tiny scale. Nor had the end of the Cold War actually bought peace. If anything, the world was more volatile, albeit perhaps on less apocalyptic scale. That did not reduce the human cost; and all these were issues that New Zealand had to tackle as the twenty-first century unfolded.

The fundamental strategic issue, however, remained unchanged: New Zealand was an island nation with far-flung trading links. The threat, both in peacetime and perhaps more directly in war, was not to the country itself but to those fragile over-ocean trade threads linking New Zealand with the world. Protecting them implied a blue-water navy, able to take steps to protect those links all the way from New Zealand's ports to their destinations; or to join international forces on the task. This reality, although initially not well-perceived by New Zealand defence thinkers, had been a constant ever since the first thoughts of naval defence emerged in the 1870s. It had largely guided the way that naval policy then emerged over the next 130 years. And the problem, as always, was finding ways — as a small island nation — of paying for the naval forces needed to do the job.

That had always been the challenge, and the technologies of the twenty-first century did not much alter that calculation. But what had changed was New Zealand's perception of itself; from a self-view as an appurtenance of Britain, a scion of Empire, the country had evolved by the early twenty-first century into a different nation, a place which saw itself as an independent, and highly innovative small nation on the world stage. That perspective was new; and, inevitably, it flowed into the way defence thinking was then expressed. For the navy, it meant something different from what had shaped the force during the twentieth century.

But that, as they say, is another story.

Endnotes

Chapter One
1   *Southern Cross*, 17 February 1873.
2   Glynn Barratt, *Russophobia in New Zealand*, p. 78.
3   *Auckland Weekly News*, 2 May 1885.
4   *New Zealand Herald*, 17 March 1885.
5   W.F.D. Jervois, 'The Defence of New Zealand', p. 21.
6   *Appendices to the Journals of the House of Representatives* (*AJHR*) 1885, A-6.
7   *New Zealand Herald*, 11 June 1886.
8   Matthew Wright, *New Zealand's Engineering Heritage*, Reed Publishing New Zealand Ltd, Auckland, 1999, pp. 46–47.
9   *New Zealand Statutes 1887*, 51 Vict, pp. 129–31.
10 *New Zealand Parliamentary Debates* (*NZPD*) 1909, Vol. 148, p. 809.
11 Arthur Marder, *The Anatomy of British Sea Power*, p. 106, quoting Lord George Hamilton, First Sea Lord.
12 See, for example, NA G2/16, Despatch No. 696/09, 'Proceedings', p. 50.
13 G.W. Monger, *The End of Isolation*, Thomas Nelson & Sons, London, 1963, pp. 10–11.
14 G. Greenwood & C. Grimshad (eds), *Documents on Australian International Affairs, 1901–1918* (DA), p. 109.
15 DA, pp. 115–19.
16 *NZPD* 1909, Vol. 148, p. 809; also CD 4948 'Conference', p. 26.
17 DA, pp. 143–45.
18 NA G48/F/4, Confidential Enclosure.
19 *New Zealand Herald*, 3 July 1905, p. 4.
20 *NZPD* 1908, Vol. 143, pp. 554–89.
21 *Evening Post*, editorial, 12 August 1908.
22 P.K. Kemp (ed.), *The Fisher Papers*, Vol. I, p. 19.
23 H.H. Asquith, *The Genesis of the War*, London, 1923, p. 112.
24 W.S. Churchill, *The World Crisis 1911–1918*, Four Square, London, 1960, p. 65.
25 *Fisher Papers*, Vol. I, p. 17.
26 Ibid, Vol. I, p. 159.
27 Ibid, Vol. II, p. 81. Fisher's italics.

28 Arthur Marder (ed.), *Fear God and Dread Nought*, Vol. II, p. 85.
29 *Fisher Papers*, Vol. I, pp. 160–61.
30 Marder, *Fear God and Dread Nought*, Vol. II, p. 59.
31 Maurice Hankey, *The Supreme Command*, Vol. I, p. 27.
32 CD 3524 'Papers Laid before the Imperial Conference, 1907', p. 48, Document 1, 'Report of the Committee of Imperial Defence on the Question of a General Scheme of Defence for Australia — May 1906', p. 48.
33 Ibid, pp. 40, 48. See also NA G48/34, 'Defence Scheme of New Zealand 1906'.
34 DA, p. 143.
35 A.R. Barclay, 'The Premier and his troubles', p. 11.
36 NA Allen Papers, 'Naval Defence — General', unnumbered file, letter 12 February 1914, Allen to Australian Minister of Defence.
37 Neville Meaney, *The Search for Security in the Pacific I*, p. 177.
38 The 1904 Japanese ships were completed with mixed armament in the end. R.A. Burt, *British Battleships of World War One*, Arms and Armour Press, London, 1986, pp. 19–20.
39 Jon Tetsuro Sumida, 'British Capital Ship Design and Fire Control in the Dreadnought Era: Sir John Fisher, Arthur Hungerford Pollen, and the Battle Cruiser', *Journal of Modern History*, Vol. 51, June 1979; Arthur Pollen, *The Navy in Battle*, pp. 95–105.
40 Burt, *British Battleships of World War One*, pp. 39, 43.
41 F.L.W. Wood, *New Zealand in the World*, Department of Internal Affairs, Wellington, 1940, pp. 82–85.
42 R.A. Loughmann, *Life of Sir Joseph Ward*, Dunedin, 1928, pp. 50, 145–46.
43 CD 3523 'Minutes of the Proceedings of the Colonial Conference, 1907', pp. 134–36, 153–55.
44 Ibid, p 134.
45 NA G2/17, 'Dominions No. 5', 'Correspondence relating to the Imperial Conference', pp. 136–37.
46 CD 4325 'Correspondence relating to the naval defence of Australia and New Zealand', p. 5.
47 NA G2/17, 'Dominions No. 5', p. 142.
48 DA, p. 160.
49 CD 4325, p. 40.
50 NA G2/17, 'Dominions No. 5', p. 176.
51 Despatch No. 696/09, pp. 4–7.
52 NA G2/17, 'Dominions No. 7', pp. 70, 175–78.
53 A. Temple-Patterson, (ed.), *The Jellicoe Papers*, Vol. I, p. 16.
54 Peter Padfield, *The Great Naval Race*, Hart-Davis, London, 1974, pp. 194–232; W.S. Churchill, *The World Crisis*, p. 31.
55 *NZPD* 1909, Vol. 146, pp. 154–69; *AJHR* 1909, A-5, p. 20; NA N1/22/6/9, 'Naval Defence', statement by Massey.
56 'Governor-General's Secret Quarterly Report', May 1909, p. 6.
57 *Evening Post*, 18–22 March 1909.
58 *Evening Post*, 22–27 March 1909; CD 4948, p. 3.
59 *Evening Post*, 31 March, 1 April 1909.

60 CD 4948, 'Conference'.
61 NA G2/16, Despatch No. 696/09, 'Dominions No. 16', pp. 7–8.
62 NA G2/17, Despatch No. 696/09, 'Dominions No. 17', p. 30.
63 CD 4949, 'Conference', pp. 19, 26.
64 NA G2/17, Despatch No. 696/09, 'Proceedings of the Imperial Conference on Naval and Military Affairs', pp. 47–50. Ward may have adopted the idea of 'starvation' not 'invasion' from the First Sea Lord, Sir John Fisher, who had expounded the same opinion in 1904.
65 CD 4949, 'Conference', p. 26.
66 These ships were variously called 'dreadnought cruisers', 'battleship cruisers' and 'armoured cruisers'. Arthur Marder, in *Fear God and Dread Nought*, Vol. 2, p. 277, suggests Fisher first referred to them as 'battlecruisers' in November 1909.
67 F.T. Jane (ed.), *Jane's Fighting Ships 1914*, pp. 44–45. The first figure translates to about $16,500 per ton in late twentieth century New Zealand currency.
68 Quoted in Parkes, p. 512.
69 J.P., Vol. I, p. 14. Reduced armour included 4-inch plate on the *Indefatigables*, which had been 6-inch plate on the earlier *Invincibles*. See Burt, *British Battleships of World War One*, p. 93.
70 J.P., Vol. I, p. 13. This probably referred to *Moltke* and *Goeben*. N.J.M. Campbell, *Battlecruisers*, pp. 13, 26, 32; Parkes, pp. 513–17.
71 Ian Sturton, *Conway's All The World's Battleships 1906 to the Present*, Conway Maritime Press, London, 1987, p. 62.
72 J.P., Vol. I, p. 13.
73 Preston, p. 128. The foreign ships were *Minaes Geraes* and *Sao Paulo* for Brazil, *Espana* and *Alfonso XIII* for Spain. *Jane's Fighting Ships 1914*, pp, 392, 435.
74 WTu fMS-195, 'HMS *New Zealand* Ship's Book'. The guns and mountings were: A turret R, gun #380, maker EOC; A turret L, gun #383, maker EOC; P turret R, gun #374, maker VSM; P turret L, gun #375, maker VSM; Q turret R, gun #382, maker EOC; Q turret L, gun #381, maker EOC; X turret R, gun #370, maker VSM; X turret L, gun #373, maker VSM.
75 CD 5135, 'Report of the Dominions Department of the Colonial Office 1910', pp. 51–52.
76 *New Zealand Yearbook 1914*, p. 270.
77 NA IA Series 71/1, 1913/661, Part 1.
78 Ibid, Parts I–IV. This comment about the armour was not strictly true.
79 Ibid, Parts I–IV.
80 See, for example, memo by Churchill to Cabinet, 22 June 1912, R.S. Churchill (ed.), *W.S. Churchill Companion Volume III*, Part 3, pp. 1570–71.
81 R.S. Churchill, *W.S. Churchill Volume II: The Young Statesman, 1901–14*, pp. 518–19.
82 R.S. Churchill (ed.), *W.S. Churchill Companion Volume III*, Part 3, p. 1504.
83 Ibid, pp. 1508, 1512.
84 NA IA Series 71/1, 1913/661, Part III.
85 R.S. Churchill (ed.), *W.S. Churchill Companion Volume III*, Part 3, p. 1758.
86 NA G40/10, Secret Paper 442M.

87 *Opunake Times*, 8 December 1912; *Nelson's Colonist*, 21 November 1912; *Wanganui Herald*, 29 November 1912. From clippings in NA Allen Papers, Box 14 (Newspapers).
88 NA Allen Papers, Naval Defence — General, unnumbered file, letter 12 February 1914 to the Australian Minister of Defence.
89 R.S. Churchill (ed.), *W.S. Churchill Companion Volume III*, Part 3, p. 1759.
90 Sir James Allen, 'New Zealand and Naval Defence', p. 5.
91 NA G48/N17, 'Extract from the Minutes of the 123rd Meeting of the CID held on 11th April 1913'; NA G48/N17, 'Imperial Naval Policy of New Zealand', CID Paper 25th April 1913, with letter by Harcourt.
92 NA Allen Papers, Naval Defence (General), Allen to Massey, 21 February 1913.
93 R.S. Churchill (ed.), *W.S. Churchill Companion Volume III*, Part 3, p. 1758.
94 NA 6/1/11, memo, Liverpool to Massey, 3 October 1913; NA N1/22/6/9, 'Naval Defence' statement by Massey, p. 3.
95 NA Allen Papers, Creswell to Allen, 13 December 1914.
96 WTu Micro MS Coll 5, ADM 116/1285 Case 177/1, Voyage of HMS *New Zealand* to New Zealand and other Dominions and Colonies 1912–13. Halsey to Sir Graham (?) 19/10/1912.
97 Ibid, misc. correspondence Admiralty–High Commission -/11/12.
98 Ibid, Minute sheet 17/10/12.
99 *Daily Telegraph*, 25 April 1913.
100 WTu Micro MS-99, Halsey, Sir Lionel, 1872–1949, personal papers 1905–1923, Lionel Halsey to his mother, 1 June 1913.
101 *Wanganui Chronicle*, 17 June 1913.
102 WTu Micro MS-99, Lionel Halsey to William Jordan, 17 February 1939.
103 WTu Micro MS-99, Lionel Halsey to his father, 15 May 1913.

Chapter Two
1 Canterbury Museum MSS 199/75 Folder 698, Diary of Captain (Lt Commander) A.D. Boyle, Royal Navy, 1914–15, February–July 1919; 30 July 1914. Hereafter referenced as Boyle.
2 *Daily Telegraph*, 25 April 1913.
3 Boyle, 27 July 1914.
4 Ibid, 28 July 1914.
5 Ibid, 29 July 1914.
6 W.S. Churchill, *The World Crisis*, p. 130.
7 Boyle, 30 July 1914.
8 W. S. Churchill, *The World Crisis*, p. 133.
9 Boyle, 1 August 1914.
10 Ibid, 4 August 1914.
11 NA 49/1, HMS *Philomel*. Telegrams HMS *Psyche* 22 October 1913 to 19 January 1915.
12 W. S. Churchill, *The World Crisis 1911–1918*, Landsborough, London 1930, p. 210.
13 NA 41/1, HMS *Philomel*, Signals and Telegram Logs 1914–1917, 'Report on

	Landing Party in Vicinity of Alexandretta', 17 February 1915.
14	Ibid.
15	Ibid, 'Report of Proceedings' 28 April 1915.
16	Ibid, 'Report of Proceedings' 10 November 1915.
17	Ibid, 'V. Rolling, Report on Condition of Hull' 14 January 1917.
18	Ibid, H.W. Stedston, Engineer L. Commander, 13 January 1917.
19	MoD Library, 'Official List, New Zealanders (Officers and men) serving in the Royal Navy, the R.N.R., and the R.N.V.R., up to September 1918.'
20	Boyle, 4 August 1914.
21	HMS *Benbow*, HMS *Emperor of India*, HMS *Erin* (ex-*Reshadieh*), HMS *Agincourt* (ex-*Sultan Osman I*), HMS *Tiger*. Preston, pp. 139–146.
22	Boyle, 9 August 1914.
23	W.S. Churchill, *The World Crisis*, p. 197.
24	William Guy Carr, *Brass Hats and Bell Bottom Trousers*, pp. 44–71.
25	Boyle, 28 August 1914.
26	Arthur Marder, *From the Dreadnought to Scapa Flow*, Vol II, p. 52
27	WTu Micro MS-99, Lionel Halsey to William Jordan 17 February 1939.
28	Cited in Carr, *Brass Hats and Bell Bottom Trousers*, pp. 53–54.
29	WTu MS Papers qMS 545, E.G.B. Coore diary, 28 August 1914.
30	Boyle, 28 August 1914.
31	Ibid.
32	Ibid.
33	WTu MS Papers qMS 545, E.G.B. Coore diary, 28 August 1914.
34	'Kia Ora HMS *New Zealand*,' p. 13.
35	Boyle, 28 August 1914.
36	W.S. Churchill, *The World Crisis*, p. 250.
37	H.C. Wright MSS, author collection. Wright settled in New Zealand after the war.
38	Ibid. HMS *Erin* was the Turkish super-dreadnought *Reshadieh*, taken over by the British when war broke out. The appropriation of both this ship and *Agincourt* was one of the reasons why the Turks sided with Germany.
39	Boyle, 3 November 1914.
40	W.S. Churchill, *The World Crisis*, p. 259.
41	H.C. Wright MSS. HMS *King George V* (1912) was the first battleship of that name and one of the second class of super-dreadnoughts.
42	W.S. Churchill, *The World Crisis*, p. 377.
43	SMS *Blücher* was a product of Fisher's misinformation campaign. It was difficult for him to hide the fact that Britain was building cruisers of unprecedented size, but he 'leaked' the idea that they were armed with 9.2-inch guns. The Germans responded with a similarly armed vessel.
44	Campbell, *Battlecruisers*, p. 18.
45	WTu Micro MS-99, Lionel Halsey to Jordan [New Zealand High Commissioner] 17 February 1939.
46	'Kia Ora HMS *New Zealand*', p. 14.
47	W. S. Churchill, in *The World Crisis*, p. 387, suggested 250 survivors and a seaplane; 'Kia Ora HMS *New Zealand*,' p. 16, based on HMS *New Zealand*'s

	logs, suggested 180 survivors and a Zeppelin.
48	Felix von Luckner cited in Lowell Thomas, *The Sea Devil's Fo'csle*, William Heinemann, London, 1930, p. 223. Von Luckner was a raconteur; this description varies from other accounts, but conveys the surprise the Germans got when they blew the ship up.
49	'Kia Ora HMS *New Zealand*', p. 20.
50	Ibid, pp. 18, 20.
51	WTu MS papers 283, Nick Barcroft letters to Miss Bell Irving, 15 June 1916.
52	Cited in Thomas, *The Sea Devil's Fo'csle*, p. 225.
53	'Kia Ora HMS *New Zealand*', p. 18.
54	Cited in Thomas, *The Sea Devil's Fo'csle*, p. 227.
55	'Kia Ora HMS *New Zealand*,' p. 21.
56	Admiral Sir Reginald Bacon, *The Life of John Rushworth, Earl Jellicoe*, pp. 270–74.
57	Felix von Luckner cited in Thomas, *The Sea Devil's Fo'csle*, p. 229. Only one British cruiser, HMS *Defence*, blew up. The second, *Warrior*, sank later, and the third, *Black Prince*, was sunk that night when she ran into the High Seas Fleet.
58	Literally, 'absolutely into the sausage boiler'), Reginald Bacon, *The Jutland Scandal*, p. 119.
59	WTu MS papers 283, Nick Barcroft letters to Miss Bell Irving, 15 June 1916. No German pre-dreadnought was sunk during this brief encounter.
60	Voices of reason were rare. See, for example, Reginald Bacon, *The Jutland Scandal*; also *The Life of John Rushworth, Earl Jellicoe*, pp. 243–332; and pro-Beatty arguments by long-time anti-Fisherite Arthur Hungerford Pollen, *The Navy in Battle*, pp. 276–353.
61	Thomas, *The Sea Devil's Fo'csle*, p. 232.
62	WTu fMS-195, HMS *New Zealand* Ship's Book.
63	Lord Fisher of Kilverstone, *Records*, pp. 212–13.
64	Roy Alexander, *The Cruise of the Raider Wolf*, p. 17.
65	Ibid, pp. 22–23.
66	Ibid, p. 105.
67	Ibid, p. 63.
68	Ibid, p. 91.
69	Ibid, p. 297.
70	Lowell Thomas, *Raiders of the Deep*, William Heinemann, London, 1930.
71	Alexander, *The Cruise of the Raider Wolf*, p. 312.
72	Felix von Luckner cited in Thomas, *The Sea Devil's Fo'csle*, p. 250.
73	When Von Luckner toured New Zealand in 1937 his party trick involved ripping telephone directories in half with his bare hands. Piet van Asch, pers. comm.
74	Felix von Luckner cited in Thomas, *The Sea Devil's Fo'csle*, pp. 294–300.

Chapter Three

1	Cited in Bacon, *The Life of John Rushworth, Earl Jellicoe*, p. 432.
2	Bacon, *The Life of John Rushworth, Earl Jellicoe*, pp. 408–11.
3	Ibid, pp. 417–30.

4   NA Navy Department 22/5, 'Missions: Lord Jellicoe's Visit to New Zealand 1919', Air Proposals, undated minute.
5   For full details see Matthew Wright, *Kiwi Air Power*, Reed Publishing New Zealand Ltd, Auckland, 1998, pp. 12–18.
6   NA Navy Department 22/5, 'Missions: Lord Jellicoe's Visit to New Zealand 1919'; 'Secret — New Zealand Naval Estimates'.
7   *NZPD* CXCI, 13 October 1921, pp. 506–7.
8   *AJHR* 1922, A-5 'Conference on the Limitation of Armaments', p. 15.
9   Ibid, pp. 12–13.
10 Ibid, p. 9.
11 Ibid, p. 19.
12 Ibid, Appendix 1, p. 23.
13 Ibid, p. 5.
14 *Dreadnought* was sold for scrap on 9 May 1921, though dismantling did not begin until January 1923. Burt, *British Battleships of World War One*, pp. 38, 58; see also Alan Raven & John Roberts, *British Battleships of World War Two*, Arms & Armour Press, London, 1976, p. 76; *AJHR* 1922, A-5 'Conference on the Limitation of Armaments', Appendix 1.
15 Burt, *British Battleships of World War One*, p. 103; also WTu fMS-195, *New Zealand* Ship's Book. These dates correct those given in other sources.
16 WTu fMS-195, *New Zealand* Ship's Book.
17 T.D. Taylor, *New Zealand's Naval Story*, A.H. & A.W. Reed, Wellington, 1948, p. 54.
18 NA Navy Department N10/7. 'CID Reports August 1922, Washington Treaty', Secret CID Memo 176c 'Committee of the Imperial Defence. The Washington Conference and its Effect Upon Empire Naval Policy and Co-Operation.' August 1922.
19 Ibid.
20 See, for example, Bacon, *The Life of John Rushworth, Earl Jellicoe*, pp. 434–50; Bacon, *The Jutland Scandal*.
21 *NZPD* CLXXXVIII, 6 August 1920, pp. 14–15.
22 *NZPD* CXCV, 1 August 1922, p. 861.
23 *Evening Post*, 29 April 1924.
24 NA Navy Department N1 6/1/4, 'Addition of Third Cruiser', *Evening Post* clipping, 24 September 1925.
25 For discussion see L.F. Luxton, 'Rockie Matelot — A Short History of the Royal Naval Volunteer Reserve, New Zealand Division,' University of Canterbury, 1987.
26 Op cit, *New Zealand Times* clipping, 17 July 1926.
27 *AJHR* 1927, A-7 'Singapore and Naval Defence', p. 2.
28 *AJHR* 1927, A-6 'Imperial Conference 1926: Summary of Proceedings', p. 21.
29 *AJHR* 1927, A-7 'Singapore and Naval Defence', p. 2.
30 For further details see Matthew Wright, *Quake — Hawke's Bay 1931*, Reed Publishing New Zealand Ltd, Auckland, 2001.
31 Wright, *Kiwi Air Power*, p. 18.
32 *Hawke's Bay — Before and After*, p. 85.

33 *New Zealand Herald*, 6 February 1931.
34 *Hawke's Bay — Before and After*, p. 85.
35 Ibid, p. 149.
36 *New Zealand Herald*, 4 February 1931.
37 *Hawke's Bay — Before and After*, p. 84.
38 *New Zealand Herald*, 4 March 1931.
39 Ibid, 5 March 1931.
40 WTu MS Papers 3359, *Taranaki* (ship), radio logs.
41 Ibid.
42 *New Zealand Herald*, 4 February 1931.
43 Ibid, 6 February 1931.
44 EPR, George Brown memoir.
45 *Hawke's Bay — Before and After*, p. 86.
46 EPR, Mary Hunter memoir.
47 *Hawke's Bay — Before and After*, p. 77.
48 RNZN Museum Oral History DLA0040, Able Seaman A.E. Ball-Guymer.
49 Ibid.
50 *Hawke's Bay — Before and After*, p. 153.
51 Noted in McDougall, *New Zealand Naval Vessels*, p. 18.
52 See, for example, Tony Simpson, *The Sugarbag Years*, p. 13.
53 Laurie Barber, *New Zealand — A Short History*, Century Hutchinson, Auckland, 1989, p. 131. See also Matthew Wright, *Havelock North — The History of a Village*, p. 191.
54 *NZPD* Vol. 246, p. 539.

Chapter Four
1 NA Navy Department N13/14a, 'Achilles' signals at River Plate', Harwood to *Cumberland* 7.12 a.m., 13 December 1939.
2 RNZN Museum Oral History DLA 0008, Lieutenant K.F. Connew.
3 RNZN Museum Oral History DLA 0010, Able Seaman H.H. Beesley.
4 Ibid.
5 RNZN Museum Oral History DLA 0008, Lieutenant K.F. Connew.
6 Ibid.
7 RNZN Museum Oral History DLA 0078, R.B. Harvey.
8 RNZN Museum Oral History DLA 0008, Lieutenant K.F. Connew.
9 Ibid.
10 Ibid.
11 RNZN Museum Oral History DLA 0010, Able Seaman H.H. Beesley.
12 NA Navy Department 48/82, HMS *Achilles*, Ship's Log for December 1939, entry 13 December 1939.
13 Ibid.
14 RNZN Museum Oral History DLA 0008, Lieutenant K.F. Connew.
15 RNZN Museum Oral History DLA 0078, R.B. Harvey.
16 NA Navy Department 48/82, HMS Achilles, Ship's Log for December 1939, entry 13 December 1939.
17 RNZN Museum Oral History DLA 0010, Able Seaman H.H. Beesley.

18   NA Navy Department Series 1 62/27/6, 'Ships and repairs: HMS *Achilles*, report of damage', CO HMS *Achilles* 22 January 1940.
19   Ibid.
20   Cited in S.D. Waters, *Achilles at the River Plate*, p. 25.
21   RNZN Museum Oral History DLA 0010, Able Seaman H.H. Beesley.
22   NA Navy Department Series 1 62/27/6, 'Ships and repairs: HMS Achilles, report of damage', CO HMS *Achilles* 22 January 1940.
23   RNZN Museum Oral History DLA 0008, Lieutenant K.F. Connew.
24   NA Navy Department 48/82, HMS *Achilles*, Ship's Log for December 1939, entry 13 December 1939.
25   RNZN Museum Oral History DLA 0078, R.B. Harvey.
26   Ibid.
27   Waters, *Achilles at the River Plate*, p. 30.
28   RNZN Museum Oral History DLA 0010, Able Seaman H.H. Beesley.
29   NA Navy Department 48/82, HMS Achilles, Ship's Log for December 1939, entry 13 December 1939.
30   NA Navy Department 13/14a, 'Achilles' signals at River Plate', *Graf Spee* to *Achilles* and *Ajax*, 11.06 a.m.
31   'With all despatch' meant 90% power. See, for example, listings in NA Navy Department 48/82, HMS *Achilles*, Ship's Log for December 1939.
32   RNZN Museum Oral History DLA 0008, Lieutenant K.F. Connew.
33   NA Navy Department 48/82, HMS *Achilles*, Ship's Log for December 1939, 13 December 1939.
34   Ibid, 14 December 1939.
35   NA Navy Department Series 1 13/33/10, War Casualties — HMNZS *Achilles* in action with *Graf Spee*, Naval Secretary N.T.P. Cooper to Mrs E.M. Martinson 29 December 1939; and other letters in file.
36   NA Navy Department Series 1 62/27/6, 'Ships and repairs: HMS *Achilles*, report of damage', CO HMS *Achilles* to Rear Admiral Commanding South America Division, 22 January 1940.
37   Cited in Geoffrey Bennett, *Naval Battles of World War II*, p. 13.
38   RNZN Museum Oral History DLA 0008, Lieutenant K.F. Connew.
39   RNZN Museum Oral History DLA 0010, Able Seaman H.H. Beesley.
40   RNZN Museum Oral History DLA 0008, Lieutenant K.F. Connew.
41   RNZN Museum Oral History DLA 0021, Commodore L.S. Stanners CBE.
42   RNZN Museum Oral History DLA 0010, Able Seaman H.H. Beesley.
43   Ibid; mileage in Waters, *Achilles* at the River Plate, p. 32.
44   Hastings Borough Council, Stewart & White Ltd to Town Clerk, Hastings, 28 February 1940.
45   NA Navy Department 13/14a, 'Achilles' signals at River Plate', Air Dept. to All Units, 22 February 1940.
46   RNZN Museum Oral History DLA 0008, Lieutenant K.F. Connew
47   According to official historian S.D. Waters, the *Erlangen* was caught by the war with insufficient coal to cross the Pacific to Chile, and her crew spent some time cutting down 400 tons of wood and fabricating sails to let them make the crossing. Waters, *Achilles at the River Plate*, pp. 75–76.

48   NA Navy Department Series 1 62/27/6, 'Ships and repairs: HMS *Achilles*, report of damage', messages 15 March 1940.
49   Governor-General to Secretary of State for the Dominions, 15 June 1940, Documents relating to New Zealand's participation in the Second World War, Vol. III, War History Branch, Department of Internal Affairs, Wellington, 1963, No. 184, p. 206. Hereafter cited as Documents.
50   Governor-General to Secretary of State for the Dominions, 3 August 1940, Documents III, No. 185, p. 207.
51   RNZN Museum Oral History DLA 0007, Lieutenant Commander S.W. Hicks.
52   Fraser to Churchill, 28 November 1940, Documents III, No. 189, p. 213.
53   NA Navy Department Series 1 16/8/30, Operations: raider activity at Nauru and Ocean Islands, DNI Melbourne, note dated 13 January 1941.
54   Fraser to Churchill, 28 November 1940, Documents III.
55   Ibid.
56   RNZN Museum Oral History DLA 0007, Lieutenant Commander S.W. Hicks.
57   NA Navy Department Series 1 16/8/30, Operations: raider activity at Nauru and Ocean Islands, 'My impressions as a prisoner aboard the *Manyo Maru* and the *Tokyo Maru* by G.W. Dillon, passenger to Nauru per Triadic.' Hereafter cited as Dillon.
58   Ibid, 'Notes on experiences aboard German raiders by G.R. Ferguson, passenger to Nauru per *Triadic*.' Hereafter cited as Ferguson.
59   Dillon.
60   Ibid.
61   Ferguson.
62   Dillon.
63   Ibid.
64   Ferguson.
65   Ibid.
66   Dillon
67   NA Navy Department Series 1 16/8/30, Operations: raider activity at Nauru and Ocean Islands, Report K.W. Goodridge — survivor from SS *Triaster* 11/1/44.
68   Ibid, clipping, *Evening Post*, 28 December 1940.
69   Ibid, ACNB to Adm. C in C China, etc, 28 December 1940.
70   Ibid, clipping, *Evening Post*, 30 December 1940.
71   Ibid, New Zealand Commissioner to A.H. Cockayne, Director-General of Agriculture, 3 January 1941.
72   RNZN Museum Oral History DLA 0074, Instructor Commander S.J.F. Hermans.
73   NA Navy Department Series 1 16/8/32, Operations: HMAS *Canberra* and HMS *Leander*, encounter with Italian Armed Ship *Ramb*-1, February 1941. Report: Captain Leander to C in C East Indies Station 28/2/1941. Details of this official account differ from events given in McDougall, New Zealand Naval Vessels, p. 28.

Endnotes

74 RNZN Museum Oral History DLA 0074, Instructor Commander S.J.F. Hermans.
75 Ibid.
76 Ibid.
77 Ibid. The reference to scuttling charges corrects McDougall, p. 28.
78 NA Navy Department Series 1 16/8/32, Report: Captain *Leander* to C in C East Indies Station 28/2/1941.
79 RNZN Museum Oral History DLA 0074, Instructor Commander S.J.F. Hermans.
80 NA Navy Department Series 1 16/8/32, NZNB to C in C East Indies Station 28 February 1941.
81 Ibid, Admiralty to NZNB 8 April 1941.
82 Ibid, NZNB to Prime Minister's Office, 27 June 1941.
83 RNZN Museum Oral History DLA 0074, Instructor Commander S.J.F. Hermans.
84 NA Navy Department Series 1 16/8/32, High Commissioner to Fraser, 5 March 1941.
85 Ibid, Admiralty to NZNB and others, 6 March 1941.
86 Ibid, Fraser to High Commissioner London, 7 March 1941.
87 NA Navy Department 13/14a, *Achilles*' signals at River Plate, Memo to CO *Leander* 23 March 1941.
88 Ibid.
89 RNZN Museum Oral History DLA 0024, Chief Petty Officer W.M. Gibbs BEM.
90 Documents I, No. 419, Fraser to Nash, 23 May 1941. For further details see Matthew Wright, *A Near-Run Affair*, Reed Publishing New Zealand Ltd, Auckland, 2000.
91 RNZN Museum Oral History DLA 0074, Instructor Commander S.J.F. Hermans.
92 Andrew Cunningham, *A Sailor's Odyssey — The Autobiography of Admiral of the Fleet Viscount Cunningham of Hyndhope*, p. 387. This was also the 25th anniversary of the Battle of Jutland.
93 RNZN Museum Oral History DLA 0074, Instructor Commander S.J.F. Hermans.
94 Ibid.
95 Ibid.
96 Ibid.
97 RNZN Museum Oral History DLA 0024, Chief Petty Officer W.M. Gibbs BEM.
98 Ian Wards, 'Peter Fraser, Warrior Prime Minister', in Margaret Clark (ed.) *Peter Fraser, Master Politician*, pp. 153–55.
99 Wright, *A Near-Run Affair*, p. 100.
100 Documents I, No. 447, Fraser to Nash, 7 June 1941
101 *New Zealand Gazette*, 1 October 1941.
102 RNZN Museum Oral History DLA 0007, Lieutenant Commander S.W. Hicks.

103 Cunningham, *A Sailor's Odyssey*, pp. 429–33; Waters, *Achilles at the River Plate*, pp. 190–92.
104 Garzke & Dulin, *Axis and Neutral Battleships in World War II*, pp. 265–67.

Chapter Five
1 Wright, *Kiwi Air Power*, pp. 64–68.
2 Churchill, III, p. 525.
3 Ibid, pp. 527, 534.
4 W.H. Garzke & R.O. Dulin, *British, Soviet, French and Dutch Battleships of World War II*, Jane's, London, 1980, pp. 192–208, 244–45.
5 Paul Harrison et al., *The Golden Age of New Zealand Flying Boats*, p. 91.
6 Ibid.
7 RNZN Museum Oral History DLA 0079, Warrant Mechanician R.W. Kirkwood.
8 RNZN Museum Oral History DLA 0073, Able Seaman L.C. Hurndell.
9 Ibid.
10 Ibid.
11 Ibid
12 RNZN Museum Oral History DLA 0007, Lieutenant Commander S.W. Hicks.
13 Ibid.
14 Ibid.
15 NA Navy Department Series 1 16/8/35, Operations: HMNZS *Monowai*, encounter with submarine and aircraft, January 1942. 'Report of action between HMNZS *Monowai* and U-boat.'
16 Ibid.
17 Ibid, I/O minute, n.d.
18 Ibid, NZNB to CO *Monowai* 28/1/42.
19 MoD Library Vertical File, J.F. McKenzie, 'Report on the RNZN, 21 March 1944.'
20 Warren F. Kimball (ed.), *Churchill & Roosevelt, The Complete Correspondence*, Vol. I, p. 321.
21 Ibid, Roosevelt to Former Naval Person, 30 January 1942, pp. 336–37.
22 Ibid, to the Former Naval Person, p. 398.
23 Ibid, Former Naval Person to the President, 20 March 1942, p. 425.
24 RNZN Museum Oral History DLA 0028, Sergeant P.H. Stapleton.
25 RNZN Museum Oral History DLA 0079, Warrant Mechanician R.W. Kirkwood.
26 Ibid.
27 NA Navy Department Series 1 16/8/40, Operations: HMNZS *Achilles*, encounter with Japanese dive bomber, January 1943. CO HMNZS *Achilles* to Naval Secretary 17 May 1943.
28 Ibid, Acting CO HMNZS *Achilles* to Naval Secretary, Report on Damage, 5 January 1943.
29 RNZN Museum Oral History DLA 0028, Sergeant P.H. Stapleton. The description varies from Waters, *Achilles at the River Plate*, p. 306.

Endnotes

30 NA Navy Department Series 1 16/8/40, CO HMNZS *Achilles* to Naval Secretary 17 May 1943.
31 Ibid, CO HMNZS *Achilles* to Naval Secretary 17 May 1943, Appendix 2.
32 RNZN Museum Oral History DLA 0029, Chief Mechanical Engineer M. Seyb.
33 NA Navy Department Series 1 16/8/40, CO HMNZS *Achilles* to Naval Secretary 17 May 1943.
34 RNZN Museum Oral History DLA 0028, Sergeant P.H. Stapleton.
35 NA Navy Department Series 1 16/8/40, Acting CO HMNZS *Achilles* to Naval Secretary, Report on Damage, 5 January 1943.
36 RNZN Museum Oral History DLA 0079, Warrant Mechanician R.W. Kirkwood.
37 Op cit, CO HMNZS *Achilles* to Naval Secretary 17 May 1943, Appendix 3.
38 Op cit, Naval OC *Philomel* to Navy Office Wellington, 13 January 1943.
39 RNZN Museum Oral History DLA 0079, Warrant Mechanician R.W. Kirkwood.
40 Ibid.
41 RNZN Museum Oral History DLA 0098, Leading Seaman E.C. McVinnie.
42 Ibid.
43 Ibid.
44 RNZN Museum Oral History DLB 0004, Yeoman of Signals J.L.W. Salter BEM, MID.
45 Ibid.
46 NA Navy Department Series 1 6/36/2, Ships and repairs: loss of HMNZS *Moa* due to enemy action. 'Report on Loss of *Moa* 12 March [sic] 1943'.
47 Ibid.
48 Ibid.
49 Ibid, Naval Secretary to Accountant Officer RNZN Advanced Base, 1 July 1943.
50 Ibid, 'Report on Loss of *Moa* 12 March [sic] 1943'.
51 RNZN Museum Oral History DLA0078, R.B. Harvey BEM.
52 RNZN Museum Oral History DLA 0013, Commander G. Mitchell MBE.
53 RNZN Museum Oral History DLA 0024, Chief Petty Officer W.M. Gibbs BEM.
54 RNZN Museum Oral History DLA 0013, Commander G. Mitchell MBE.
55 Ibid.
56 RNZN Museum Oral History DLA0078, R.B. Harvey BEM.
57 Ibid.
58 NA Navy Department Series 1 16/8/43, Operations: HMNZS *Leander*, encounter with Japanese naval forces, Kula Gulf, July 1943. CO HMNZS *Leander* to Naval Secretary, Navy Office: 'Report of action against Japanese naval forces', 13 July 1943.
59 RNZN Museum Oral History DLA 0078, Chief Electrician R.B. Harvey BEM.
60 NA Navy Department Series 1 16/8/43, CO HMNZS *Leander* to Naval Secretary, Navy Office: 'Report of action against Japanese naval forces', 13 July

	1943.
61	RNZN Museum Oral History DLA 0078, Chief Electrician R.B. Harvey BEM.
62	Not seven as noted in Waters, *Achilles at the River Plate*, p. 321. Op cit, Navy Office to Registrar Births Deaths and Marriages 25 September 1944. The men were: Able Seaman James F. Beattie, Able Seaman George G. Dryland, Stoker 1st Class G.C. Edwards, Able Seaman Frank W. Hooke, Able Seaman Robert G. Morris, Stoker 1st Class Maurice W. O'Neill, Acting Leading Seaman Raymond A. Rolston, all of the RNZN, and Royal Navy Able Seaman William D. Clyde.
63	RNZN Museum Oral History DLA 0078, Chief Electrician R.B. Harvey BEM.
64	NA Navy Department Series 1 16/8/43, CO HMNZS *Leander* to Naval Secretary, Navy Office: 'Report of action against Japanese naval forces', 13 July 1943.
65	RNZN Museum Oral History DLA 0078, Chief Electrician R.B. Harvey BEM.
66	Ibid.
67	Ibid.
68	NA Navy Department Series 1 16/8/43, CO HMNZS *Leander* to Naval Secretary, Navy Office: 'Report of action against Japanese naval forces', 13 July 1943.
69	Ibid.
70	Ibid.
71	RNZN Museum Oral History DLA 0078, Chief Electrician R.B. Harvey BEM.
72	Ibid.
73	Ibid.
74	Ibid.
75	Ibid, Appendix 1.
76	NA Navy Department Series 1 16/8/43, CO HMNZS *Leander* to Naval Secretary, Navy Office: 'Report of action against Japanese naval forces', 13 July 1943.
77	Ibid.
78	RNZN Museum Oral History DLA 0013, Commander G. Mitchell MBE.
79	RNZN Museum Oral History DLA 0078, Chief Electrician R.B. Harvey BEM.
80	NA Navy Department Series 1 16/8/43, CO HMNZS *Leander* to Naval Secretary, Navy Office: 'Report of action against Japanese naval forces', 13 July 1943.
81	Ibid.
82	Ibid; Navy Office to Registrar Births Deaths and Marriages 25 September 1944.
83	Ibid, CNS to NZNB 2 August 1943.
84	Ibid.
85	Ibid, Admiralty to NZNB, 3 August 1943.

86	RNZN Museum Oral History DLA 0079, Warrant Mechanician R.W. Kirkwood.
87	NA Navy Department 48/61, HMS *Achilles*, Ship's Log for January 1944.
88	NA Navy Department Series 1 16/8/43, CNS to NZNB.
89	NA Navy Department Series 1 6/1/25, Conditions of Transfer of *Gambia*.
90	Ibid, Navy Office Wgtn to Minister of Defence 1 December 1943.
91	Ibid.
92	RNZN Museum Oral History DLA 0024, Chief Petty Officer W.M. Gibbs NEM.
93	NA Navy Department Series 1 16/8/44, Operations: Report of submarine in Cook Strait, November 1943, NZNB to NOCW 30/11/43.
94	Ibid, 'ASDIC efficiency of Fairmiles during operations on night of 3rd–4th November 1943 — report.'
95	Ibid, Senior Officer 81st ML Flotilla to NOCW 4/11/43.
96	Ibid, NOCW to NZNB 10/11/43.
97	Ibid, NZNB to NOCW 30/11/43.
98	Ibid, NOCW to NZNB 10/11/43.
99	Ibid, NZNB to NOCW 30/11/43.
100	Ibid, NZNB to NOCW 14/1/44.
101	Ibid, NZNB to NOCW 26/12/43.
102	Cited in M.P. Lissington, *New Zealand and the United States*, p. 83. It was signed on 21 January.
103	Op cit, Doc. 84, p. 206.
104	Op cit, Doc. 87, pp. 208–9.
105	Op cit, Doc. 90, p. 211.
106	*Documents* III, No. 428, Army Headquarters to Admiral Newton, p. 444.
107	MoD Library Vertical File, 'Report on the RNZN, 31 March 1944'.
108	Cited in David Stevens, *U-Boat Far from Home*, p. 182.
109	Details of shipping and Napier entertainments are in the *Daily Telegraph*, 14–16 February 1945.
110	This story was verified to the author by the family of the crew member.
111	NA Navy Department Series 1 6/1/25, Conditions of Transfer of *Gambia*, Secret NZNB Memo for Minister of Defence, 7 September 1944.
112	Ibid, minute sheet n.d. 1944.
113	Cunningham, *A Sailor's Odyssey*, p. 606.
114	Lyon, *Warships*, p. 148. These battleships had been surrendered to Britain in September 1943 and had been laid up since in Egyptian waters.
115	MoD Library Vertical File, 'Paper on Royal New Zealand Navy and Naval Facilities in New Zealand 1945'. The dock had been lengthened earlier in the war.
116	MoD Library Vertical File, 'Report on the Royal New Zealand Navy — 31st March 1944'.
117	RNZN Museum Oral History DLA 0078, Chief Electrician R.B. Harvey BEM.
118	Ibid.
119	Ibid.

120 Ibid.
121 Ibid.
122 Ibid. See also NA Navy Department 67/16, HMNZS *Gambia*, Ship's Log, August 1945, entry 9 August 1945.
123 See, for example, *Documents* III, pp. 458–509.
124 RNZN, 'Report of the New Zealand Naval Board for the period 1st April 1945 to 31st March 1946', p. 3.
125 Ibid.
126 RNZN Museum Oral History DLA 0078, Chief Electrician R.B. Harvey BEM.
127 NA Navy Department 67/16, HMNZS *Gambia*, Ship's Log, August 1945, entry 27 August 1945.
128 RNZN Museum Oral History DLA 0078, Chief Electrician R.B. Harvey BEM.
129 NA Navy Department 67/16, HMNZS *Gambia*, Ship's Log, August 1945, 31 August 1945.

Chapter Six
1 NA Navy Department Series 1 6/46, Ships and repairs: 'Loch' class frigates general, August 1947–June 1949, Hon. F. Jones 'New Zealand Defence Policy', 5 April 1948.
2 NA Navy Department Series 1 22/6/14, Naval Board and Policy, RNZN Post-War Planning, draft memo n.d. 'The Royal New Zealand Navy — Policy. Need for a statement on policy'.
3 'Report of the New Zealand Naval Board for the period 1st April 1945 to 31st March 1946'.
4 RNZN Museum Oral History DLA 0020, Lieutenant Commander C.V. Harris BEM.
5 NA Navy Department Series 1 22/6/14, Naval Board and Policy: RNZN Post-war planning, memo NZNB to MoD, 11 July 1945.
6 Ibid, memo NZNB to MoD, 15 December 1945.
7 Ibid, draft memo n.d. 'The Royal New Zealand Navy — Policy. Need for a statement on policy'.
8 Ibid, memo for MoD, 26 March 1946.
9 Ibid, memo for MoD, 13 May 1946.
10 NA Navy Department Series 1 6/1/27, Relief of *Achilles* and *Gambia*.
11 *New Zealand Herald*, 1 July 1946, clipping in NA Navy Department Series 1 6/1/27, Relief of *Achilles* and *Gambia*.
12 NA Navy Department Series 1 6/1/27, misc. messages.
13 Ibid, *Black Prince* to NZNB, 1 June 1946.
14 Ibid, C.S. Auckland to NZNB, 24 May 1946.
15 Ibid, C.S. Auckland to NZNB, 6 June 1946.
16 NA Navy Department Series 1 6/45, Ships and repairs: *Dido* class cruisers general, 'Restricted Memo', NZNB to High Commissioner, 4 November 1946.
17 Ibid, correspondence, e.g. CO NZ Squadron to NZNB, 4 April 1951.
18 Ibid, NZNB to CO NZ Squadron, 11 January 1951.

ENDNOTES

19   Ibid.
20   RNZN Museum Oral History DLA 0004, Commander A.V. Kempthorne OBE.
21   RNZN Museum Oral History DLA 0020, Lieutenant Commander C.V. Harris BEM.
22   *Auckland Star*, 2 April 1947.
23   *New Zealand Herald*, 2 April 1947.
24   *New Zealand Herald*, n.d., April 1947.
25   *Southern Cross*, 29 April 1947.
26   *Auckland Star*, 26 April 1947.
27   *New Zealand Herald*, 26 April 1947.
28   NA 13/21/10, Discipline: mutiny and unrest in HMNZS Philomel following new pay code 1947, minuted clipping sheet, Truth, 13 August 1947.
29   *New Zealand Herald*, 10 May 1947.
30   *Dominion*, 10 July 1947.
31   NA 13/21/10, Naval Secretary to Minister of Defence 30 June 1948.
32   Ibid.
33   NA Series 1 6/46, Ships and repairs: 'Loch' class frigates general, August 1947–June 1949, Hon. F. Jones 'New Zealand Defence Policy', 5 April 1948.
34   Martin Walker, *The Cold War*, Vintage, London, 1994, pp. 29–31.
35   *Documents* II, Fraser to Acting Prime Minister, 14 May 1945, pp. 415–16.
36   Churchill, *The Second World War*, VI, p. 578.
37   Ibid, pp. 579–580; see also Walker, *The Cold War*, pp. 23–24, 29–58.
38   NA Series 1 6/46, Secretary NZ Government offices London to Secretary Navy Office, 25 August 1947.
39   Ibid, W.J. Jordan, New Zealand High Commissioner, to Minister of Defence, 4 February 1948, (enclosures).
40   Ibid.
41   Ibid, Naval Secretary to Minister of Defence, 9 March 1948.
42   Ibid, Secretary to Treasury to Acting Minister of Finance, 18 March 1948.
43   Ibid, appended note, 12 March 1948.
44   Ibid, Hon. F. Jones 'New Zealand Defence Policy', 5 April 1948.
45   Ibid.
46   Ibid.
47   *Dunedin Evening Star*, 19 April 1948.
48   *Truth*, 12 January 1949.
49   Not Morlich as reported in McDougall, *New Zealand Naval Vessels*, p. 38.
50   NA Series 1 6/46, memo 11 April 1949.
51   RNZN Museum Oral History DLA 0004, Commander A.V. Kempthorne OBE.
52   NA Series 1 6/46, John McKay to NZNB 6 May 1949.
53   'Remembering the Korean War — and a romance by radio', Vice Admiral Sir Neil Anderson talks to Richard Jackson. MS, R.T. Jackson Collection.
54   Walker, *The Cold War*, pp. 73–79.
55   'Remembering the Korean War — the First Kiwi in Action', Tom Riddell talks to Richard Jackson. MS, R.T. Jackson collection.

56 *Encyclopaedia of New Zealand*, Vol. III, p. 580.
57 'Report of the New Zealand Naval Board for the period 1st April 1950 to 31st March 1951', p. 2.
58 'Report of the New Zealand Naval Board for the period 1 April 1951 to 31 March 1952', p. 4.
59 *Royal New Zealand Navy in the Korean War*, Navy Office, revised edition, c. 1955.
60 'Remembering the Korean War — the First Kiwi in Action', Tom Riddell talks to Richard Jackson. MS, R.T. Jackson collection.
61 Ibid.
62 'Remembering the Korean War — and a romance by radio', Vice Admiral Sir Neil Anderson talks to Richard Jackson. MS, R.T. Jackson collection.
63 'Remembering the Korean War — the First Kiwi in Action', Tom Riddell talks to Richard Jackson. R.T. Jackson. MS, R.T. Jackson collection.
64 'Remembering the Korean War — and a romance by radio', Vice Admiral Sir Neil Anderson talks to Richard Jackson. MS, R.T. Jackson Collection.
65 RNZN Museum Oral History DLA 0114, Leading Cook T.W. Abbott QSM.
66 'Remembering the Korean War — and a romance by radio', Vice Admiral Sir Neil Anderson talks to Richard Jackson. MS, R.T. Jackson Collection.
67 *Royal New Zealand Navy in the Korean War*, p. 5.
68 'Remembering the Korean War — and a romance by radio', Vice Admiral Sir Neil Anderson talks to Richard Jackson. MS, R.T. Jackson Collection.
69 RNZN Museum Oral History DLA 0004, Commander A.V. Kempthorne OBE.
70 'Remembering the Korean War — the First Kiwi in Action', Tom Riddell talks to Richard Jackson. R.T. Jackson Collection.
71 Ibid.
72 RNZN Museum Oral History DLA 0152, Instructor Lieutenant A.G. Long.
73 RNZN Museum Oral History DLA 0004, Commander A.V. Kempthorne OBE.
74 RNZN Museum Oral History DLA 0013, Commander G. Mitchell MBE.
75 RNZN Museum Oral History DLA 0134, Lieutenant Commander D.E.C. Barratt MBE.
76 RNZN Museum Oral History DLA 0152, Instructor Lieutenant A.G. Long.
77 RNZN Museum Oral History DLA 0134, Lieutenant Commander D.E C. Barratt MBE.
78 RNZN Museum Oral History DLA 0152, Instructor Lieutenant A.G. Long.
79 Ibid.
80 RNZN Museum Oral History DLA 0134, Lieutenant Commander D.E.C. Barratt MBE.
81 Ibid.
82 RNZN Museum Oral History DLA 0114, Leading Cook T.W. Abbott QSM.
83 'Report of the New Zealand Naval Board for the period 1 April 1953 to 31 March 1954'.

Chapter Seven
1   'Report of the New Zealand Naval Board for the period 1 April 1949 to 31 March 1950', p. 2.
2   'Report of the New Zealand Naval Board for the period 1 April 1952 to 31 March 1953', p. 3.
3   'Report of the New Zealand Naval Board for the period 1 April 1951 to 31 March 1952', p. 3.
4   RNZN Museum Oral History DLA 0065, Rear-Admiral G.S. Ritchie CB, DSC.
5   Laurie Barber, *New Zealand — A Short History*, pp. 166–68.
6   'Report of the New Zealand Naval Board for the period 1 April 1951 to 31 March 1952', p. 2.
7   RNZN Museum Oral History DLA 0114, Leading Cook T.W. Abbott QSM.
8   'Report of the New Zealand Naval Board for the period 1 April 1953 to 31 March 1954', pp. 7–8.
9   Wright, *New Zealand's Engineering Heritage*, pp. 44–45.
10   RNZN Museum Oral History DLA 0114, Leading Cook T.W. Abbott QSM.
11   'Report of the New Zealand Naval Board for the period 1 April 1953 to 31 March 1954', pp. 7–8.
12   NA Navy Department Series 1 6/45, NZNB from FOCAF, 27 February 1951.
13   'Report of the New Zealand Naval Board for the period 1st April 1949 to 31st March 1950', p. 2.
14   'Report of the New Zealand Naval Board for the period 1st April 1950 to 31st March 1951', p. 2.
15   RNZN Museum Oral History DLA 0103, Rear Admiral D.B. Domett CB, CBE.
16   Ibid.
17   Ibid.
18   MoD Library Vertical File, 'Past ships of the RNZN', typescript, p. 12. Also cited as 880 tons, NA Navy Department Series 1 16/31/8, Trans-Antarctic Expedition, Publicity 1958–60.
19   Ibid, *Endeavour* to NZNB 1/1/57 and 3/1/57.
20   Ibid, Sitrep 4, 11 January 1957.
21   Ibid, Sitrep 10 (n.d.) (January 1957).
22   RNZN Museum Oral History DLA 0103, Rear Admiral D.B. Domett CB, CBE.
23   NA Navy Department Series 1 16/31/8, Sitrep 12, 28 January 1957.
24   Ibid, *Endeavour* to NZNB 22 February 1957.
25   Ibid, *Endeavour* to NZNB 26 February 1957.
26   Ibid, Sitrep 10, 23 February 1958.
27   RNZN Museum Oral History DLA 0103, Rear Admiral D.B. Domett CB, CBE.
28   Ibid.
29   NA Navy Department Series 1 16/31/8, Sitrep 6, 21 January 1958.
30   Ibid, *Endeavour* to NZNB 2 March 1958.
31   RNZN Museum Oral History DLA 0103, Rear Admiral D.B. Domett CB,

CBE.
32   The other *Endeavours* were: a merchant that won battle honours at Cadiz (1596); a 36-gun vessel (1652–56); a 59-ton bomb vessel (1694–95); an 18-ton hoy (1694–1705); a 211-ton transport (1707–13); a 55-ton armed cutter (1763–68); a bark (1768–75); a schooner (1775–1780s); a hired gunboat (1804–1913); a survey ship (1912–1946); and a net layer (1956–61). Not all were called *Endeavour* for their whole careers. See ibid pp. 4–5.
33   *New Zealand Herald*, 24 June 1954.
34   Barber, *New Zealand — A Short History*, p. 174.
35   *New Zealand Herald*, 30 May 1962.
36   RNZN Museum, Captain T.M. O'Brien OBE, interview 1993.
37   Ibid.
38   Ibid.
39   Ibid.
40   Ibid.
41   Ibid.
42   Ibid.
43   Noted in Howard, pp. 92–93.
44   RNZN Museum, Captain T.M. O'Brien OBE, interview 1993.
45   Ibid.
46   Noted in McDougall, *New Zealand Naval Vessels*, p. 84.
47   *Dominion*, 10 January 1979.
48   *Evening Post*, 6 October 1981.
49   Ibid.
50   MoD Library Vertical File, 'Leander Frigates for New Zealand', news release 19 October 1981; *Evening Post*, 17 August 1983.
51   MoD Library Vertical File, 'Leander Frigates for New Zealand', news release 19 October 1981.
52   *Evening Post*, 8 June 1981.
53   Ibid, 22 December 1983.
54   Ibid, 26 August 1988.
55   *Dominion*, 27 August 1988.
56   *Evening Post*, 17 August 1983.
57   *Dominion*, 17 October 1983.
58   *New Zealand Times*, 13 January 1985.

Chapter Eight
1   See, for example, Paul Harris & Linda Twiname, *First Knights*, Howling at the Moon Press, Auckland, 1998, pp. 209–213.
2   White Paper, 1997, p. 18.
3   'The Defence of New Zealand', White Paper, 1991, p. 88.
4   Ministry of Defence, 'The Anzac Frigates', pamphlet 1995, p. 3.
5   *The Frigate Debate*, Pacific Institute of Resource Management, 1989, p. 17.
6   *Dominion*, 20 March 1997.
7   Ministry of Defence, 'The Anzac Frigates', pp. 3, 12.
8   Health expenditure in 1994 was $4602.0 milion, 15.5% of all government

expenditure. Comparable defence expenditure the same year was $1216.8 million, 4.1% of all government expenditure. The total ANZAC frigate programme cost signed up in 1989 was $1262 million, intermittently spread over successive financial years with a guaranteed payback of $800 million to industry. See Thorns & Sedgwick, p. 114.

9   Wright, *New Zealand's Engineering Heritage*, p. 163.
10   *Evening Post*, 1 March 1997.
11   *Sunday Star-Times*, 26 October 1997.
12   Ibid, 5 October 1997.
13   *Dominion*, 16 April 1997.
14   *Evening Post*, 9 June 1997.
15   Judith Martin, 'Hell's Kitchen', *New Zealand Defence Quarterly*, No. 27, Summer 1999.
16   Judith Martin, 'High Seas Hunter', *New Zealand Defence Quarterly*, No. 25, Winter 1999.
17   *Navy Today*, No. 53, March 2001.
18   *Dominion*, 20 March 2001.

Glossary

ANZAC	Australia and New Zealand Army Corps.
ASDIC	underwater sound detection system developed in 1917–18 and extensively refined since; known to the US as SONAR.
AWACS	Airborne Warning and Control System.
barbette	the structure beneath a gun-house containing ammunition and hoists.
BPDMS	Basic Point Defence Missile System, e.g. Sparrow.
Button	Second World War code name for Espiritu Santo.
Cactus	Second World War code name for Guadalcanal.
CNS	Chief of Naval Staff.
CODOG	Combined Diesel Or Gas (propulsion).
DP	Dual Purpose, guns able to engage air and sea targets.
DSC	Distinguished Service Cross.
DSO	Distinguished Service Order.
First Lord	the political head of the Royal Navy, a Cabinet post.
First Sea Lord	the naval head of the Royal Navy, held by a ranking officer.
gun-house	the rotating above-deck structure protecting the guns.
HSK	*Hilfskreuzer* (Auxiliary Cruiser).
HA	High Angle, usually referring to anti-aircraft guns.
IFF	Identify Friend or Foe radio transmission system.
MBES	multi-beam echo sounders.
NZNB	New Zealand Naval Board.
Oerlikon	20-mm machine gun commonly fitted to warships.

pocket battleship	popular term for the armoured ships produced by Germany 1927–36.
pom pom	British 2-pounder AA cannon deployed during World War Two.
RAS	Replenishment At Sea.
reserve buoyancy	the excess of buoyancy over sinkage.
RFA	Royal Fleet Auxiliary.
RN	Royal Navy.
RNZAF	Royal New Zealand Air Force.
RNZN	Royal New Zealand Navy.
RNZNVR	Royal New Zealand Navy Volunteer Reserve.
SAM	Surface to Air Missile.
WRNZNS	Women's Royal New Zealand Naval Service.

Bibliography

Primary Sources

Alexander Turnbull Library (WTu)
fMS-195 HMS *New Zealand* Ship's Book
fMS Papers-3925 Plans of HMS *New Zealand*
qMS Papers-545 E.G.B. Coore diary 1913–14
MS-Papers-283 Nick Barcroft letters to Miss Bell Irving, 1914, 1916
MS Papers-0378, 1437 R.H. Fitzherbert, letters on Jutland
MS-Papers-2297 R.F. Mackie Collection
Micro MS-99 Halsey, Sir Lionel 1872–1949, personal papers 1905–23 (Australian Joint Copying Project M1179; Hertfordshire County Record Office, Hertford, England)

Archives New Zealand (NA)
Colonial Office
209/270
Governor [-General]
Series G2/17 'Dominions No.5', 'Dominions No.7', 'Dominions No.16'
Despatch No. 696/09
Series G40/10, G40/N16
Series G1/1, G48/34
Series G48/F/4, G48/N17

Internal Affairs
Series 71/1, 1913/661 (Parts I–IV)

Navy Department
Series 1 1/7/8 Australasian Squadron maintenance 1902–14
1/34 HMS *New Zealand* Prizes Fund, General Correspondence 1914–45
6/1/11 *Bristol* class cruisers 1906–14
6/9 HMS *New Zealand* general correspondence 1913
6/45 Ships and repairs: *Dido* class cruisers general
6/46 Ships and repairs: 'Loch' class frigates general August 1947–June 1949
6/1/14 Addition of third cruiser
6/1/25 Conditions of transfer of *Gambia*
6/1/27 Relief of *Achilles* and *Gambia*
6/31/8 Publicity 1953–60 (Trans-Antarctic)
6/35/2 Ships and repairs: loss of HMNZS *Moa* due to enemy action
6/46/27 Specifications and drawings 1948–58: 'Loch' class frigates
6/51/1 *Whitby* class frigates general
8/12/22a Report of waterfront strike
10/1 Defence Scheme 1908
10/2 Report by Lord Jellicoe on his naval mission to New Zealand
10/7 CID Reports August 1922, Washington Treaty
13/14a HMS *Achilles*' signals at River Plate
13/21/10 Discipline: mutiny and unrest in HMNZS *Philomel* following new pay code 1947
13/33/10 War Casualties: HMNZS *Achilles* in action with *Graf Spee*
16/8/30 Operations: raider activity at Nauru and Ocean Islands
16/8/32 Operations: HMAS *Canberra* and HMS *Leander*, encounter with Italian armed ship Ramb-1, February 1941
16/8/35 Operations: HMNZS *Monowai*, encounter with submarine and aircraft, January 1942
16/8/40 Operations: HMNZS *Achilles*, encounter with Japanese dive bomber, January 1943
16/8/43 Operations: HMNZS *Leander*, encounter with Japanese naval forces, Kula Gulf, July 1943
16/8/44 Operations: Report of submarine in Cook Strait, November 1943
18/2 Naval Defence Act 1913, General

22/5 Missions: Lord Jellicoe's visit to New Zealand 1919
22/6/1 Policy of Naval Board Pt 1, 1913–29
22/6/16 Naval Board and Policy: RNZN Post-war planning
25/2/1 HMS *New Zealand* Trophies 1911–61
41/1 HMS *Philomel*: signals and telegrams 1914–1917
62/27/6 Ships and repairs: HMS *Achilles*, report of damage
Series 48/42 HMS *Achilles*, Ship's Log for November and December 1939
Series 67/16 HMNZS *Gambia*, Ship's Log, August 1945
Series 109/59 HMS *Royalist*, Captain's Ship's Book
General Assembly Library
'Great Britain, Imperial Accounts and Papers'
CD 3523 'Minutes of the Proceedings of the Colonial Conference, 1907'
CD 3524 'Papers Laid before the Imperial Conference, 1907'
CD 4325 'Correspondence relating to the naval defence of Australia and New Zealand'
CD 4948 'Conference with the Representatives of the self-governing Dominions on the Naval and Military Defence of the Empire, 1909'
CD 5135 'Report of the Dominions Department of the Colonial Office'
National Library
New Zealand Parliamentary Debates (NZPD)
Appendices to the Journals of the House of Representatives (AJHR)

Canterbury Museum
Diary of Captain (Lt Commander) A.D. Boyle, Royal Navy, 1914–15, February–July 1919
Ministry of Defence Library
Newspaper files
Vertical files
'Royal New Zealand Navy in the Korean War'
Cornwall, J.P.M., 'The Tyler Case' MSS
Royal New Zealand Navy

Richard Jackson Collection
'Remembering the Korean War — The First Kiwi in Action', Tom Riddell talks to Richard Jackson.

RNZN Museum Oral Histories
DLA 0114 Leading Cook T.W. Abbott, QSM, RNZN (Rtd)
DLA 0040 Able Seaman A.E. Ball-Guymer, RNZN (Rtd)
DLA 0134 Lieutenant Commander D.E.C. Barratt, MBE, RNZN (Rtd)
DLA 0010 Able Seaman H.H. Beesley RNZN (Rtd)
DLA 0008 Lieutenant K.F. Connew, BEM, RNZN (Rtd)
DLA 0103 Rear Admiral D.B. Domett, CB, CBE, RNZN (Rtd)
DLA 0024 Chief Petty Officer W.M. Gibbs, BEM, RNZN (Rtd)
DLA 0016 Senior Commissioned Engineer Officer H.W. Harris, MBE, RNZN (Rtd)
DLA 0020 Lieutenant Commander C.V. Harris, BEM, RNZN (Rtd)
DLA 0078 Chief Electrician R.B. Harvey, BEM, RNZN (Rtd)
DLA 0074 Instructor Commander S.J.F. Hermans, RNZN (Rtd)
DLA 0007 Lieutenant Commander S.W. Hicks, RNZN (Rtd)
DLA 0073 Able Seaman L.C. Hurndell
DLA 0004 Commander A.V. Kempthorne OBE, RNZN (Rtd)
DLA 0079 Warrant Mechanician R.W. Kirkwood, RNZN (Rtd)
DLA 0066 Surgeon Captain (D) T.H. Logan, MBE, RNZN (Rtd)
DLA 0152 Instructor Lieutenant A.G. Long, RNZN (Rtd)
DLA 0098 Leading Seaman E.C. McVinnie, MID
DLA 0013 Commander G. Mitchell MBE, RNZN (Rtd)
DLA 0110 Captain T.M. O'Brien, OBE, RNZN
DLA 0065 Rear Admiral G.S. Ritchie, CB, DSC, RN (Rtd)
DLB 0004 Yeoman of Signals J.L.W. Salter, BEM, MID, RNZNVR (Rtd)
DLA 0029 Chief Mechanical Engineer M. Seyb, RNZN (Rtd)
DLA 0021 Commodore L.S. Stanners, CBE, RNZN (Rtd)
DLA 0028 Sergeant P.H. Stapleton, RM (Rtd)

Published Primary Sources

Barclay, A.R. 'The Premier and his troubles', S. Lister, Printer, Dunedin, 1909.
Beresford, Admiral Lord Charles, *The Betrayal*, London, 1912.
Brett, M.V. (ed.), *The Journals and Letters of Viscount Esher*, 4 vols, London, 1934–38.
Churchill, R.S. (ed.), *W.S. Churchill, Companion Volume III*, Part 3, William

Heinemann Ltd, London, 1969.
Gooch, G.P. & Temperley, Harold (eds), *British Documents on the Origins of the War*, 10 vols, London, 1927–35.
Greenwood, G. & Grimshaw, C. (eds), *Documents on Australian International Affairs*, 1901–1918, Thomas Nelson (Australia) Ltd, Melbourne, 1977.
Hankey, Maurice, *The Supreme Command*, 2 vols, London, 1961.
Jane, Fred T. (ed.), *Jane's Fighting Ships 1914*, Sampson Low Marston & Co., London, 1914: David & Charles Reprints 1969.
Jervois, W.F.D., 'The Defence of New Zealand', New Zealand Institute, Wellington, 1884.
Kemp, P.K. (ed), *The Fisher Papers*, (2 vols), Navy Records Society, London, 1960 & 1964.
Kimball, Warren F. (ed.), *Churchill & Roosevelt, The Complete Correspondence*, Princeton University Press, Princeton, New Jersey, 1984.
Laby, T.H., *New Zealand's Naval Policy*, The Dominion General Printing House, Wellington, 1913.
Marder, Arthur J. (ed.), *Fear God and Dread Nought*, 3 vols, Jonathan Cape, London, 1952–59.
Temple-Patterson, A. (ed), *The Jellicoe Papers*, 2 vols, Navy Records Society, London, 1966.

Newspapers

The Daily Southern Cross
The Evening Post
New Zealand Herald
New Zealand Truth

Secondary Sources

—   *The Anzac Frigate Debate*, Pacific Institute of Resource Management, Wellington, 1989.
—   *The Anzac Frigates*, Ministry of Defence, 1995.
—   *Navy — Royal New Zealand Navy*, NZDF, 6th Edition, 1999.

Alexander, Ray, *The Cruise of the Raider Wolf*, Angus & Robertson, Sydney, 1940.

Allen, Colonel Sir James, 'New Zealand and Naval Defence', New Zealand Historical Association, Wellington, 1929.

Archibald, E.H.H., *The Metal Fighting Ship*, Blandford Press, London, 1971.

Bacon, Reginald, *The Jutland Scandal*, 5th Edition, Hutchinson & Co., London, 1933.

Bacon, Reginald, *The Life of John Rushworth, Earl Jellicoe*, Cassell & Co., London, 1936.

Barratt, Glynn, *Russophobia in New Zealand, 1838–1904*, Dunmore Press, Palmerston North, 1981.

Bennett, Geoffrey, *Naval Battles of World War II*, David McKay, New York, 1975.

Bennett, Neville, 'Consultation or information? Great Britain, The Dominions, and the Renewal of the Anglo-Japanese Alliance, 1911', *New Zealand Journal of History*, Vol. 4, No. 2, October 1970.

Callahan, Raymond, 'The Illusion of Security: Singapore 1919–1942', *Journal of Contemporary History*, Vol. 9, No. 2, April 1976.

Campbell, N.J.M., *Battlecruisers*, Conway Maritime Press, London, 1978.

Carr, William Guy, *Brass Hats and Bell Bottom Trousers*, Hutchinson & Co., London, 1939.

Clark, Margaret (ed.), *Peter Fraser, Master Politician*, Dunmore Press, Palmerston North, 1998.

Crawford, John, *New Zealand's Pacific Frontline: Guadalcanal — Solomon Islands Campaign 1942–45*, NZDF, Wellington, 1992.

Crawford, John, *Atlantic Kiwis — New Zealanders and the Battle of the Atlantic*, NZDF, Wellington, 1993.

Gibbons, Tony, *The Complete Encyclopedia of Battleships and Battlecruisers*, Salamander Books, London, 1983.

Gordon, D.C., 'The Admiralty and Dominion Navies, 1902–14', *Journal of Modern History* Vol. 33, No. 4, December 1961.

Gowen, R.J., 'British Legerdemain at the 1911 Imperial Conference: The Dominions, Defence Planning and the Renewal of the Anglo-Japanese Alliance', *Journal of Modern History*, Vol. 52, No. 3, August 1980.

Haggie, Paul, 'The Royal Navy and War Planning in the Fisher Era', *Journal of Contemporary History*, Vol. 8, No. 3, July 1973.

Harker, Jack S., *Well Done Leander*, Collins Bros, Auckland, 1971.
Harker, Jack S., *HMNZS Achilles*, William Collins, Auckland, 1980.
Howard, Grant, *The Navy in New Zealand — An Illustrated History*, A.H. & A.W. Reed Ltd, Wellington, 1981.
Howard, N.G., 'New Zealand Naval Policy 1885–1921', unpublished MA Hons Thesis, University of Otago, 1952.
Lissington, M.P., *New Zealand and Japan, 1900–1941*, New Zealand Government Printer, Wellington, 1972.
Mackay, Ruddock F., 'The Admiralty, The German Navy, and the Re-Distribution of the British Fleet, 1904–05', *Mariner's Mirror*, Vol. 56, No. 3, August 1970.
Mackay, Ruddock F., *Fisher of Kilverstone*, Clarendon Press, Oxford, 1973.
Mackay, Ruddock F., 'Historical Re-interpretations of the Anglo-German Naval Rivalry', in Gerald Jordan (ed.), *Naval Warfare in the Twentieth Century*, Croom-Helm, London, 1977.
Mackintosh J.P., 'The Role of the Committee of Imperial Defence before 1914', *English Historical Review* Vol. 77, July 1962.
Marder, Arthur J., *The Anatomy of British Sea Power*, London, 1940.
Marder, Arthur J., *From the Dreadnought to Scapa Flow*, 5 Vols, London, 1960–70.
Maynard, Jeff, *Niagara's Gold*, Kangaroo Press, Kenthurst, 1996.
McDougall, R.J., *New Zealand Naval Vessels*, Government Print, Wellington, 1989.
Meaney, Neville, *The Search for Security in the Pacific*, Vol. I, Sydney University Press, Sydney, 1976.
Nish, I.H., 'Australia and the Anglo-Japanese Alliance', *Australian Journal of Politics and History*, Vol. 9, No. 2, November 1963.
Nish, I.H., *Alliance in Decline*, The Athlone Press, University of London, London 1966, 1968 reprint.
Nish, I.H., *The Anglo Japanese Alliance*, The Athlone Press, University of London, London, 1966, 1968 reprint.
Nish, I.H., 'Admiral Jerram and the German Pacific Fleet, 1913–15', *Mariner's Mirror*, Vol. 56, No. 4, November 1970.
Pollen, Arthur Hungerford, *The Navy in Battle*, Chatto & Windus, London, 1919.
Sumida, Jon Tetsuro, 'British Capital Ship Design and Fire Control in the

Dreadnought Era: Sir John Fisher, Arthur Hungerford Pollen, and the Battle Cruiser', *Journal of Modern History*, Vol. 51, June 1979.

Stevens, David, *U-Boat Far from Home*, Allen & Unwin, Sydney, 1997.

Stevens, David (ed.), *Maritime Power in the Twentieth Century — The Australian Experience*, Allen and Unwin, St Leonards, 1998.

Templeton, Malcolm, *Ties of Blood and Empire*, Auckland University Press, Auckland, 1994.

Towle, P.A., 'The Effect of the Russo-Japanese War on British Naval Policy', *Mariner's Mirror*, Vol. 60, No. 4, November 1970.

Waters, S.D., *Achilles at the River Plate*, War History Branch, Department of Internal Affairs, Wellington, 1948.

Waters, S.D., *The Royal New Zealand Navy*, War History Branch, Department of Internal Affairs, Wellington 1956.

Weir, T.G., 'New Zealand's Naval Policy, 1909–14', unpub. MA Thesis, Canterbury University, 1973.

Wood, F.L.W., 'Why did New Zealand not join the Australian Commonwealth in 1900–01?', *New Zealand Journal of History*, Vol. 2 No. 2, October 1968.

Wright, Matthew, 'Admiral Sir John Fisher and the Strategic Redistribution of the British Battle Fleets, 1904–1909', unpub. BA Hons Research Essay, Victoria University of Wellington, 1984.

— 'Australia, New Zealand and Imperial Naval Defence 1902–1913', MA Thesis, Massey University, Palmerston North, 1986.

— 'Sir Joseph Ward and New Zealand Naval Defence, 1907–13', *Political Science*, July 1989.

— 'Supership', *New Zealand Listener*, 18 December 1989.

-'Dissenter in the Admiralty', *New Zealand Listener*, 23 April 1990.

— 'HMS *New Zealand* — The Naming of a Battlecruiser', *New Zealand Navy News*, Vol. 16 No.1, Autumn 1990.

— 'Public adoration heralded birth of military might', *Daily Telegraph*, 6 October 1990.

— 'Big hurrahs for HMS *New Zealand*', *The Press*, 13 October 1990.

— 'When we bought our first battleship', *Dominion*, 27 December 1990.

— 'Patriotic gift to homeland made Kiwis proud', *Otago Daily Times*, 19 January 1991.

— 'Von Luckner — the gentleman warrior', *Dominion Sunday Times*, 17 March 1991.

— 'NZ Defence Review of crucial importance to region', *Australian Aviation*, September 1991.
— 'Military adopt corporate plan to keep the peace', *Dominion*, 16 November 1992.
— 'Nuclear navy fleets dwindling away', *Dominion*, 4 January 1993.
— 'Australian co-operation essential to New Zealand Defence Policy', *Australian Aviation*, No. 90, September 1993.
— 'Sealift for the soldiers', *New Zealand Defence Quarterly*, No. 8, Autumn 1995.
— 'British ships visit after "no-nukes" assurance', *Daily Telegraph*, 17 June 1995.
— 'Navy choices', *New Zealand Wings*, November 1995.
— 'New details uncovered — U boat attack in Napier', *Daily Telegraph*, 26 June 1997.

Index

Abyssinian crisis, 73
Achilles, HMS (HMNZS after October 1941), 1, 74-84, 86-89, 91, 96, 112, 114, 119-124, 127, 136, 137, 144-147, 151-153
Aden, 12, 35, 36, 97, 102, 103
Admiralstab (German Admiralty), 51
Admiralty, Royal Navy, 7, 9, 10, 13, 16, 19, 20, 22-26, 31-35, 38, 42, 44, 51, 60-62, 65-68, 72, 74, 75, 78, 87, 90, 96, 100-102, 111, 136, 137, 143, 152, 153, 157-159
Afghanistan, 7
Africa, 26, 35, 97, 106, 107, 109, 191
Agincourt, HMS, 64
Ahuriri harbour, 69
Ainsworth, Rear-Admiral Walden L. (USN), 127, 129, 130
Aitutaki, 55
Ajax, HMS, 76, 78-80, 82-84, 86, 103, 106
Akaroa, 28
Akitio, 142
Alderton, Ivan, 77
Alexandria, 103, 106, 107
Allen, Colonel James, 13, 14, 22, 25, 35, 60, 61
Allingham, Lieutenant J. D., 148
Altenfjord, 109
Amethyst, HMS, 167, 170
Amokura, HMS (former HMS *Sparrow*), 11
Aquitania, SS (liner), 88, 114
Arabis, HMNZS, 145, 158, 159
Arbuthnot, Rear-Admiral Sir Robert, 42
Arethusa, HMS, 39
Argentina, 83
Ariadne, SMS, 39, 188

237

Atlantis (German HSK), 96, 98, 101
Auckland, 8, 9, 12, 29, 34, 56, 57, 61, 65, 69-71, 74, 87, 88, 91, 92, 97, 100, 108, 117, 118, 121, 124, 126, 136, 142, 159, 161, 165, 172, 183-185, 187, 189, 190, 201
Audacious, HMS, 41
Aurora, HMS, 107
Australia, 1, 2, 7, 9-11, 13-21, 26-28, 34, 44, 59-62, 65, 66, 72, 88-90, 95, 100, 101, 105, 106, 119, 120, 136, 140, 141, 144, 151, 153, 156, 161, 187, 188, 190, 193-195
Australian 6, 7, 9, 14-20, 24, 28, 35, 44, 53, 60, 62, 69, 70, 88-90, 103, 114, 119, 120, 144, 151, 153, 165, 176, 187, 190, 192, 194, 195, 197, 200-203
Avenger, HMS, 55, 109
Awarua (flying boat), 89, 91
Bacchante, HMS, 189
Baldwin, Stanley, 67
Ball-Guymer, Able-Seaman A.E., 71
Banda Alula, 97
Barcroft, Penrose L. ('Nick'), 32, 37, 46, 49
Bayntun, HMS, 108
Beatty, Vice-Admiral Sir David, 38-40, 42-48, 66
Beesley, Able Seaman H. H., 76, 79, 81, 83, 86, 87
Beirut, 104, 105
Bellona, HMS, 153, 154, 156, 158, 161, 176, 182, 183
Berendsen, Carl, 105
Bernhard 96
Bevan, Captain Robert, 97-100, 103
Blücher, SMS, 43, 44
Bordeaux, 95
Boston, 138, 143
Bougainville, 201
Boyle, Lieutenant-Commander Alexander D., 31-33, 37-41
Bridson, Gordon, 126
Brisbane, 114, 119, 184
Brunei, 192
Buchanan, Signalman C. H., 125
Buenos Aires, 86

Callao, 77
Cambodia, 201
Canada, 18, 28, 60, 61, 65, 66, 105
Canterbury, HMNZS (frigate), 185-187, 189, 196-202

Canterbury, HMNZS (logistic ship), 200
Caribbean, 76
Chatham, HMS, 65-67
Chinnamp'o, 165, 166
Christchurch, 42
Churchill, Winston, 12, 23-25, 31-33, 38, 41-44, 66, 91, 92, 105, 106, 111, 112, 118-120, 140, 157
Coore, Midshipman Edward G. B., 32, 39, 40, 42
Coronel, battle of, 42
Cradock, Rear-Admiral Christopher, 42
Cremer, Peter, 108
Creswell, Captain William, 10, 13
Crete, 102, 103, 105, 197
Crimean War, 6, 7
Cromarty, 41
Cumberland, HMS, 78, 84, 86
Cunningham, Admiral Sir Andrew Browne, 102, 103, 106, 144
Cyprus, 105
Czechoslovakia, 74

Darwin, 118
Denmark, 44, 200
Derfflinger, SMS, 43, 46, 48
Devonport, 56, 65-68, 73, 75, 88, 118, 121, 124, 127, 136, 139, 153, 155, 158, 185-188, 200
Diadem, HMS, 152, 153
Diamond, HMS, 9
Dido class cruiser, 152-154.
Dido, HMS (frigate),189
Dillon, G. W., 93-95
Diomede, HMS, 67, 71, 72, 74
Doenitz, Admiral Karl, 141
Duke of York, HMS, 148
Dunedin, HMS, 67, 68, 71, 74

East Timor, 198, 201, 202
Egypt, 35, 102, 105
Electra, HMS, 113
Erin, HMS, 41
Esher, Lord (Reginald Brett), 21
Espiritu Santo, 121, 128
Esquimalt, 12

Evan-Thomas, Rear-Admiral Hugh, 45-47
Exeter, HMS, 76, 79, 80, 83

Fairmile Class B launch, 139, 145
Fairmiles 90, 139, 140
Falkland Islands, 84, 86, 178, 189, 190
Fanshawe, Vice-Admiral A. D., 11
Ferguson, G. R., 93, 94
Fiji, 55, 56, 89, 116, 119-121, 127, 162, 174, 184, 201
Fisher, Admiral Sir John Arbuthnot, 11, 12, 13, 14-16, 18, 19, 20, 21, 23, 24, 33, 44, 51
Fisher, Andrew, 16
Five Power Defence Arrangement (FPDA), 188, 192, 202
Forrest, Sir John, 10
Foxton, Colonel J. F. G., 19
Fraser, Peter, 2, 89, 91, 92, 96, 102, 103, 105, 106, 111, 119, 120, 137, 141, 144, 155-157, 187

Gambia, HMS (HMNZS), 137, 141, 143-148, 151-153, 161
Germany, 12, 14, 16, 23, 31, 33, 34, 50, 51, 54, 57, 74, 75, 85, 88, 96, 101, 141, 142, 157
Ghormley, Vice-Admiral Robert L., 120
Gibraltar, 12
Gisborne, 28, 142
Glennie, Captain I. G., 74
Gniesenau (KM), 90
Godley Head, 64
Goeben, SMS, 32, 79
Goodenough, Commodore William, 38-39
Great Britain, 1, 2, 6-8, 10-12, 16, 19, 23-25, 30, 32, 33, 49-52, 59, 60, 62-66, 68, 71, 72, 75, 88, 89, 102, 105, 106, 111, 144, 149-151, 153, 155, 157-159, 161, 174, 178, 185, 186, 188, 189, 195, 204

Hall-Thompson, Captain P. H., 26, 35, 36
Halsey, Captain Lionel, 26-29, 39, 43
Halsey, Admiral William, 141, 148.
Hamaguchi Osachi, 72, 73
Hamakaze, IJN, 130
Hankey, Maurice, 13
Harwich, 38, 39
Harwood, Commodore Henry, 76, 78, 79, 82-86
Hatsuyuki, JMSDF, 195
Hauraki Gulf, 56, 198
Havelock North, 27, 109
Hawea, HMNZS, 159, 166-172, 177, 178, 187
Hawke's Bay Club, 27
Hawkes Bay earthquake, 68, 70, 71
Hawke's Bay, 27, 42, 68, 142, 174

Heligoland, 38, 49
Herrick, Commodore L. E., 163
Hurndell, Able Seaman L. E., 114, 115

Ibuki, IJN, 35
Ikara anti-submarine missile launcher, 189
Inchon 163-167
Indefatigable, HMS, 20-22, 27, 45, 109, 148
Indonesia, 186, 192
Ingenohl, Vice-Admiral Frederich von, 37
Invincible, HMS, 15, 20, 21, 38, 40, 47
Irirangi, HMNZS, 175, 176

Jakarta, 141
Japan, 1, 8, 10-12, 14, 24, 59, 62, 63, 68, 72-74, 88, 89, 92, 96, 111, 118, 120, 121, 139-141, 145, 146, 148, 151, 160 161, 165, 195
Java, 115
Jellicoe, Admiral Sir John Rushworth, 16, 21, 22, 33, 37, 38, 42-45, 47-51, 60-62, 65, 67, 68, 72
Jervis Bay, 176
Johnston, Lieutenant-Commander F. N. F., 166
Jordan, W. J., 101, 137
Joylands Cabaret, 142
Jutland, 44, 50

Kamaishi Iron Works, 146
Kaman Aerospace SH-2G Seasprite, 198
Kandahar, HMS, 107
Kaskowiski (Russian cruiser), 5, 6
Katafanga, 55
Kavieng, 95
Kempthorne, A. V., 155, 167, 168
Kermadecs 53, 56, 89, 92
Kidd, Doug, 190
Kimberley, HMS, 97, 106
Kirk, Norman, 187
Kirkwood, R. W., 114, 122, 124, 136,
Kirkwood, Captain Henry, 178, 179
Kolombangara, battle of, 128
Kongo, IJN, 49, 112
Kuantan, 112
Kulmerland (HSK), 90, 94, 95

Laburnum, HMS, 65, 70
Lachlan, HMNZS, 174, 175, 184, 199
Langsdorf, *Kapitän zur See* Hans, 78, 80, 83-86

241

Leach, Captain John, 113
Leander, HMS (HMNZS after October 1941), 74, 87, 88, 95-103, 105, 119-121, 127-131, 134-138, 143, 182, 188, 189, 194 198,
Lexington, USS, 119
Leyte Gulf, 145
Lowestoft, 187
Luckner, Count Felix von, 47, 48, 54-58
Luftwaffe, 104
Lunga, 120, 139
Lutzow, SMS, 45.
Lutzow, (KM), 108
Lyttelton, 8, 28, 52, 91, 96, 174

MacArthur, Douglas, 163, 164, 196
Mackay, Able Seaman Malcolm J., 116
Mahia Peninsula, 174
Makambo, 128
Malaya, 111, 165,
Malaysia, 188, 192
Manawanui, HMNZS, 201
Manchuria, 73, 160
Maniapoto, Rewi, 8
Mansergh, Captain Cecil, 122-124, 128, 134, 135
Manus Island, 145, 147, 183
Maori, 8, 23, 29, 140, 159
Marianas, 34
Marjoribanks, Edward, see Tweedmouth, Lord, 10
Mbennga passage, 117
McMurdo Sound, 179
McVinnie, Leading Seaman E. C., 125
Mediterranean Sea, 12, 32, 74, 79, 102, 103, 106, 109, 161, 177
Melbourne, 18, 19, 194, 197
Milburn, Ordinary Telegraphist N. J., 81
Millington-Drake, Eugene, 85
Minneapolis, USS, 121
Minotaur, HMS, 14, 15, 35
Missouri, USS, 148
Moltke, SMS, 43, 46
Montevideo, 1, 83, 84, 87
Mopelia Island, 55, 57
Morgan, Captain Horace L., 69, 70, 112, 113
Moscow, 161
Muldoon, Robert, 189
Murchison, HMAS, 168
Murmansk, 109
Mururoa Atoll, 187, 199

Mutsu, IJN, 63

Nagasaki, 147
Nakamagon, USS, 181
Nash, Walter, 102, 105, 141
Nauru, 92, 93, 95, 96
Neptune, HMS, 102, 106-108
New Georgia, 121, 127, 128, 139
New Guinea, 54, 114, 120, 143, 201
New Zealand, 1-3, 6-11, 13, 14, 16-20, 22-35, 37-47, 49-68, 71-76, 78, 79, 84, 87-92, 96, 97, 100-103, 105, 106, 108, 109, 111, 112, 117-120, 124, 126-128, 137-154, 156-159, 161-163, 165-167, 170-174, 177-180, 184-195, 197-204
Niagara, SS, 88
Nimitz, Admiral Chester W., 119, 120
Nordmeyer, Arnold, 182
North Carolina, USS, 121
Northumberland, SS, 69, 70
Noumea, 34, 119, 126, 138
Nowra, NAS, 176
Nuku'alofa, 121

Oamaru, 28
Ohakune, 137
Okinawa, 145, 146
Olympic, SS, 41, 147
Onehunga, 8
Orion, HMS [1910] 22, 41, 42,
Orion (HSK), 88-92, 94, 96
Osaka, 185
Otago, 28, 174,
Otago, HMNZS, 181, 187-189

P-3K Orion, 201
Pacific Ocean, 2, 7, 8, 10-13, 19, 20, 23, 26, 34, 54, 55, 59, 60, 62-66, 73, 74, 76, 88-90, 96, 108, 111, 116, 118-120, 127, 133, 137, 140, 141, 143-145, 149, 151, 152, 156-160, 186, 191, 199, 202
Paengyong-do, 171
Palmerston North, 196
Panama, 90, 120, 124, 138
Parry, Captain W. E., 75, 79, 81, 83, 84, 87, 88, 90, 112
Pass of Bahama, see also *Seeadler*, 54
Penang, 141
Pernambuco, 72
Philippines, 11, 120, 192
Philomel, HMS [cruiser] 26, 33-36, 59, 61, 65, 69
Philomel, HMS (HMNZS from October 1941), land base, 154, 156

243

Phoebe, HMS, 103
Polynesia, 187
Prince of Wales, HMS, 112-113
Pyramus, HMS, 25, 28, 34, 35

Queensland, 10
Quick, Walter H., 131
Quigley Review, 194

Ramb-1, 98, 100
Ramilles, HMS, 88
Rangitane, SS, 91, 92
Raoul Island, 162
Rawalpindi, SS, 90
Rendova, USS, 168
Repulse, HMS, 111-113
Rodney, HMS, 111
Roosevelt, Franklin, 112, 118, 119, 120, 140
Roskill, Commander Stephen Wentworth, 129, 132, 134
Rotoiti, HMNZS, 159-161, 165-168, 170-172, 177, 187
Royalist, HMNZS, 173, 182-185
Russia, 5-8, 11, 12, 14, 33, 74, 160
Rutherford, Ernest, (Lord Rutherford of Nelson), 51

Safaja, 36
Sagami Wan, 148
Saigon, 112, 113
Sakishima Gunto, 145
Salmond, Sir John, 63
Samoa, 10, 34, 56, 68, 120, 162
San Francisco, 120
Santa Cruz Islands, 120
Sarajevo, 31
Sasebo, 162, 163, 165, 168
Scapa Flow, 32, 33, 43
Scharnhorst, (KM), 90, 108
Scotland, 90
Scratchley, Colonel Peter, 7, 8
Seeadler, 54, 55, 57
Selbourne, Lord, 12, 16
Sembawang, 114
Seoul, 161, 163, 166
Seydlitz, SMS, 43, 45, 46, 50
Shantung, 72
Sheerness, 74
Sinclair-Burgess, Colonel W. L. H., 73
Singora, 112

INDEX

Solomon Islands, 120, 121, 128, 138-140, 199
Somalialand, 97, 98
Somerville, Admiral Sir James, 143
Songjin Island, 170
Sphakia, 103
Spratly Islands, 192
Stapleton, Sergeant P. H., 122, 123
Straits of Magellan, 78
Sumatra, 143, 144
Surabaya, 143
Swiftsure, HMS, 153
Sydney, 6, 7, 18, 20, 35, 61, 88, 89, 91, 142, 144, 145, 151, 172
Syria, 103, 104, 105

Taiwan, 192
Taiwanese 188
Tangiwai disaster, 175
Taradale, 27
Taroona, SS, 116, 117
Tasman Sea, 1, 11, 18, 19, 35, 53, 88-90, 101, 118, 181, 192
Taupo, HMNZS, 159, 170, 171, 175, 177, 187, 198
Tauranga, HMS, 9
Tenix Group, 197
Thailand, 192
Timaru, 28, 137
Tirpitz, Admiral Alfred von, 23, 24
Tirpitz, (KM), 109, 110
Tokyo, 73, 74, 92, 121, 129, 147, 148
Tongatapu, 119
Townsville, 95
Tripoli, 107
Tromso, 110
Troubridge, Vice-Admiral Sir Ernest, 79, 85
Truman, President Harry S., 157
Tryon, Rear-Admiral Sir George, 9
Tsingtao, 34
Tsushima, battle of, 12
Tudor-Boddam, Lieutenant-Colonel Edmund Meyer, 9
Tulagi, 120, 127-129, 134
Turakina, SS, 89
Tyrwhitt, Commodore Reginald, 38, 39

Upham, Charles, 200
Uruguay, 83, 85
Uruguayan 85

Valentine, Stoker First Class E., 137

Valparaiso, 77
Vandegrift, Major-General A. A>, 121
Veronica, HMS, 65, 69-71
Vigor-Brown, John, 27
von Egidy, Kapitän zur See Moritz, 46

Waikato, HMNZS, 187, 189, 201
Waiouru, 175, 176
Wairuna, SS, 53, 56
Waitemata Harbour, 5
Wakakura, HMS, 67
Wakaya Island, 55
Wallingford, Flight Lieutenant Sidney, 68
Walsh, Commander John, 66
Ward, Joseph, 13-23, 25, 44, 49, 50, 60, 61, 72
Washbourn, Gunnery Officer W. E., 81, 185
Wellington, 3, 8, 23, 25, 27, 34, 35, 37, 49, 56, 61, 65, 75, 87, 89, 91, 92, 96, 108, 117-119, 121, 139, 140, 142, 144, 159, 160, 174, 187, 190, 197-199, 201
Wellington, HMNZS, 189
Westall, J. C., 71
Westland Wasp, 182, 198
Westport, 54, 87, 175
Weyher, Kurt, 88, 89, 91, 95
Whangaehu River, 175
Whangarei, 196, 199
White-Parsons, H., 69
Whitmore, Colonel-General Sir George, 7
Wilhelmshaven, 24, 37
William-Powlett, Captain N. J. W., 143
Wilson, Admiral Sir Arthur, 23
Wonsan, 164
Woodville, 17

Yagodnik, 110
Yangtse River, 167, 170
Yarmouth, 42
Yarra, HMAS, 97
Yukikaze, IJN, 130

Zeebrugge, 52

About the author

Matthew Wright is a New Zealand writer with over thirty years professional experience as a published author and in publishing. He has qualifications in writing, music and anthropology among other fields, and holds multiple post-graduate degrees in history. He is a Fellow of the Royal Historical Society at University College, London.

Matthew Wright's New Zealand Military Series

Collect the set

www.ingramcontent.com/pod-product-compliance
Lightning Source LLC
Chambersburg PA
CBHW061439300426
44114CB00014B/1758